TRADING

FOR BEGINNERS

LEARN TECHNICAL ANALYSIS, BUILD YOUR MINDSET AND START EARNING

Luigi Mele

All Rights Reserved - Any duplication of this document is prohibited

Copyright © 2024 by Luigi Mele – All Rights Reserved

No part of this guide may be reproduced, in any form, without the written permission of the publisher, with the exception of short quotations used for the publication of articles or reviews, which in any case must provide for the correct indication of the text of origin in the bibliography and margin of the extract.

Legal Note

The information contained in this book and its contents are not intended to replace any form of medical or professional advice, and the book itself is not intended to replace the need for medical, financial, legal, or other advice or services which may be necessary. The content and information in this book have been provided for educational, instructional and/or recreational purposes only.

The content and information contained within the book are derived from sources believed to be reliable and are accurate according to the knowledge, information, and beliefs of the Author. However, the Author cannot guarantee its accuracy and validity and therefore cannot be held responsible for any errors and/or omissions. In addition, this book may be subject to periodic changes as needed and with the intent to provide the reader with the highest quality content.

By applying the contents and information in this book, you agree to hold the Author harmless from any damages, costs and expenses, including attorneys' fees, which may result from the application of any such information. This notice applies to any loss, damage, or injury caused by the application of the contents of this book, whether directly or indirectly, in breach of contract, tort, negligence, personal injury, criminal intent, or under any other circumstances.

You agree to accept all risks derived from the use of the information presented in this book.

You agree that, by continuing to read this book, you will, when appropriate and/or necessary, consult a professional (including,

All Rights Reserved - Any duplication of this document is prohibited

but not limited to, your physician, attorney, financial advisor, or other such professional) before using the suggested remedies, techniques, and information in this book.

It should be remembered that there is a substantial risk of loss in trading on financial markets. Every investor and every Trader has the responsibility to independently evaluate the investment and specifically if it is congruent and commensurate with their financial conditions, furthermore they should only invest money that they can afford to lose.

This educational material does not represent a solicitation or recommendation to invest. The author assumes no responsibility for investments made using the techniques and methodologies discussed here, nor does it claim that following the aforementioned methodologies will automatically result in profitable trading.

TABLE OF CONTENTS

Introduction 1

Chapter 1: Make Money Consistently with Trading 7

Chapter 2: Reading Price Charts 21

Chapter 3: Interpreting Japanese Price Candles 30

Chapter 4: Correctly Identify Supports and Resistances 47

Chapter 5: How to Use Moving Averages 58

Chapter 6: How to Use Technical Indicators 80

Chapter 7: Analyze the Market Cycle 99

Chapter 8: How to Trade Trends 114

Chapter 9: Exploit Breakouts in Sideways Markets 138

Chapter 10: Price Chart Configurations 149

Chapter 11: Position Sizing.. 161

Chapter 12: Risk Management and Trade Management 169

Chapter 13: Design Your Own Trading System 176

Chapter 14: Psychology in Trading and Winning Mindset 192

Chapter 15: The 11+1 Habits of the Successful Trader 209

Chapter 16: The Process of Becoming a Trader 220

Conclusion... 230

Bonus Contents... 233

References 234

All Rights Reserved - Any duplication of this document is prohibited

Introduction

Hello Aspiring Trader, welcome to this new and fascinating world. The following text will be fully devoted to building your basic trading education.

First, I would like to congratulate you on taking your first step into the world of professional trading. With this book, I will try to convey the knowledge necessary to make you successfully navigate the financial crises, which are cyclically repeated in world markets.

Financial crises are comparable to hellish journeys where, in the worst situations and in the most varied difficulties, one really learns how to operate on the markets. During crises, we learn to be not only smarter Traders but also deepen our knowledge of human nature, which is directly reflected in price trends. The experience that comes from these complex, fascinating and dangerous moments will benefit you for the rest of your days as a Trader.

The main objective of this book is to teach you how to protect your capital, helping you to lay the necessary foundations to avoid painful losses of money, often quantifiable in thousands of US Dollars.

Through these contents you can avoid, at least at the beginning, engaging in expensive basic training courses. In these pages, you will find everything you need to start being an aware and profitable Trader in the financial markets. I guarantee it!

I will teach you the fundamentals and crucial knowledge related to the technical analysis of financial markets, so you can start trading professionally.

You will become familiar with the *"Statistical Advantage"* concept and learn the basics of reading price charts and market structure.

We will observe some particular configurations of the same graphs, called *"Patterns,"* which recur frequently.

We will then proceed to understand the concepts related to risk management, I will help you understand what a *"Trading System"* is and how to build one, your first and personal Trading System.

We will also address the crucial concept of *"Trading Psychology"* and how this component can silently influence our choices, hindering our business.

At the end of this course of study, which I sincerely hope you will face with due seriousness and the utmost respect, I can guarantee that the skills acquired will ensure that you have the same technical perspective as a Professional Trader. You will also develop the confidence to enter and survive the financial markets with real money.

If you have never heard of Trading before and you are a complete neophyte in the sector, you will have to consider spending a lot of your time consolidating the foundations before starting to have substantial economic returns from your operation.

In any case, this book will definitively open the doors to a training course designed to lead you to be profitable while protecting your basic capital.

The book was mainly written for Trader Neophytes, people who want to learn how to analyze the financial markets to have an economic return but who, at the same time, realizing their inexperience, decide to delve into the subject humbly, aware of the need to acquire a more professional technical approach.

When I address the reader with the term Neophyte Trader, I am essentially referring to a person who can belong to one of the following three major groups of people, classified according to their current knowledge of the subject:

- o Those who have never carried out a market transaction in their life but have heard of it and are eager to learn much more about this world;
- o Those who have begun to operate in the markets but not having consolidated their knowledge are still unable to juggle effectively in various situations;
- o Those who have already carried out numerous operations but, despite the experience now acquired, fail to be able to generate consistent returns from this type of business.

If you belong to one of these three categories of people, I can assure you that this book is tailor-made for you.

With regard to the financial markets to which we will refer, we will mainly deal with Stocks and Commodities. But be careful, everything you will learn on these pages will still be applicable to any type of market, from the FOREX currency market to Sector Indices and even Cryptocurrencies.

As far as I'm concerned, my trading style is essentially short-medium term, I prefer Day Trading, which consists in opening a position with the aim of concluding it on the same day, Multi-Day Trading, with operations extended to a few days, up to Swing Trading, which takes place over a few weeks. This preference of mine means that I prefer charts with four-hour, daily and weekly periodicity. You will be able to apply this information even if your style is more long-term oriented, through Position Trading strategies, or if you prefer faster exchanges typical of Day Trading.

I would also like to give a little emphasis on something that I think is important to anticipate, this book is not suitable for some groups of people.

The book is not aimed at the group of those who would like to become long-term investors, such as Value Investors or Growth Investors, for whom operations typically have a multi-year nature and are based on decisions deriving from fundamental analyzes of companies and markets. Therefore, if you see yourself in this last description, I can only suggest that you continue reading with the hope that, perhaps, the information contained in these pages can be added to your analysis methodology, giving you the opportunity to compose through them a clearer picture of the financial instrument you would like to trade in the near future.

It is not excluded that in the future, for this specific group of people, I will write a book dedicated precisely to fundamental analysis.

The book is also not suitable for anyone who thinks they can get rich quickly, effortlessly, and without commitment. I am sorry to inform this category of people that, in the financial markets, money is made in large quantities but over a long period of time and is lost, in even greater quantities, in an extremely shorter time.

Trading is certainly one of the most complex and difficult activities to learn, but with the will, commitment and methodical attitude, I assure you that it can become one of your most profitable activities.

Within the pages of this book, a didactic Trading System will be introduced, a useful example for the realization of your personal Trading strategies, designed to minimize the damage you could incur by operating in the markets carelessly.

However, I must anticipate that a system, however well functioning and structured, must necessarily be understood in all its parts.

Running a System Trading blindly, without understanding exactly what you are doing, will be a recipe for financial disaster for you. The markets are constantly changing, therefore you will always have the burden of making equally rapid decisions about the use, modification, or even the elimination of a Trading System from your portfolio of strategies precisely because each system is designed with specific rules and limitations that inevitably limit its effectiveness.

This information will not make you a millionaire if you intend to invest only $5,000 in this business. Those who speak of such unbalanced returns are not honest with those who listen to them and are only trying to sell smoke.

Professional Traders never speak in monetary terms but always and only in terms of returns, risks and probabilities.

Before starting your journey, to get the most out of the information that will be sent to you, I recommend getting a demo account on any Online Trading platform. It doesn't matter which one it is, any broker that gives you the opportunity to observe price charts of financial instruments will do just fine. Among the best-known platforms, there is certainly TradingView, which I will use to extract graphs related to the topics discussed.

Regardless of the platform you choose, I advise you to draw up a list of ten elements, chosen at your discretion among the various types of financial instruments, as your Watchlist. If you prefer stocks, choose your ten favorite companies, if you are more interested in currencies or commodities, do the same with these. No one will forbid you to create a promiscuous list, but since you're at the beginning, I personally recommend that you start delving into one category at a time.

Whenever you find yourself learning a new concept on these pages, you will observe the securities in your list, accessing the platform to observe the graphs and apply the new concepts to them.

My advice is to proceed methodically in reading the book, avoiding skipping entire chapters just because they apparently deal with trivial concepts for you.

The book is structured in an organic way, what is expressed in the various chapters often concatenates into the following chapters, progressively creating a basic formation necessary for the understanding of subsequent concepts.

While studying these concepts, you will also learn something about yourself and your personality. Know right away that the higher your level of self-criticism on what you learn, produce and apply, the better the development of your Trading Systems will be and, therefore, their effectiveness.

Trading is a subject whose study requires a lifetime of constant application and concentration.

Trading is a journey, not a destination, and on this journey, I will be happy to patiently show you the first steps in the right direction.

Chapter 1:

Make Money Consistently with Trading

"Can a Trader really make profits consistently and continuously?" You've probably wondered this more than once while watching videos and reading articles. Let's start by saying that most people consider Traders, even those who trade regularly and professionally, as a type of bettor or gambler. When each person observes the world, he filters and perceives it subjectively based on his own experience and knowledge; precisely for this reason, he does not associate Trading with a job of skill and responsibility but exclusively with an opaque activity conducted by serial bettors.

Without digressing further and returning to the question:

"Can a Trader really make profits consistently and continuously?"

I can give you two answers, in the short answer, I can confirm that a Trader can indeed be capable of generating profits.

In answering more extensively and precisely, a Trader can achieve this result only if he has developed at least one strategy that guarantees a positive economic return deriving from a certain Statistical Advantage in a reasonable amount of time.

The study of the strengths and weaknesses of the market to obtain a Statistical Advantage is exactly the area of which the technical analysis of the financial markets deals.

Technical analysis is nothing more than a huge and complicated tool created to help Traders and investors increase their chances of carrying out a successful operation. In the long term, the relationship between operations with a positive return will be evident compared to the total operations.

Technical analysis gives us the ability to generate consistent profits as well as the ability to discern the complexity of different market scenarios and different markets in general.

Let's explore the concept of the Trader's Statistical Advantage. We can say that a Trader achieves a Statistical Advantage on the market when he can adequately identify the entry and exit points of a specific operation so that, over a fair number of operations, the total profit deriving from winning Trades is greater than the loss total deriving from the losing Trades, added to the total of the operating commissions.

This definition highlights three key elements that need attention:

- The Trader must have an adequate technical approach that indicates when to enter and when to exit the market;
- The Trader needs to carry out an adequate number of trades before having the possibility to observe any Statistical Advantage deriving from his specific strategy;
- The Statistical Advantage must not be understood exclusively in terms of the quantity of profit or loss trades, rather, it is strictly correlated with the differential of the value generated between Winning Trades and Losing Trades.

There is a mathematical method, quite simple actually, but really useful to clarify this last sentence, the Expected Value formula:

$$Va(X) = X_1P_1 + X_2P_2 + X_3P_3 + \ldots + X_kP_k$$

The symbol K is representative of the number of possible scenarios that can arise. In Trading, the value of K is equal to 2 because it is possible to close a transaction either in profit or in loss.

If it is objected that we can also obtain a draw closing as a third result, we assume that this result is not actually a result. Personally, in these rare cases, I include it as a count among profit operations to underestimate my earning probabilities and be more relaxed in evaluations.

With the symbol X, we represent the value of your total return in each possible scenario. Applying it to Trading, we can use the X_1

value to indicate the total number of Profit Trades and the X_2 value to indicate the total number of Loss Trades.

With the symbol P, we indicate the probability connected to each specific scenario, therefore, we will have the probability of winning P_1 and, in a complementary way, the probability of losing P_2.

The overall probability will be P_t, which will obviously include 100% of the cases.

A numerical example will clarify these mathematical abstractions.

Numerical Example

Imagine observing two Traders, whom we will call Anthony and Bert. Anthony, through his strategy, has a 50% probability of executing a profitable trade and, of course, also has a 50% probability of executing a losing trade. Both when he wins and when he loses, Anthony expects his balance to vary by $100.

Trader Bert has the same win rate with a 50% probability, but unlike Anthony, when he wins, he earns twice as much as when he loses, respectively $200 in profit and $100 in loss.

Could you tell me with this information which of the two is the more capable Trader?

To clarify this mathematically, we apply the Expected Value formula for the case of Anthony and Bert.

Trader Anthony:

$$Va(X) = X_1P_1 + X_2P_2$$

$$Va = (100) * 50\% + (-100) * 50\% =$$

$$= 100 * 0{,}5 - 100 * 0{,}5 = 0 \text{ USD}$$

Trader Bert:

$$Va(X) = X_1P_1 + X_2P_2$$

$$Va = (200) * 50\% + (-100) * 50\% =$$

$$= 200 * 0{,}5 - 100 * 0{,}5 = 50 \text{ USD}$$

From this simple equation, we can understand that, for the Trader Antonio, the expected probable value deriving from each single Trade is equal to $0, while Bert, the second Trader, can probably expect an average profit of $50 for every single operation.

I would say that it is evident that Bert is the more capable Trader of the two.

Strategy Evaluation

Let's dive into some more facets of the expected value formula. You must always remember that the probability value can only be defined with adequate reliability if it is evaluated over a wide range of measures, therefore it will be your responsibility to carry out an adequate number of executions before being able to prove or disprove the effectiveness of the Statistical Advantage deriving from your strategy.

The ideal number of trades will purely depend on your Trading Style. For Traders who prefer the short term, such as swing Traders, about thirty executions can be considered a good "start" on a statistical basis.

For those who prefer the day trading approach, it is also possible to increase the start of the statistical base to fifty or one hundred operations.

It is also important not to interrupt the evaluation of the performance of one's strategies, but on the contrary, to maintain one's own historical document, which contains at least:

- The date of each completed transaction.
- The security, unit or currency traded.
- The result obtained, regardless of whether it is in profit or loss.
- Any commission charges applied, if they are not automatically included in the overall value of the Trade.

If you prefer, you can use the Excel file I have prepared for you, downloadable for free from the Bonus Section of this book.

Through this information, you can start monitoring the performance of your strategy correctly and day after day, and then process your personal statistics.

Personally, in my spreadsheet, I have also inserted an evaluation of the daily performance, an average of the values of the operations of the day, and a moving average calculated on the basis of the number of operations that I consider representative.

Remember that, well before starting to use your strategy with real money in the market, it is always advisable to carry out a test based on historical price data, that is to say, a *"Backtest."*

A Backtest is nothing more than a test methodology created to evaluate the effectiveness of a strategy that exploits the past behavior of a security or a currency over a given period of time.

Through this method, you will not have to wait for the real market times, i.e., for the conditions defined by you in the strategy to occur, but you will simply have to apply the same conditions based on the price history. Once you have carried out a number of operations that you deem appropriate, you will be able to obtain an accurate estimate of the effectiveness of your strategy.

Returning to the formula of the Expected Value, the simultaneous presence of two variables, the probability P and the value X, must be taken into consideration. These variables, in essence, represent the two possible ways a Trader can technically intervene in his operations.

Some Traders focus on increasing the probabilities linked to a single Trade, while others prefer to increase the disparity between the expected value for Profit Trades and the value for Loss Trades, effectively regulating their risk/reward ratio.

There is no right or wrong way, you have to find the right middle ground that can work for your specific character.

Professional Traders are not the only ones to use the Expected Value Formula, but it is also widely used in many other industries. The evaluation of the total prize of the lotteries or of the prize amount of the scratch cards is expertly calculated so that, from a statistical point of view, the issuing body always has a positive balance.

Having learned the concept of expected value, which I would say is vital for a Trader's long-term profitability, we can give a new, very simplified definition of the Trader's Statistical Advantage.

A Trader has a Statistical Advantage on the market when he can adequately identify entry and exit points of a specific trade such that, over a fair number of trades, the expected total amount of profits and losses, net of trading fees is greater than zero.

Said in the form of an Expression:

$$Va\ (X) > 0.$$

When a Trader achieves a Statistical Advantage on the market, his specific strategy generates a positive expected value, therefore is mathematically profitable.

Now that you understand the importance of securing a statistical edge in the market, you will have begun to imagine how professional Traders make consistent and repeated profits.

When I said that other industries use the expected value formula as well, I also mentioned lotteries and scratch cards, but there is one huge industry that I have not mentioned yet, the Gambling Industry.

I said clearly earlier that people from the outside see Traders as gamblers, but in fact, a Trader has many more facets in common with casino managers.

A gambling house manager, or casino if you prefer, knows in detail every single game present, active, and offered to his audience. For each game, he knows the rules and, in some cases, defines them himself, evaluates and intervenes where possible to vary the odds of each game to his own advantage.

Exactly as we defined in the Expected Value formula, they will do everything in their power to guarantee themselves a positive expected value and, therefore, effectively secure themselves a Statistical Advantage over the bets of their customers.

The Statistical Advantage for the casino, in the long run, and after millions of bets, has a Positive expected value while the expected value of the gamblers is always Negative.

Another aspect concerns emotionality, the players suffer a disadvantage due to their human nature, which causes the constant alternation between Fears and Greed. Fears can be the most diverse, but among the main ones are the fear of losing money and the "F.O.M.O." Fear of Missing Out the winning chance if you don't play immediately. On the other side of the table, casino owners are totally emotionless. They define the rules of the game with strategic intelligence and a priori, after which they apply them slavishly. Their effort takes shape when they hire people who respect and enforce the rules.

Gambling house owners understand the law of large numbers better than anyone else, this is why in casinos there are free drinks and food, discounted hotel rooms, and many other specially designed features and benefits to attract a customer for as long as possible. Having more customers for longer mathematically translates into more bets, which in turn translates into more profits for the casino.

An immediate way to introduce the logic of probabilities of casinos is to illustrate the functioning of the most common and famous in this sector, the Roulette.

Most people believe that, in this specific game, the probability of winning is 50%, depending on whether you choose Black or Red, Even or Odd, with progressively decreasing probabilities based on the quantity of numbered boxes covered by the bet and, therefore, progressively more attractive prizes.

In reality, the game includes at least one green box with the value 0 indicated on it, often the box 00 is also present. By adding these figures to the total numbers, they create a higher Statistical Advantage in their favor by reducing the probability of victory of their players at the table.

n.1 – Roulette wheel example

In a roulette table, it is possible to count from a minimum of 37 numbers up to a maximum of 38. Eighteen numbers will have a red base color, eighteen will have a black base color and up to two boxes will have a green base color, respectively, the zero and double zero. In the case of 38 boxes, if we did a short calculation, we would discover that, with each spin of the wheel, the table has a 52.6% win probability rate and the players will have a 47.4%

win rate. The Statistical Advantage of the casino in this specific game is 5.2%.

You may think 5.2% is small but try to imagine a large number of plays at this table. For every $1,000 wagered by patrons, the dealer will almost automatically earn $52.

We apply the Expected Value formula to mathematically calculate this assumption:

$$Va = (1000) * 52,6\% + (-1000) * 47,4\% =$$

$$= 1000 * 0,526 - 1000 * 0,474 =$$

$$= 526 - 474 = 52 \text{ USD}$$

The specific profit is obviously scalable and if, for example, bets were made for a value of $1,000,000 in a casino, the corresponding profit would be equal to $52,000.

Now how can we, as Traders, take advantage of this mathematical peculiarity?

It is essential that the Trader, even before making his first Trade in the real market, equips himself with a Trading System that ensures him an adequate Statistical Advantage. Just like the owners of casinos, we define in principle the rules we must abide by and respect them religiously to obtain our Statistical Advantage.

A Trading System must be structured with two main components:

- Technical component, necessary to build the specific strategy;
- Methodological component, which provides for adequate rules that regulate all the other non-technical areas of the application of the strategy itself, such as management and economic sustainability.

By means of the strategy, we will have the necessary help to identify the Trades with the highest probability of success, which will provide an indication of market entry.

The rules, on the other hand, are extremely necessary to define what will be the maximum amount that you can afford to lose in the event of failure and what the relative return will be in the event of a gain, or they could also simply be temporal rules, based on a self-imposed limit of minutes, hours or days.

Executing a strategy by tirelessly applying the rules will allow you to leave emotion out during the decision-making and executive phase.

If all this confuses you and you still don't quite understand a Trading System, relax and don't worry too much. In the following pages, I will illustrate all the elements necessary to create an adequate Trading System and how to use them.

I want to give you some more examples to clarify how these two components influence the final result.

Let's call again the Traders of the previous example, Anthony and Bert, who meet their third partner, Trader Carl.

Anthony, our first Trader, has an initial capital of $10,000 and, in applying his own Trading System, decides to risk 1% of this sum each time, corresponding to $100. The risk/return ratio is 1:3, this means that every time a market order is entered, the order always sets the value of its risk percentage, 1%, as the maximum tolerable loss limit.

On the contrary, when the operation makes a profit, it will be closed by limiting its maximum profit to $300, equivalent to 3% of the base capital. This is a self-imposing risk management rule to limit the impact of a negative trade on your entire account.

In this second example, let's assume that Anthony has a 60% chance of winning, resulting from the technical component of the Trading System. In 3 months of operation, Anthony carries out and concludes 100 operations.

With the information we have, we apply the expected value formula:

$$Va = (300) * 60\% + (-100) * 40\% =$$

$$= 300 * 0{,}60 - 100 * 0{,}40 =$$

$$= 180 - 40 = 140 \text{ USD}$$

The expected value for Anthony will therefore be $140 for each single Trade, and out of 100 completed operations, Anthony's system can generate an expected gross profit of $14,000. Anthony's return on initial capital at risk is 140%, which is not bad.

In the same period, Bert also carried out operations on the financial markets. Let's imagine that Bert has the same initial capital as Anthony, $10,000; his risk/return ratio is always equal to 1:3, and he always risks 1% of his own capital each time. So far, everything is absolutely identical to what we saw for Trader Anthony.

However, Bert's strategy has some technical differences, leading to a lower probability of winning, equal to 30%. Bert has built a strategy that appears much less effective than Anthony's strategy, for every 10 transactions concluded, seven of these will be at a loss.

So, let's look at what happened to Bert's expected value:

$$Va = (300) * 30\% + (-100) * 70\% =$$

$$= 300 * 0{,}30 - 100 * 0{,}70 =$$

$$= 90 - 70 = 20 \text{ USD}$$

The expected value for each operation, based on the strategy and rules of Trader Bert, is equal to $20. At the end of his 100 Trades, Bert will have a total gross profit of $2,000 corresponding to a return on the initial capital of 20%.

At this moment, you'll wonder what I'm writing, that maybe I'm wrong and you'll feel confused. Even if the math clearly demonstrates it, how is it possible to still make money even if you lose 70% of the time?

The answer is that Trader Bert, like Trader Anthony, has made the choice to operate with an extremely advantageous risk/return ratio. Each time he loses, he loses relatively little compared to the possible gain in cases of Trade in Profit. What you have just read is, in fact, the true Statistical Advantage of the Trader.

Our third Trader, Carl, is a beginner who has decided to risk the same initial capital of $10,000 and the same level of risk per Trade of 1%. He made this choice only because, having had a chat with Anthony and Bert, he is convinced that they are the right parameters without investigating the reason in depth.

Unfortunately, unlike the other two friends, Carl is very emotional and, due to the thrill of having more frequent wins or out of simple fear, he is content to earn only $50 each time he wins. In this example, the risk/reward ratio is 2:1, risk twice as much to get a small return.

This humbler level of pretensions of him allows him to have a high probability of winning, equal to Anthony, 60%, and this causes him to have an illusory perception of being a capable Trader.

Let's apply the expected value formula one last time to see how things have changed:

$$Va = (50) * 60\% + (-100) * 40\% =$$

$$= 50 * 0,60 - 100 * 0,40 =$$

$$= 30 - 40 = -10 \text{ USD}$$

It is clear that Trader Carl, despite the odds in his clear favor, fails to be profitable and consistent in the long run due to the risk/return ratio deliberately to his disadvantage. At the end of the 100 Trades, Carl lost $1,000, and in percentage terms, he achieved a return on the initial capital of -10%.

Always remember that no matter how likely you are to win, if the risk/reward ratio is unfavorable to you, in the long run, the market will be your gambling house and you will be, in spite of yourself, the naive bettor.

The last example makes us understand that the best way to maximize profits in Trading is to do what a real Trader does:

"A Trader looks for the best opportunities on the market, those that guarantee him an excellent Statistical Advantage, operates conservatively by reducing the maximum risk for each operation and imposes a risk/return ratio unbalanced in his favor."

However, returning to the real world, leaving out didactic examples, the application of these simple concepts is quite difficult for beginners. Our nature is human, we are not always logical and often subject to a third silent and intangible component, the psychological component.

The psychological component is a complex mental system that can either help or hinder the Trader.

An expert Trader, who consistently and diligently follows the rules of his Trading System without emotional interference, has the right psychological attitude to be profitable in the long term.

Just like when you learn to drive a car, on paper it is possible to learn the technique, the procedures, the components, the rules, define routes, and know the road signs. All of this certainly provides a basis, but, once sitting in the driver's seat for the first time, you can find yourself agitated, nervous, and in the throes of fear of accidents or hurting someone. Your unconscious kicks in almost unexpectedly and can cause much damage.

With experience, our driving becomes more confident, calm and we know what to do in every single situation. Technically, a novice driver who drives his vehicle at 100 kilometers per hour exposes himself to the same potential risk as an experienced driver would, the driver will make the real difference.

Think of the learning process of Trading in the same way, you are in a potentially dangerous environment and, if you don't know what to do, you risk damaging your wallet. You can study and learn proper risk management, and your newly learned skills will give a first scaling to the level of possible harm. Over time, with the sedimentation of knowledge within you, with the mental automation of some decision-making processes and the security of experience, the risk will once again undergo an enormous reduction. As an experienced motorist can enjoy his car ride, an experienced Trader can enjoy the experience of trading in the market.

In this chapter, we have given a general overview of the three main components of Professional Trading, the "Three Cornerstones" that a Trader must develop to the maximum if he seriously wants to approach this world in a professional way.

Let me summarize them briefly:

1. A Trader must look for market opportunities that, according to his strategy, guarantee a high probability of success and a Statistical Advantage. This is possible by applying a Trading System equipped with appropriate rules;
2. A Trader must always guarantee himself an asymmetrical risk/return ratio biased in his favor. He must also contain losses with the knowledge that the possible gain will be mathematically greater than the risk;
3. A Trader must have an adequate psychological aptitude to allow him to constantly apply the self-imposed rules in the Trading System. This attitude is formed and consolidated with experience and by approaching the markets with the right mindset.

If you apply the Three Cornerstones of Professional Trading, I can assure you that your results will visibly improve in a reasonably short time.

Chapter 2:
Reading Price Charts

What is it that actually moves prices? If the price of a financial instrument didn't move, there would be no graph to read, just a continuous horizontal line that stays constant over time.

Every market has two main participants, the buyers and the sellers. Buyers imagine that prices will tend to grow in the future and therefore wait for the best moment to purchase, which is not necessarily the present moment. Once the purchase has been made, the buyers will hold their open position until they either guarantee themselves a profit or have reached their loss tolerance limit when it comes to selling.

On the other side of the market are the sellers, they imagine that prices will tend to fall in the future, and therefore, they will want to sell today at the current price. With this logic, they want to avoid the decline further affecting the value of their position.

Imagine then that buyers and sellers work and operate as two opposing forces, fighting a battle to the exhaustion in the market, pushing prices in every opposite direction.

When there are more buyers willing to buy at the current price, market prices will tend to react and change. Sellers intent on obtaining greater profits will raise the selling prices of their shares, realizing that the current market demand for that specific financial instrument is growing. The possibility of a greater profit by the sellers will push the prices higher and higher.

Exactly the opposite happens when the sellers are momentarily more than the buyers. In an attempt to get rid of their shares as soon as possible, the sellers will accept to suffer ever-increasing losses. An increasing supply will therefore be created in the market, and a race to the bottom of prices will start. On the opposite side, the buyers, observing a progressive and evident loss of value of the financial instrument, will be late in carrying out their purchase orders. Prices will continue to go down until they are generally considered worthwhile to buy again.

There is only one reason that moves the markets, and that is the simple imbalance between supply and demand, between purchasing power and selling pressure. There is nothing else, there are no tricks, there are no secret intercontinental operations, there is nothing more than the interest of sellers and buyers.

Technical analysis, which allows us to build our Statistical Advantage, is the simple result of elaborating and studying the price graphs created by the imbalance between buying pressure and selling pressure.

In everyday practice, buying and selling decisions are made by human beings when what we want to buy or sell reaches certain price levels or falls at certain chronological moments. The markets have a certain memory, and it often happens that the movement of prices in a graph, the Price Action, settles on price levels considered important in a non-random way. These price levels are called psychological thresholds.

The selling and buying pressures will cause readable and repeatable configurations to be created in the graph, which we call patterns. This characteristic of the market is a major source of our Statistical Advantage.

I want to underline that if we intend to operate as professional Traders, we will not be able to base our operations exclusively on the identification of market patterns, mechanically and without an adequate critical eye.

A Trader takes advantage of the formation of a pattern to search for its meaning, understand what produced it, and understand how the imbalance between supply and demand has caused prices to behave in that particular way. A pattern is a consequence, not a starting point.

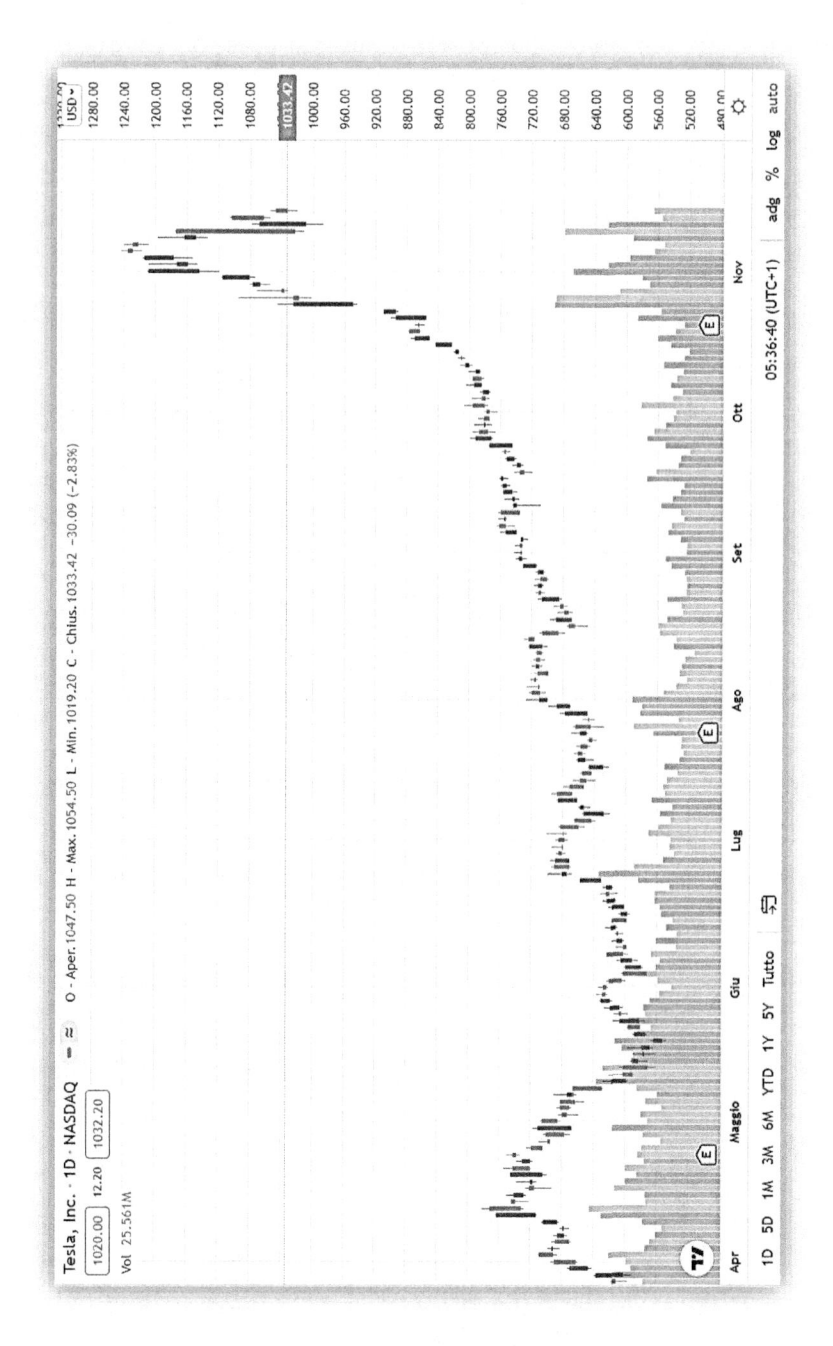

Illustration n.2 – Tesla Inc.Chart

On the previous page, I report a daily candlestick chart of Tesla Inc., extracted from TradingView, depicting the prices from April until November 2021.

Looking at the graph, what information do you think it is providing us? What do you think this graph reflects? What can you tell us about the company and the interest that the market has in it?

A graph brings with it at least three different levels of information.

At the first level, we are aware that the graph is nothing more than a tool that shows us market data in a structured and orderly form. Once the Trader has learned how to read the messages coming from the market, he will be able to understand the psychological tendencies and the imbalance present between buyers and sellers at the specific moment observed.

At the second level, the graph is a map depicting human behaviors and emotions in the market. The map suggests paths to anticipate the behavior of most of the participants.

At the third level, a price chart is a graphical display of the anticipation attempts made by market participants in the near future.

Understanding how price charts can come in handy is important, if not essential, to make the best possible choices.

In order to read a price chart we need certain conditions to be met:

1. <u>The graph must be easy to read.</u> The first thing to do is always to focus on price candles and market structures before anything else;

2. <u>The graph must be simple.</u> When you look at a chart, your intent must be to make it easy to see the price of candles as the first and most important information contained in it. When you want to apply additional chart tools, such as indicators and oscillators, remember that while very useful, they are largely always derivatives of price information. It

is important to avoid adding tools in excessive quantities to prevent them from distracting you from your analyses;

3. <u>The method by which you analyze price charts must demonstrate consistency.</u> Using consistent approaches reduces the time required to navigate between various financial instruments when analyzing a chart. Over time, the Trader develops his mind and his vision to the point of being able, with a quick observation of the price graph, to identify what is really important and what could happen in the near future;

4. <u>The method must be adequate.</u> One of the key skills of a professional Trader is to process and analyze large amounts of data in extremely short periods of time. The Trader consciously makes decisions after evaluating the risks and opportunities that can be deduced from the price chart. Professional Trader finds a combination of elements that fits their specific trading style and works well for them. The way you look at the graph, how you configure and customize it, must be appropriate for you. Many novice Traders think that by simply copying the style of other successful Traders, excellent results can be obtained effortlessly and without attention. Instead, this is one of the most serious mistakes a Trader can commit. The mind of the Trader you would like to copy, like the mind of every other person on earth, is completely different from yours. Different minds lead to different behaviors and decisions, even in all other surrounding conditions.

Initial Tips

Before you start looking at price charts on your own, there are a few tips I would like to give you.

Each graph is a representation of prices made up of a horizontal axis, where the reference time period is indicated, and a vertical axis, where the price scale of the specific financial instrument is shown. Each graph can always be displayed as a line graph or logarithmic graph. If you have opened an account on a trading platform, such as TradingView, you will notice that this possibility is always present. In TradingView, it is found in the lower right corner of the screen. As a basic rule, it is advisable to switch from linear to logarithmic display whenever you are faced with a price increase of at least 100% or when you observe a chart over a period that includes at least two years of price movements. Below are two charts of the same price instrument but with a different scale of representation. The graphs represent the price trend of Tesla over a period of approximately two years.

You will surely notice the big difference, especially on the left side of the graph. At the beginning of 2019 and until January 2020, the path traced by Tesla's prices in illustration n.3, a graph on a linear scale, appears almost horizontal. In 2020, thanks to the well-known market turbulence generated by COVID-19, large movements and large price reversals are observed compared to 2019. The fluctuations subsequently lead to a bull market that is still active.

Instead, observe the graph on a logarithmic scale, 2019 appears anything but flat and the movements that took place in 2020 appear proportionate, even if important. Even the reversal of prices that took place towards the end of August appears much less worrying. The logarithmic scale harmonizes the price variation, normalizing the explosive phases. The effective percentage fluctuation, as the price increases, decreases. This reduction in the percentage return makes the financial instrument much less attractive from the point of view of the expected short-term return, effectively expressing the reduction in volatility.

If the value of an instrument rises from US$100 to US$200 in one day and returns to US$100 the next day, the total can be expressed mathematically as +100 -100 = 0 USD.

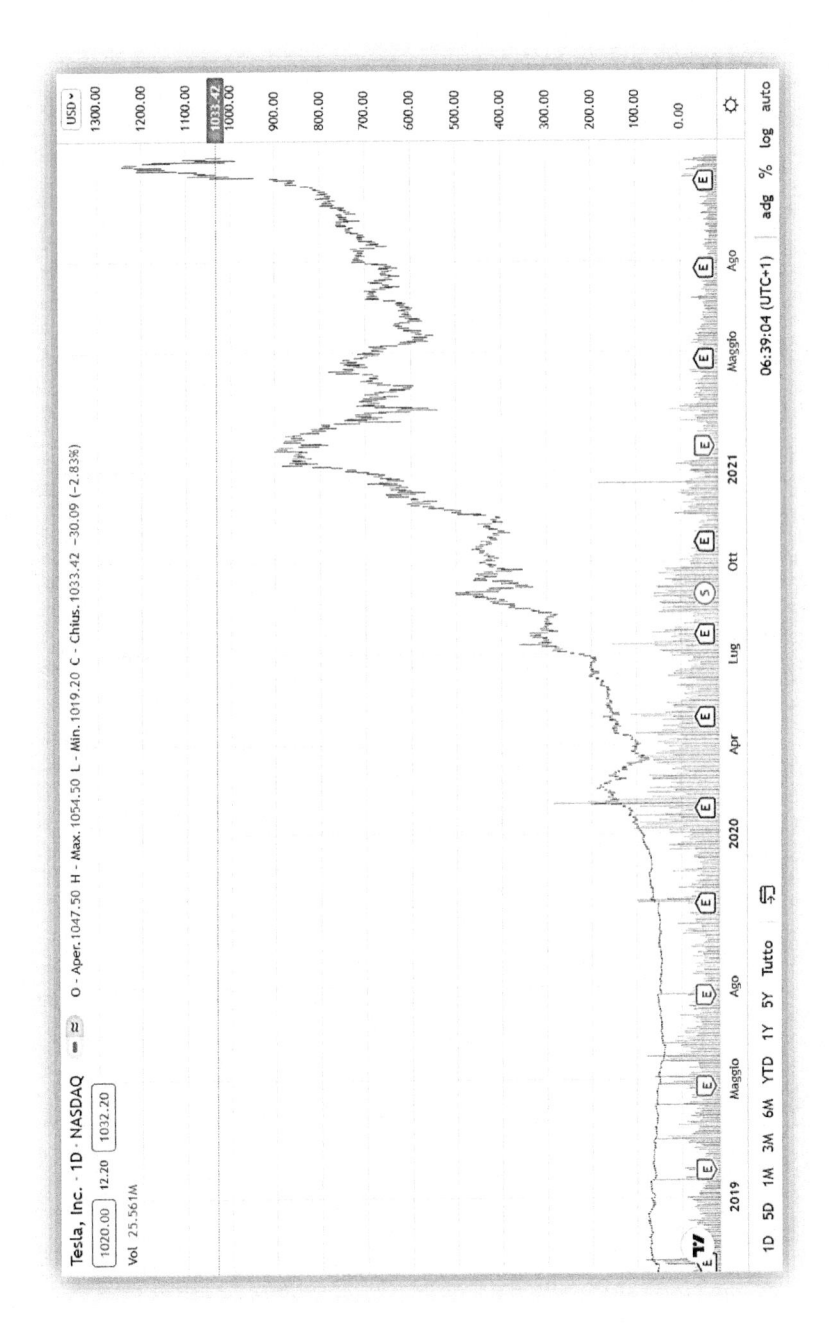

Illustration n.3 – Tesla Inc. chart in linear scale

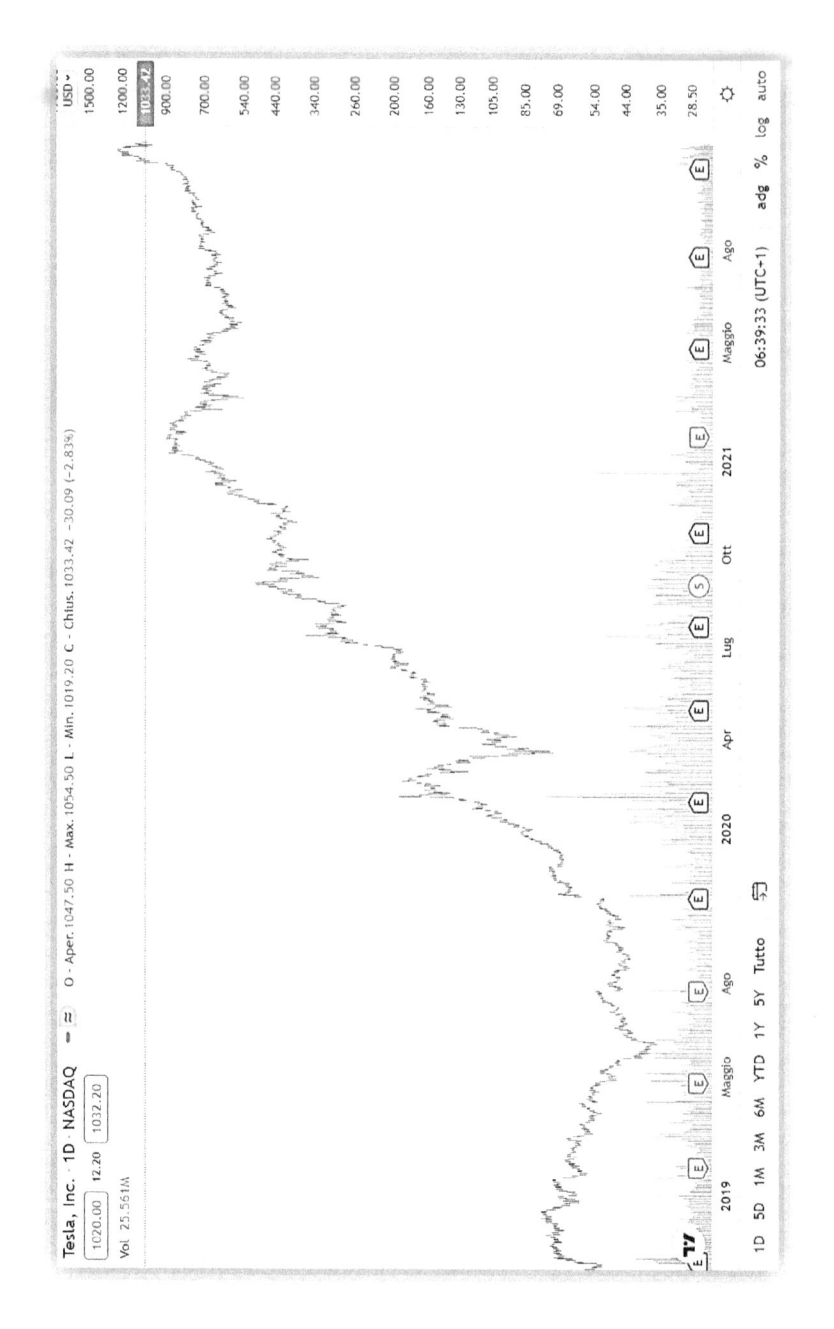

Illustration n.4 – Tesla Inc. graph in logarithmic scale

If the same increase were expressed as a percentage, my financial instrument would rise by 100% on the first day, and the next day it would lose 50% of its value.

If the value of an instrument rises from US$100 to US$200 in one day and returns to US$100 the next day, the total can be expressed mathematically as +100 -100 = 0 USD. If the same increase were expressed as a percentage, my financial instrument would rise by 100% on the first day, and the next day it would lose 50% of its value.

When instead, we find ourselves in the case of a more contained increase in value in relative terms, let's say from 1,000 dollars to 1,100 dollars, the instrument will appreciate by 10% for the same increase, to then reverse the 9.09%. Algebraically nothing has changed, yet the price behavior has changed a lot in the eyes of investors and Traders, who could make very different choices in the two scenarios.

Now let's talk about Time Frame. The possibility of observing different time frames is given to us by any Online Trading platform. Every professional Trader analyzes the price charts observing the various configurations at different time intervals. A good methodology is to observe time frames with a higher time interval to confirm the hypothesis of the formation of a new trend and then go down a level towards shorter range intervals to define an entry or exit point from the market precisely.

In general, different time frames can be correlated to each other with ratios from 3 to 5. If my operation requires, for example, observing the development of prices daily, I could observe a chart with a 4-hour periodicity to carry out my analyses and decisions. After that, with the intention of looking for a good level of detail and identifying the best time to enter the market, I would move my attention towards a graphic representation with hourly or 30-minute candles.

Chapter 3:
Interpreting Japanese Price Candles

In this chapter, you will be explained in a simple and clear way how to read Japanese price candles and, subsequently, we will see some of the most recurring price patterns in Price Action of undoubted utility in the operations of every Trader.

Price charts based on Japanese candlesticks are probably the most famous and widespread in the technical analysis of financial markets.

Classic Japanese candlesticks visually consist of a thin line at the top, called the upper shadow, another thin line at the bottom, called the lower shadow and a central rectangle that we call the body of the candle.

Japanese candles are distinguished by a color that was originally exclusively black or white. Nowadays, it is much more frequent to find the representation with green and red colors.

But what information do candles contain? How do we interpret them? What do they tell us?

Every single candle contains a total of four fundamental price pieces of information and two directly related pieces of information.

Price information:

- o Opening price of the unit of time;
- o Highest price in the unit of time;
- o Lowest price in the unit of time;
- o Closing price of the unit of time.

Related information:

- o The unit of time;
- o Positivity or Negativity.

A candle, therefore, expresses, in the selected time unit, all the information relating to the movement of the price and, at its closure, the data on the positivity or negativity.

The candle is considered positive when the opening price is lower than the closing price, in this case, its representation on the chart will be white or green.

The candle is considered negative when the opening price is higher than the closing price, in this second and last case, its representation on the chart will be black or red.

Below is a representation of Japanese candlesticks:

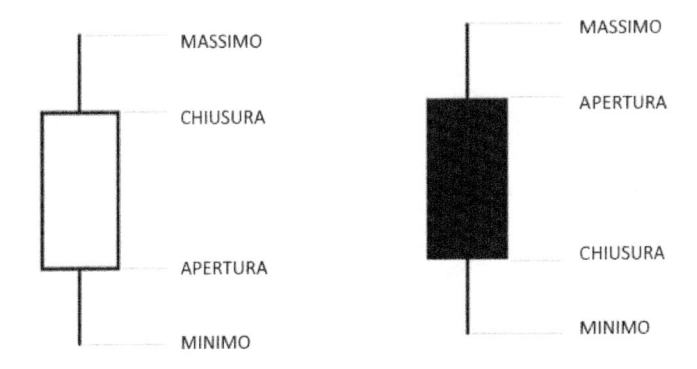

Translation: MAXIMUM – CLOSE – OPEN – MINIMUM.

Illustration n.5 – Representation of Japanese candlesticks

Through this information, anyone can get an idea at a glance of the price movement of a financial instrument in its unit of time.

By observing a price chart, we can also see the variety of different conformations a candle can take, as this basic information varies.

Japanese candlesticks vary in height, body extent, and shadow extent. Also, certain groupings of specific shaped candlesticks define what we call *"Price Patterns"*.

Patterns are not entirely random and often hide a precise indication of the mood of market participants.

Through these patterns, once able to interpret them according to the configuration and market context, we will be able to obtain new information that will contribute to the formation of our personal Statistical Advantage.

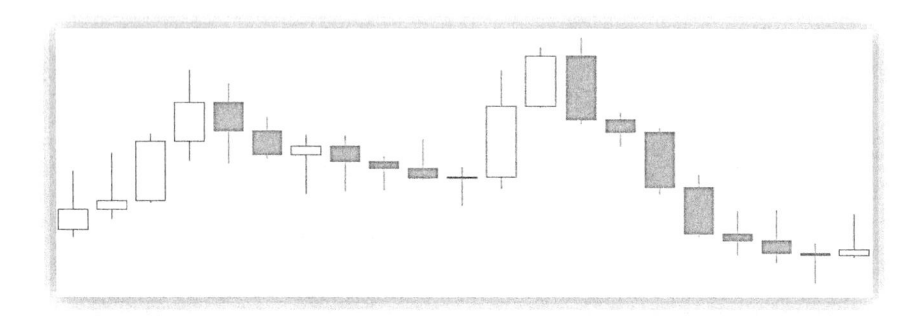

Illustration n.6 – Generic sequence of Japanese candlesticks

In the following pages, I will illustrate six of the most effective Japanese candlestick patterns that a Trader must learn to recognize and use in everyday life. Learning to readily recognize the following patterns will help you increase your chances of setting up a profitable trade.

Bullish Hammer Pattern

This pattern consists of only one candlestick of a particular conformation. It has a generally very small body and is positioned in the upper part. Its upper shadow is very small, if not absent, while the lower shadow is very evident, even twice the extent of the body.

A Hammer is, in fact, a conformation of the candle, but to be more precise the name of Hammer is specific to the candle when positive, vice versa it takes the name of Hanging Man if negative.

The fact that it takes on one color over the other varies little if we talk about patterns. A pattern is not only defined by the conformation of the specific candle but also by its particular position within a chart.

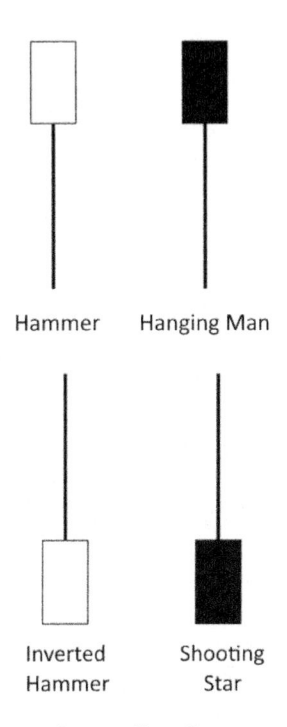

Hammer	Hanging Man
Inverted Hammer	Shooting Star

Illustration n.7 – Four types of reversal candles

Exactly as you imagine, even a single specific candlestick can be relevant to a price chart. This relevance can be explained in that a Bullish Hammer Pattern within a market is an early signal of a potential exhaustion of the selling pressure and, at the same time, it signals that the buying power begins to prevail over the selling pressure and the imminent creation of a potential imbalance in favor of the buyers is underlined.

Both of these signals are considered bullish and indicate that prices are more likely to rise in the near future.

The Bullish Hammer Pattern will give its maximum contribution to the reading of the Price Action when it appears in two specific points of the chart:

- When it forms near a support at the end of a downtrend;
- When it forms near a support level during the uptrend price growth phase.

In the second case, the support can be both static and dynamic. When the support is static, the price level previously tested by the chart can be identified via a horizontal line. When the support is of the dynamic type, it can be identified both by tracing a sloping line and by tracing a curved line from the variable price level, which can be a moving average.

On the following page, I report an example of the formation of this pattern on the Meta Platforms graph, better known as Facebook. In the graph, it is possible to observe the formation of a cycle in the period enclosed between October 2015 and January 2016. In the final phase of the cycle, the formation of a very pronounced bullish hammer, whose shadow rests on a resistance, can be observed.

In the days immediately following, a decisive recovery can be seen.

The subsequent retracement of this recovery did not invalidate the formation of a new uptrend.

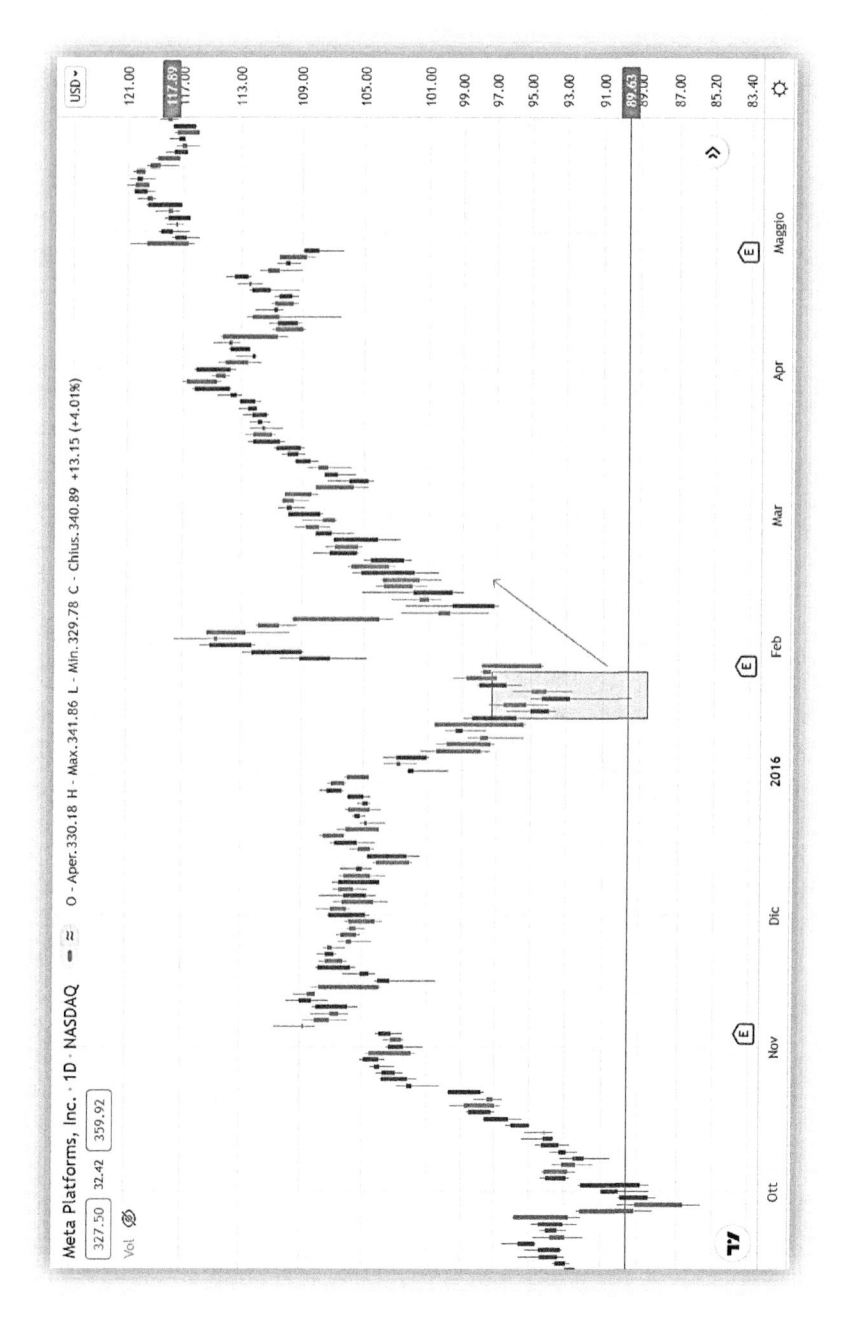

Illustration n.8 – Meta Platform Chart

Bearish Shooting Star Pattern

After introducing the Bullish Hammer Pattern, we must necessarily also deal with its exact opposite, the Bearish Shooting Star Pattern.

This pattern, like the Bullish Hammer Pattern, provides for the formation of a candle characterized by a very small body that is located, unlike what happens for the Hammer and Hanging Man in the lower part of the same. The candlestick can have a very small or no lower shadow and a very pronounced upper shadow.

Once again, candles can have positive or negative connotations and for this reason, they are respectively called Inverted Hammer and Shooting Star.

This type of candle provides the signal for two important situations:

- o The potential depletion of buyers' purchasing power.
- o Selling pressure begins to outweigh demand.

Following the formation of this type of candlestick, it is, therefore, possible that an imbalance in market conditions is created in favor of the sellers since both situations indicated signal the probable fall in prices in the immediate future.

Just like the Hammer Bullish Pattern, the Shooting Star Bearish Pattern will give its maximum contribution to the reading of the price action, thus offering us the best Statistical Advantage when it appears in two specific points of the chart:

- o When it forms near a resistance at the end of an uptrend;
- o When it forms near a static or dynamic resistance level during the price decline phase of the downtrend.

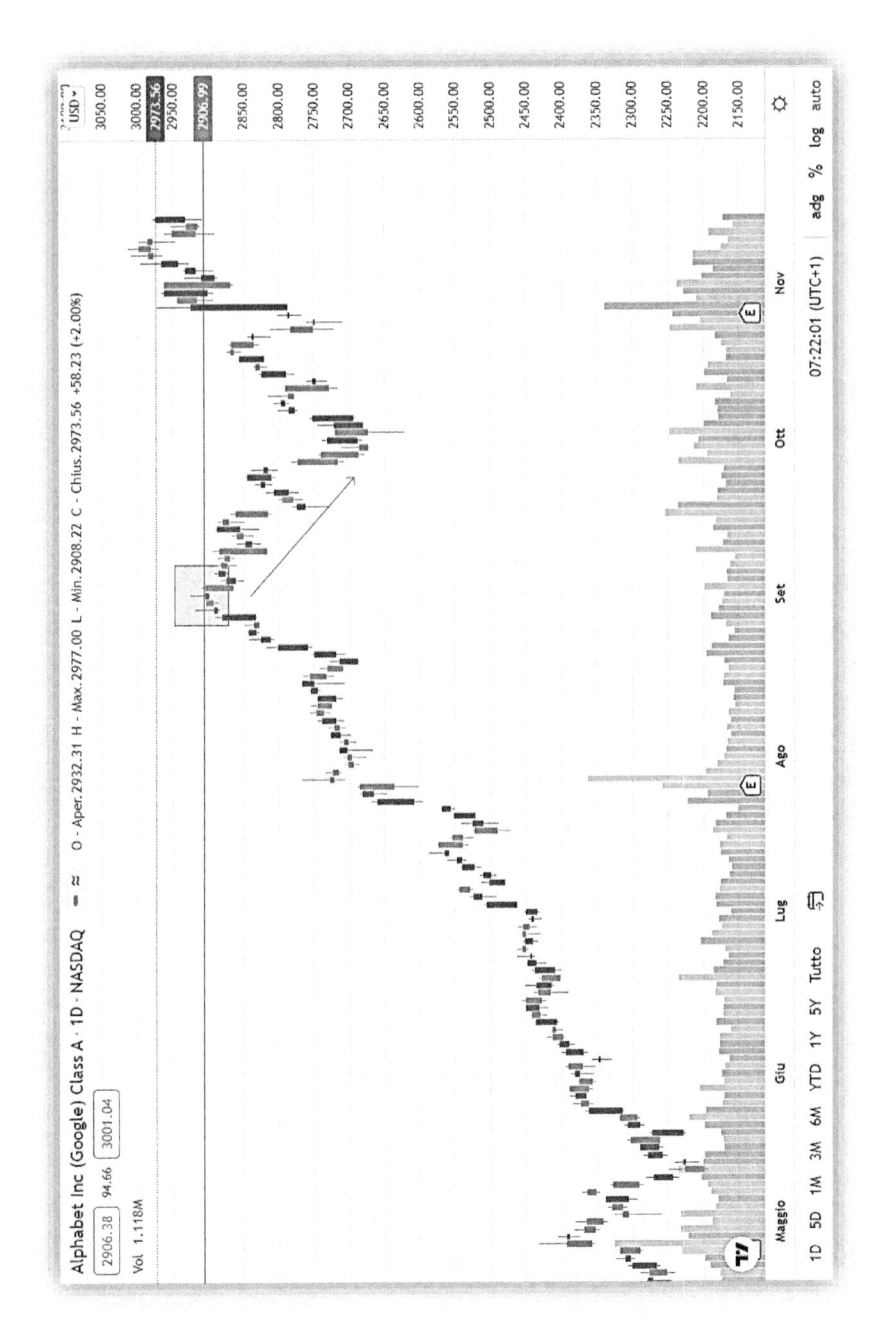

Illustration n.9 –Alphabet Chart

On the previous page, I reported an example of the formation of this pattern on the graph of the Alphabet company, which you will surely know under the name of Google.

In the graph, it is possible to clearly see a bull run that lasted more than three months and stopped in September 2021. On that date, the formation of a bearish Inverted Hammer is observed near a static resistance level.

In the days immediately following, and until the first ten days of October, the market retraced consistently, creating an extension leg comparable to about 33% of the bullish leg to resume its upward run and align with the main trend.

Bullish Engulfing Pattern

The Bullish Engulfing Pattern is a very effective pattern resulting from the combination of two candles, a first small negative candle followed by a second larger positive candle. The peculiarity of the second candle is that of having the body large enough to almost entirely cover the price range of the previous candle with the relative shadows.

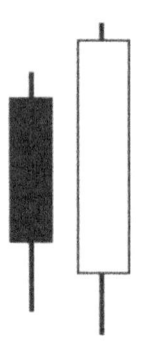

Illustration n.10 – Bullish Engulfing

The formation of this pattern is a signal of the potential exhaustion of the selling pressure and the bullying entry of the buyers into the market.

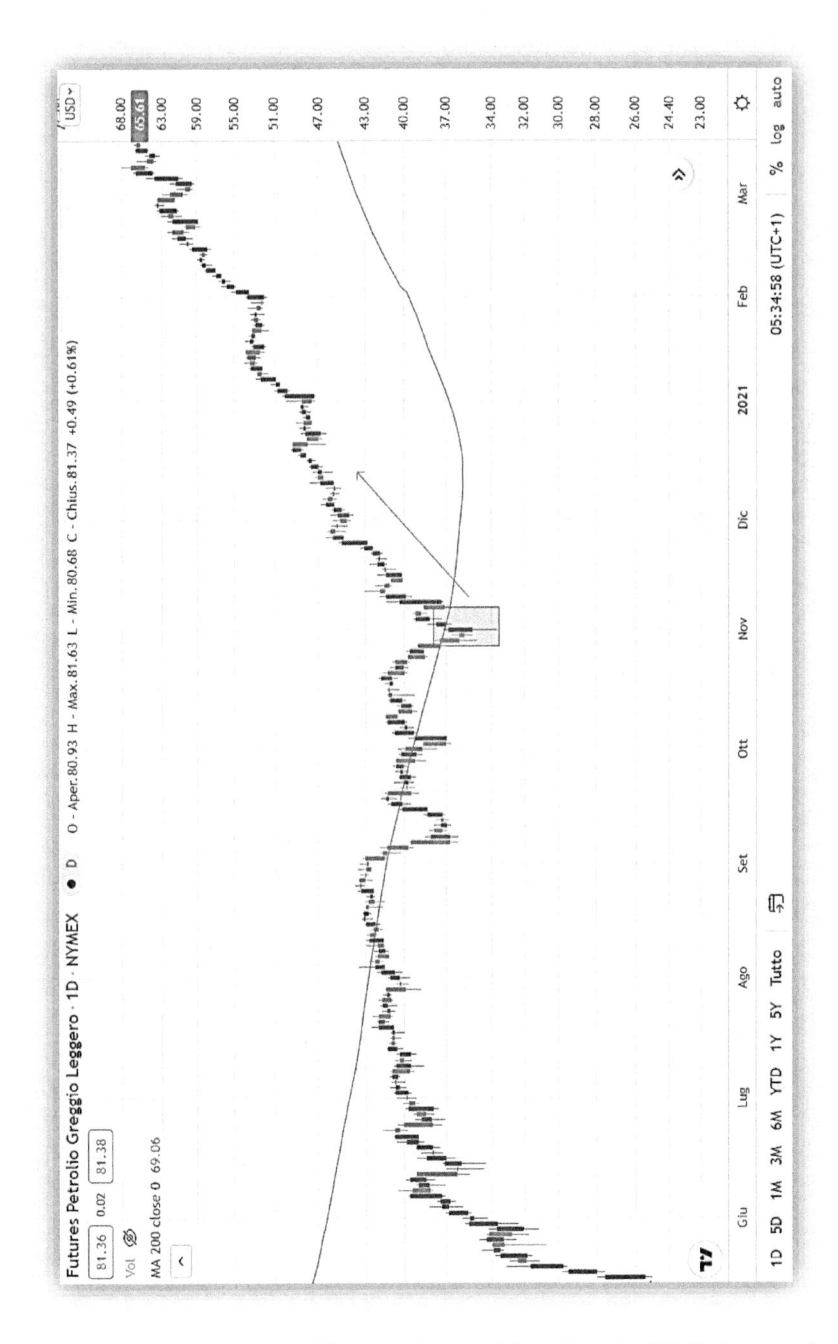

Illustration n.11 – Crude Oil Futures chart

The advent of buyers creates an imbalance in transactions in favor of the buyers themselves and turns the market in the direction of growth.

As result of this strong buying willingness, the price will have a great chance of rising. Below is an example to better clarify the use of this signal.

On the oil futures chart above, this pattern formed in November 2020. In the days following its formation, the price chart exceeded the 200-period moving average, confirming the validity of the signal and starting a new upward push in prices, which lasted almost without interruption until March 2021.

The Bullish Engulfing Pattern will give its maximum contribution to the reading of the Price Action when it appears in two specific points of the graph:

- When it forms near a support at the end of a downtrend;
- When it forms near a static or dynamic support level and precisely at the ascending Lows of an uptrend.

Bearish Engulfing Pattern

The Bearish Engulfing Pattern, the exact opposite of the Bullish Engulfing Pattern, comes from the combination of two candles. A first candle, small and positive, followed by a second candle, negative and large enough to almost entirely cover the price range of the previous candle, with relative shadows.

This pattern indicates the exhaustion of buying pressure from buyers and the increased strength of sellers to apply selling pressure on the market. Prices are being pushed down forcefully, indicating a potential price drop in the near future.

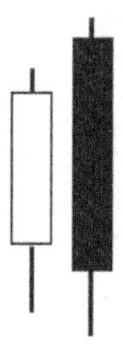

Illustration n.12 – Bearish Engulfing

The Bearish Engulfing Pattern will give its maximum contribution to the reading of the Price Action when it appears in two specific points of the chart:

- o   When it forms near resistance at the end of an uptrend;
- o   When it forms near a static or dynamic resistance level and precisely at the descending Highs points of a downtrend.

Bullish Morning Star Pattern

This pattern consists of three candles in succession having the following characteristics:

- o   The first candle is bearish and very pronounced.
- o   A very small second candlestick of indecision. Can be either positive or negative and has a small body and pronounced shadows. It generally forms near a support level.
- o   The last candle, the most important, of a bullish positive type. With a very pronounced body, this candle closes at least above the half body of the first candle. It defines the pattern in its formation.

The Bullish Morning Star Pattern is considered to be the best bullish reversal pattern. It generally provides a reliable signal when it forms near important support levels at the end of a bear market.

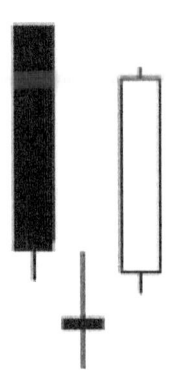

Illustration n.13 – Bullish Morning Star

On the Morningstar chart, it is possible to observe a retracement that pushes prices to lean against the resistance of $215. Taking a closer look at the price rebound, we can see the formation of the Bullish Morning Star, which suggests the generalized intention to push prices upwards.

Being able to promptly recognize the formation of this price pattern on the chart, close to a well-defined support level, will give you the right start for your new long operation, with the certainty of relying on one of the best existing signals in the technical analysis of financial markets.

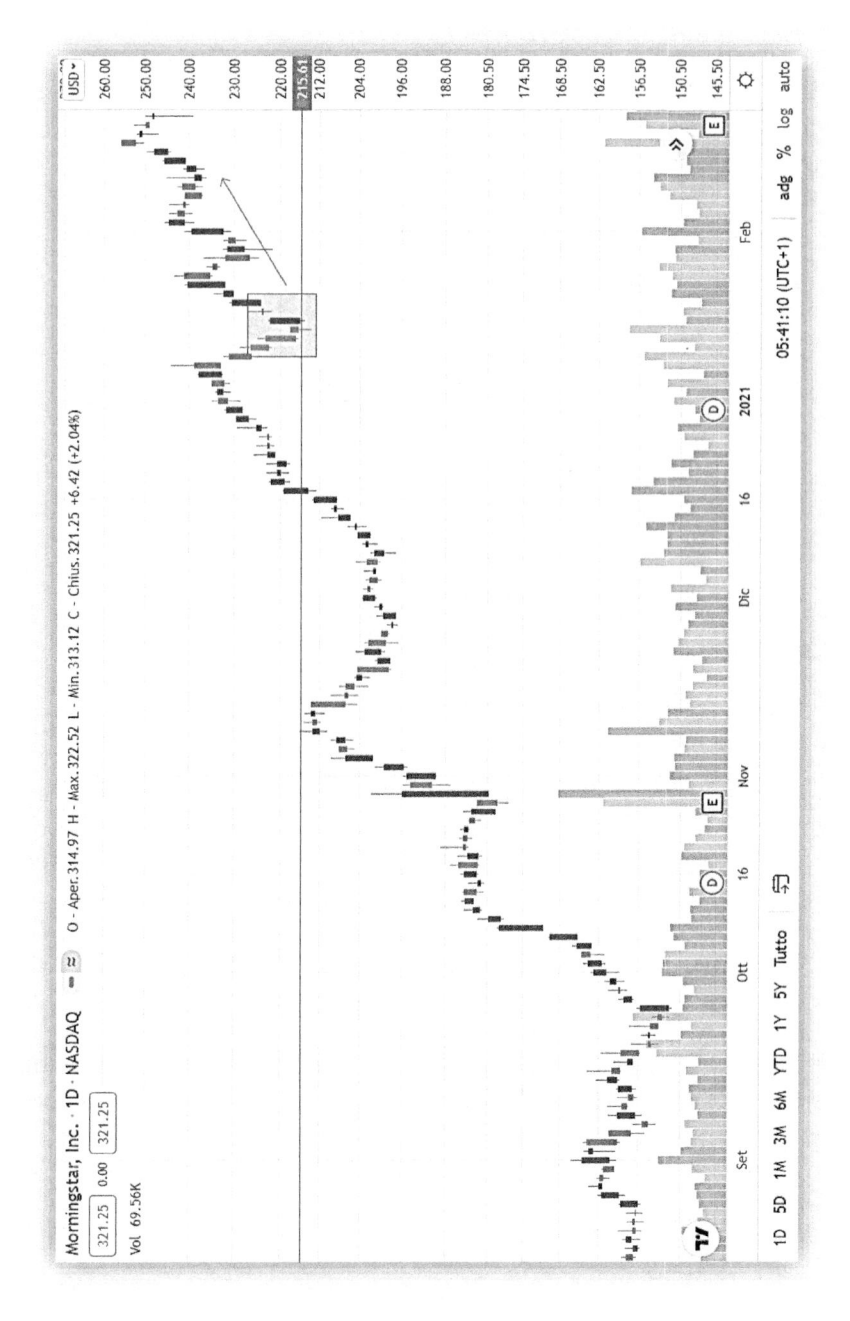

Illustration n.14 –Morningstar Inc. Graphic year 2021

Bearish Evening Star Pattern

At the opposite end of the Bullish Morning Star Pattern, also formed by three consecutive candles, is the Bearish Evening Star Pattern.

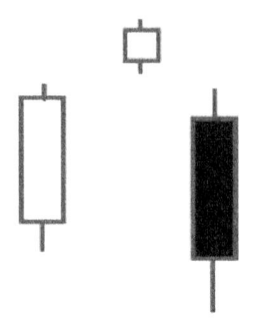

Illustration n.15 – Bearish Evening Star

This pattern consists of three candles in succession having the following characteristics:

- o The first candle encloses a good price range with an uptrend.
- o A very small second candlestick of indecision, which can be both positive and negative, with a small body and pronounced shadows. It generally forms near a price resistance level.
- o The last candle, with a negative and bearish character. With a very pronounced body, this candle closes at least below the half body of the first candle.

The Bearish Evening Star Pattern is considered to be the best bearish reversal pattern. It provides a reliable signal when it forms near important resistance levels at the end of a bull market.

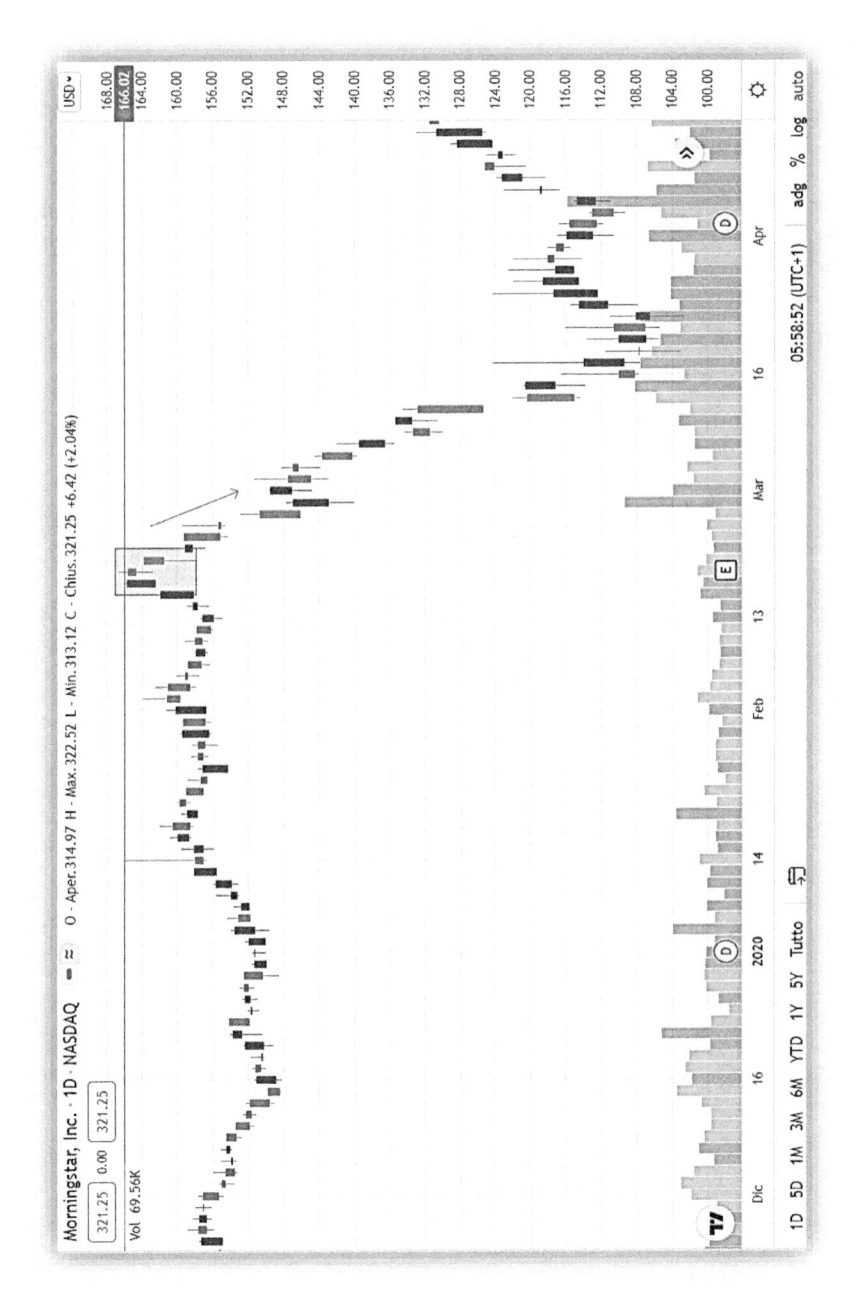

Illustration n.16 –Morningstar Inc Chart year 2020

Not being able to dwell too much on this kind of detailed explanation of further patterns, I trust that you have now understood how it is possible to interpret the meaning of the single candle within a broader context of price fluctuations.

However, I urge you to learn more about reading and interpreting Japanese candlesticks and other price patterns on your own.

In the next chapter, we will address together some advanced chart reading techniques, which include the use of moving averages and the correct identification of supports and resistances.

Chapter 4:
Correctly Identify Supports and Resistance

In the chapter you are about to study, we will discuss the concepts of price support and resistance and how, in any market, it is possible to identify these important price levels.

The ability to know how to identify supports and resistances on the chart is among the most important that a professional Trader must acquire.

Through the simple identification of these price levels, which will be of great help in validating price patterns, you will, more than anything else, realize how knowledge of these dynamics becomes a fundamental tool in the risk management phase.

So let's start with the basics, asking ourselves the right questions.

What is a support? What is a resistance?

The first thing we need to understand is what, inside the chart, we call Peak Point, Pivot Point or Reversal Point. They are in fact the basic levels of the market structure and can be divided into Pivot Highs and Pivot Lows or alternatively referred to as Swing Highs and Swing Lows.

A Swing High, which we can call a relative maximum point, is observed when the maximum price reached by a candle is higher than both the high of the candle that precedes it and the high of the candle that follows it. Buyers observe the maximum price level beyond which acquiring further market shares is not perceived as sufficiently attractive.

On the opposite side, a Swing Low, which we can call a relative minimum point with the same logic, exhibits the same concept. It is observed when the minimum price reached by a candle is lower than both the minimum of the candle that precedes it and the minimum of the candle that follows it. The sellers have reached the minimum price level beyond which there are no longer enough numbers to generate further downward pressure.

Now we will see how these characteristics of the reversal points can be useful for carrying out our analysis of the specific financial instrument.

In the Amazon daily price candlestick chart, it is possible to observe how some specific low swing points are generated on an almost regular basis, identified by me with a rectangle to make it easier to read. By joining these relative minimum points with a horizontal line, we find that this important price level currently performs the function of support. Looking at the chart further back, in March 2021, we note how the same price level had assumed a resistance function.

We can see that, around this price level, there is a lot of trading activity. When price candles get close to it, they often tend to be rejected.

In the light of what has been observed, a great way to look for potential price support or resistance lines will obviously be to connect several swing lows or swing highs formed in a specific market during a given period of time.

One of the key benefits of studying the support and resistance levels of a financial instrument is the help they can give us in identifying particular configurations of possible downward or upward breakouts in prices in the near future.

For example, if we had identified the resistance level already in March 2021 on the Amazon chart, we could have concentrated on finding a possible upward break, which then occurred in April. As you can see, once the upward breakout has taken place, prices rise with decisive force.

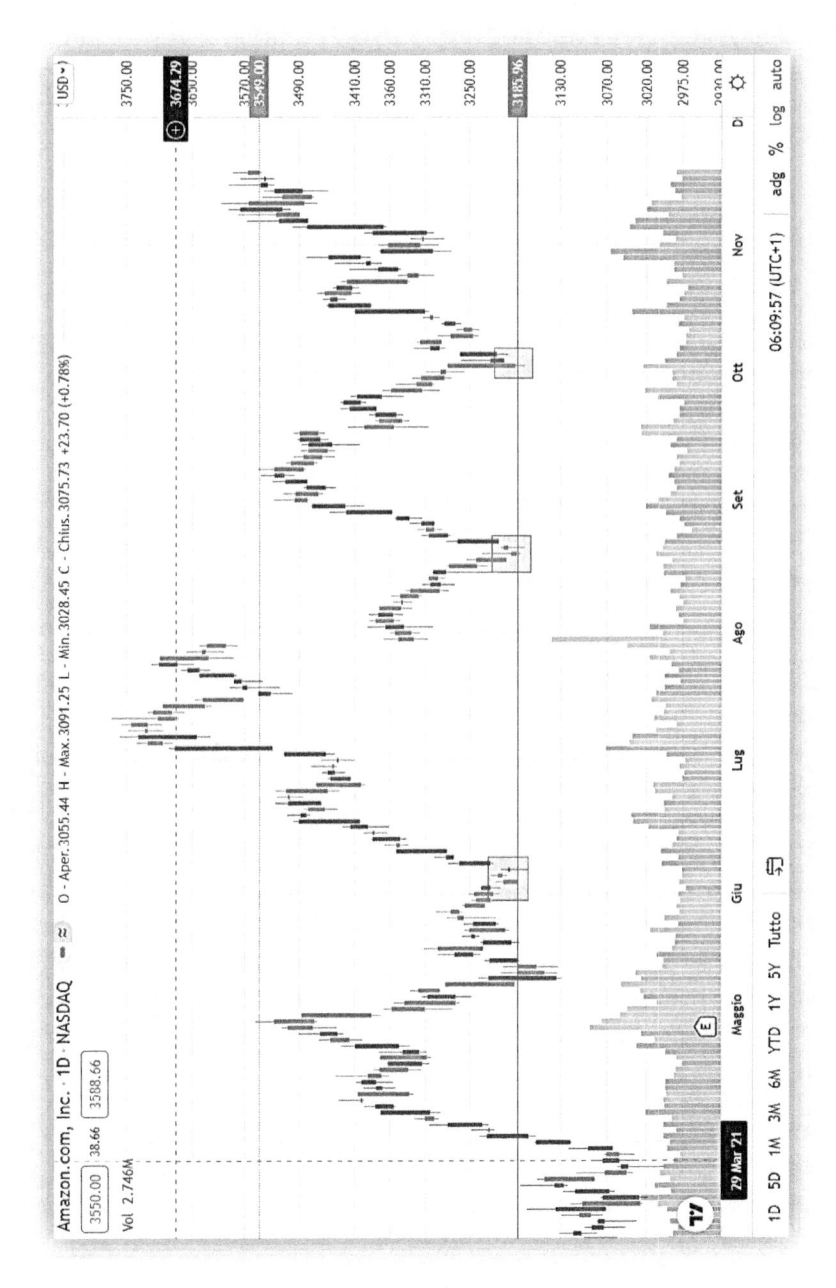

Illustration n.17 –Amazon.com Chart

Obviously, it is not enough to go beyond a price level to configure an upward breakout, but these movements must always be reflected in the traded volume of the specific session. A price breakout, confirmed by growing volumes, can be an excellent entry signal.

Let's take a look at a chart of the Euro/British Pound currency exchange, whose symbol is EUR/GBP.

We can count at least eight Swing Low points, six of which you find appropriately highlighted as being more significant.

These relative minimum points are consecutively decreasing as, from time to time, they reach new minimum price levels. By connecting at least two of the points, typically the most recent and the most distant, or only the two most recent, with a straight line, its effectiveness must then be verified by matching it with other inversion points.

When this happens, we have defined a descending dynamic support on the chart of the specific financial instrument. We, therefore, have evidence of how prices are structured and how they follow a downward but regular trend.

Therefore, from the EUR/GBP chart, it is possible to draw a hypothesis, far from risky, to expect a decisive rebound in prices whenever the candles approach this trend line. The upward bounce will generally be short-lived, as it is only necessary to provide new energy for the downward thrust. It is also likely to expect, in the short term, the achievement of a new and lower relative minimum point.

Remember that we are essentially talking about probabilities, therefore, the mere fact that prices have moved in a certain way in the past does not generate certainty of the movement in the future.

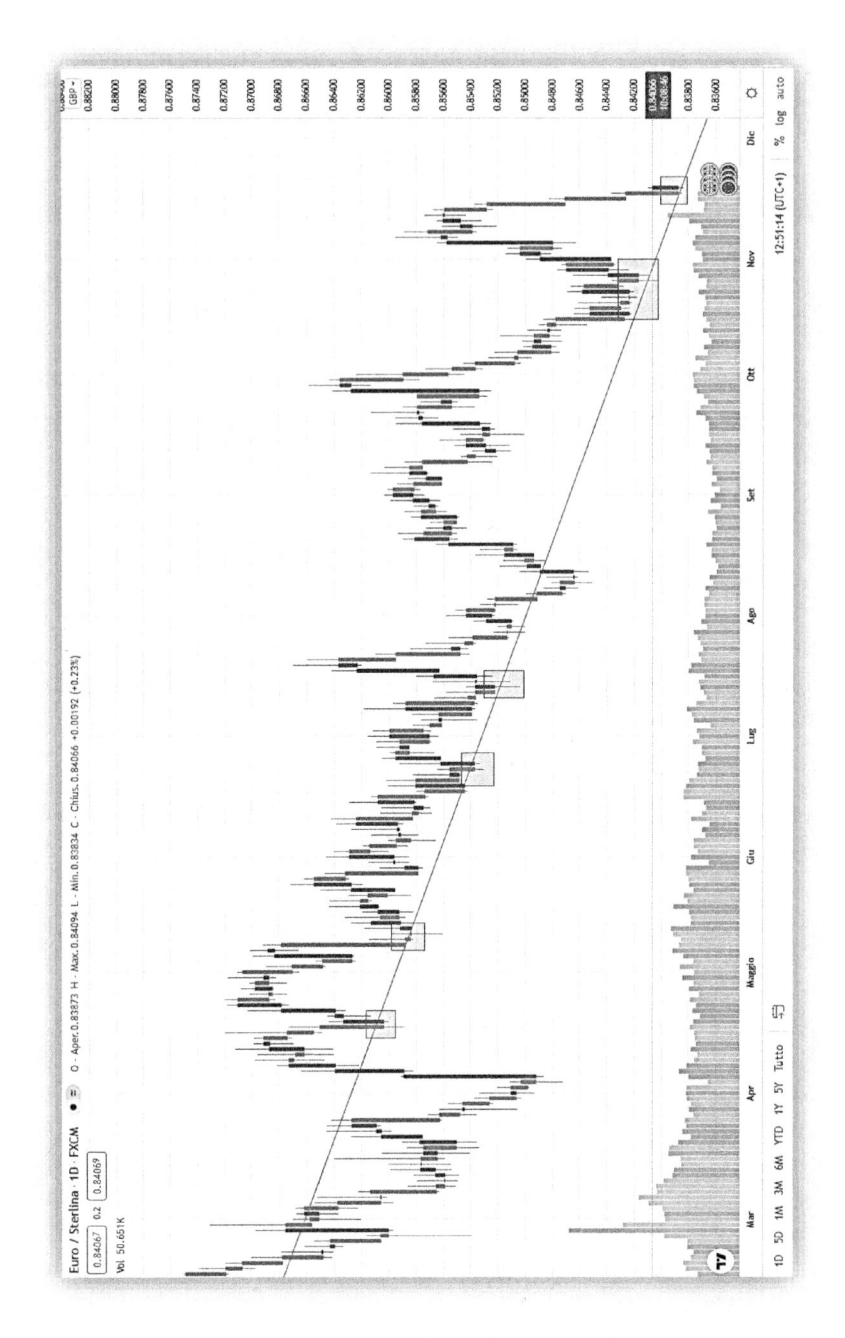

Illustration n.18 – Euro/British Pound Chart

A support, in light of what has been observed so far, is a price level on which a sufficient amount of market demand is concentrated and, for this reason, has the potential to interrupt a downward movement and bounce prices upwards.

Previously I expressed the concept that the market is nothing more than the result of the imbalance between purchasing power and selling pressure, for this assumption when it turns downwards, it will progressively attract more buyers.

When prices are deemed low enough, the group of buyers will be persuaded to purchase all the sell orders present at that given moment, also agreeing to pay a higher price for the same security, effectively starting a new phase of positive market imbalance.

So the price, even though it is heading towards a descending trend, will behave as if it hit a floor, bouncing upwards.

In an uptrend market characterized by successive higher highs and higher lows, the uptrend support line can be constructed by connecting at least three high lows with a straight line.

As for support, in similar conditions we could find a series of swing highs that, properly connected, could make us identify a static or dynamic resistance line to evaluate possible strategies and opportunities.

A resistance line, or simply resistance, is a price level at which strong selling pressure in market shares builds up, caused by a large number of sellers. For this reason, a resistance has the potential to interrupt a bullish movement.

We, therefore, understand that a resistance line is nothing more than a supply line, where sellers wait. As prices rise, sellers' desire to liquidate increases and, at a certain point, the selling pressure exceeds the buying power of the buyers, satisfying all the unexpressed demand in the market and creating a significant imbalance between the buying and selling. The selling pressure will be so high that we can see a downward bounce on the chart as if prices had hit a ceiling.

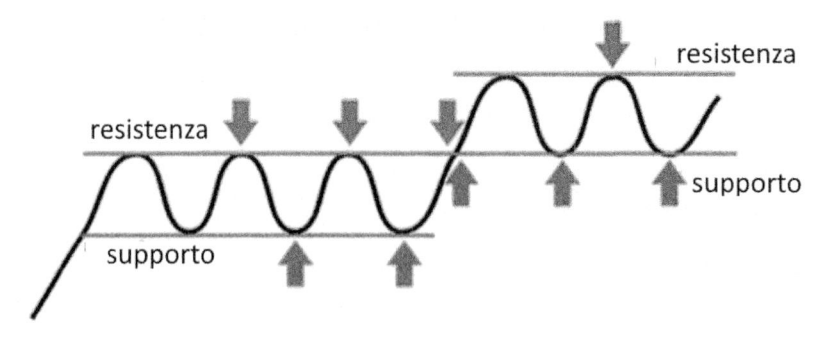

Translation: Resistance – support

Illustration n.19– Schematization of the alternation between supports and resistances

I would like to underline that a trendline is a special type of support or resistance line that is often used by Traders who prefer the trend following approach, i.e., a particular type of Trading focused on price movements characterized by marked directionality.

Traders of this type use trend lines to analyze and visualize the structure of the markets.

It is common practice for professional Traders to use support and resistance levels to help identify an ideal entry point, to correctly define the Stop Loss level, and consequently, to define the respective profit objective imposed by their strategy.

In a downtrend market characterized by successive highs and lower lows, the downtrend resistance line can be constructed by connecting at least three lower highs with a straight line.

If the market is in an uptrend, we will focus our attention more on support lines while, of course, when the market goes down we will pay more attention to the resistance lines.

In light of the above, you will now have to impress upon your mind the following very important assumptions:

"Once a resistance level has been breached to the upside by the price action, it will become potential support."

"Once a support level has been breached to the downside by price action, it will become a potential resistance."

This peculiarity of support and resistance is generated due to the behavior that market participants adopt around these specific price levels.

When approaching a resistance line, with the expectation of liquidating their shares, many Traders will enter sell orders or, if they do not have market shares, they could try to carry out short-type operations, entering short sell orders.

With this way of operating, a Trader hypothesizes that a downward retracement could occur, with a fair probability, caused precisely by the rejection of prices near the resistance line.

Unfortunately, and fortunately, prices do not always behave in such a predictable way and fail to respect the barrier provided by the resistance.

This sudden upward action of prices, beyond the resistance level, is called an upward break, and in the jargon, it is called a breakout.

All market participants will see a reversal of their forecasts. Traders eager to liquidate their positions will be eating their hands with the thought of having sold their shares too early, while those who were positioned short will be executed at a loss, in the best case scenario, if they have taken the time to set a Stop Loss.

Beyond that, the total amount of market shares continue to be important, even above the resistance level, thus increasing the demand for an increasingly popular financial instrument.

After the first upward momentum of prices, they generally retrace downwards reaching resistance again and giving rise to the rebound phenomenon, very often called Pullback.

Traders initially positioned short, who have not yet closed their operation due to absence or high distance from their Stop Loss, will have to make a choice to find themselves approximately in the breakeven condition, i.e., in breakeven with the price paid for the market shares upon entry. When the price gets close enough to resistance, they will close their positions at breakeven or cover their sell position by buying back the financial instrument again, to proceed in the opposite direction. This buying logic will strengthen the power of the former resistance, turning it into support.

This inverted imbalance, caused by the transition from high selling pressure to high buying pressure, generates the change of nature of the resistance line into a support line.

I would advise a novice Trader to pay close attention when observing this kind of transition scenario. Both because it constitutes a possible risk and because it can constitute a great profit opportunity.

With experience, this feature of the market can be easily exploited in your favor, and could make a difference in your performance.

Some quick tips:

- Support and resistance lines must connect a minimum number of three pivot points to be considered reliable;
- More recent Pivot points matter more than later ones;
- In connecting the maximum number of Pivot points, try to identify a line that connects them by minimizing the number of candlesticks cut by it;
- The best support and resistance lines are the most obvious and clearly verifiable ones, therefore avoid forcing their creation;
- Looking at charts with higher periodicity, such as daily or four-hour time frames, helps reduce market noise and allows you to draw resistances and supports more easily thanks to a clearer structure of the market;

- Using the linear graph, allows you to observe the daily closures in a cleaner way, and therefore allows an easier identification of the Pivot points.

By making adequate use of supports and resistances, it is possible to recognize some simple configurations of action.

Whenever prices approach support and resistance levels, two potential scenarios can be envisaged: a retest of the line, followed by a rebound in the opposite direction, or a breakout of the price level with the acceleration of Momentum.

Therefore the two possible scenarios, linked to the two possible conditions of support and resistance, offer a total of 4 possibilities of action to be analyzed:

- In case of Test of Support, when prices bounce upwards, the probability of being successful with a Long Buy Trade will be higher;
- In the event of failure to Test the support, with prices breaking downwards with a growing Momentum, a condition of possible bearish breakout is generated, therefore the most sensible choice is to evaluate a short-type Trade for sale;
- In case of Test of resistance, when the prices bounce down, the probability of succeeding with a short Sell Trade will be higher;
- In the event of failure to Test the resistance, with prices breaking upwards with a growing Momentum, a condition of possible bullish breakout is generated, therefore the most sensible choice is to evaluate a long-type Trade in purchase.

These simple suggestions can help you observe the price configurations generated in the market with a more critical eye.

Remember that, however, the ability to correctly identify supports and resistances is perhaps the most important of the basic knowledge that a novice Trader must acquire.

When trading with real money and on moving price charts, it is obvious that making trading decisions solely on support or resistance may not be enough to have an adequate advantage, as these considerations are never so crystal clear and linear.

Since whenever we make decisions that involve the use of our resources, we cannot afford to act with too much uncertainty, in the following chapters, I will show you other notions useful for increasing your Statistical Advantage. Once these notions have been properly combined with the knowledge of the market structure, defined through the recognition of supports and resistances, these will be an additional cause of a significant improvement in your overall performance.

Chapter 5:
How to Use Moving Averages

In this chapter, we will deal with moving averages, what they are, and how they can be useful for looking for particularly profitable price configurations.

Despite being a novice in this fascinating world of Trading, you have probably noticed that, in some price charts, curved lines are shown near the price candles, which tend to move in a manner consistent with the price trend. These curved lines are called moving averages and are widely used by all professional Traders who operate on the market with a trend following approach.

A moving average is, to all intents and purposes, an average of price values, which consolidates at regular intervals in accordance with the periodicity defined by the specific graph.

It, therefore, determines the average value of the prices and reports it on the graph by progressively drawing a curved line that represents the fluctuation of the price value calculated over a specific time interval chosen by the Trader.

In the event of sudden price changes, when a moving average is present on the chart, it is not rare to be able to find that the distance between the latter and the price candles diverges.

The moving average always represents the movement of prices, but it will be a more softened and less marked representation by its construction. This peculiarity will be all the more evident with the expansion of the time interval at the basis of its calculation.

Moving averages are among the tools most used by Traders precisely because of their disarming simplicity of understanding and their logic of use.

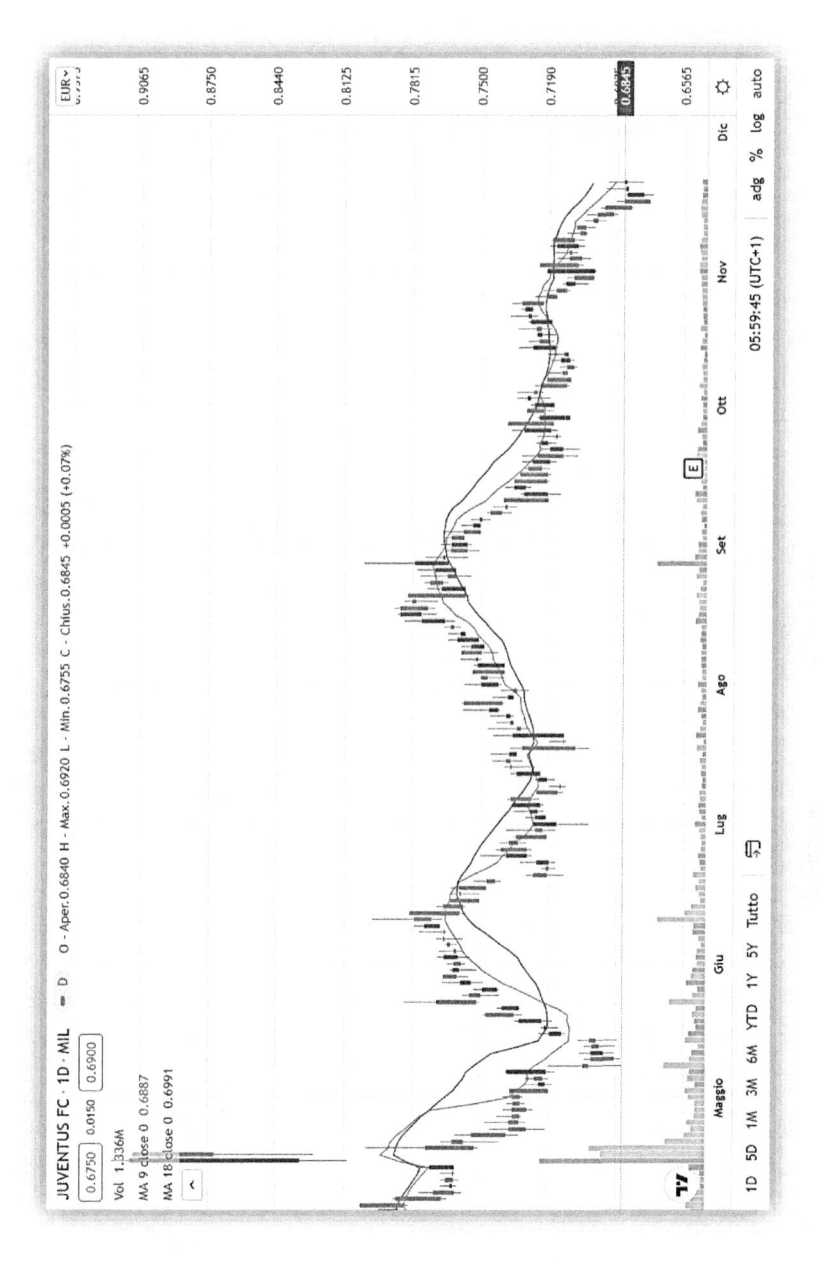

Illustration n.20– Juventus Football Club Chart for the year 2021 with moving averages

Like most of the tools available to technical analysts, moving averages can be constructed by having a series of price data, which is called the number of periods.

On a chart like the one shown above for Juventus, with a time frame of daily candlesticks, two moving averages of different periodicity were applied, respectively for 9 periods and 18 periods.

The first of the two moving averages will then be calculated as the average of the closing prices of the last 9 Japanese candles, and similarly, the second will be calculated on the basis of the last 18 candles.

The choice of the calculation period of the technical indicators is strictly linked to the preferences of the Trader and his strategies. Obviously, there are more significant periodicities linked to the greater use on a global scale, which will give rise to averages with more reliable signals than totally arbitrary values.

To clarify this concept, a Trader who used an average of 200 daily periods would make a sensible choice as it is among the most frequently used periods in the search for long-term trends. Conversely, a Trader who applies an average calculated over 239 periods to his chart would make a less significant and effective choice due to the lower frequency of use on a global scale.

Each moving average period could potentially represent a specific psychological level in the market. This last sentence hides an important notion, which can be better understood by looking at the Bitcoin price chart that I have prepared for you.

On the Bitcoin daily candlestick chart, you can observe how it has applied three distinct moving averages, differentiated only in the considered periodicity. The most jagged moving average, calculated over 5 periods, follows the price very closely and therefore reacts to market fluctuations very quickly.

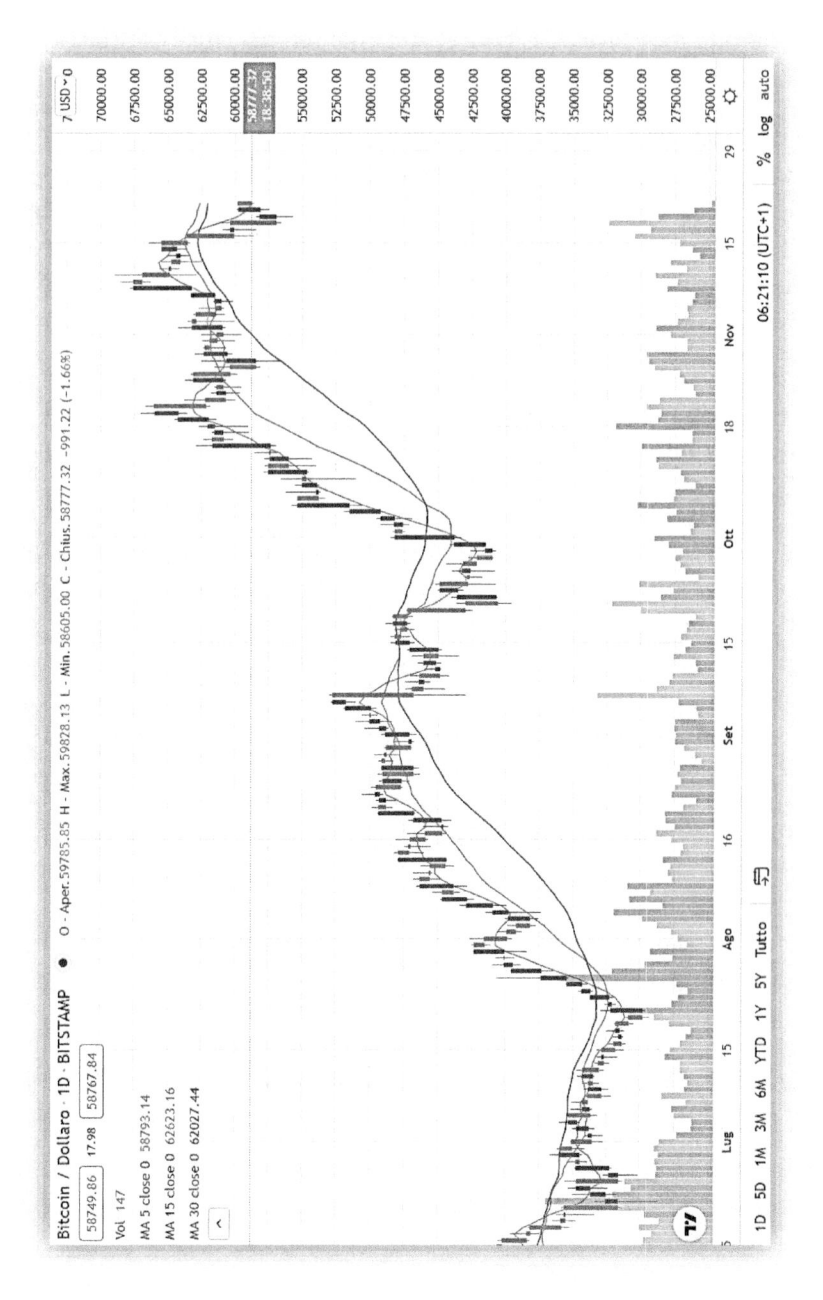

Illustration n.21– Bitcoin year 2021 chart with moving averages

A moving average of this type is useful for capturing the momentum of a financial instrument.

The second line, which deviates slightly from the price chart, is calculated over 15 periods. This second line, as can be seen at a glance, does not immediately follow the price, but in some points, as happened, for example, at the beginning of August and around August 20th, the price candles get close enough to give the impression that it acts as a dynamic support.

The third and last average, the most distant from the price candles, has been calculated on a basis of 30 periods, this means that the average price represented is calculated taking into account all the closing prices of the candles formed in the last thirty days.

It is evident that, even in the presence of significant price movements, the responsiveness of the third average is visually limited compared to the two previously mentioned averages. Yet, despite its limited reactivity, around July 20th, we can observe that the price movement rises above it, suggesting a potential bullish phase. This hypothesis is further supported by the upward crossovers generated by the two faster averages.

Therefore, in July, if we had applied these considerations, we would have been spectators of an interesting configuration for an excellent purchase entry and, with adequate patience, this operation would have ended around September 7, with the passage of the price candles below of the 30-period average and the closing of the first bullish leg.

In general, therefore, there is the possibility of building moving averages commonly used by Traders, which adapt to specific usage logics precisely due to their frequency.

Number of Periods	Usage Logic
Average of the 5 periods	Can identify a Strong Momentum of prices
Average of 10 periods	Can identify a Very Short-term Trend
Average of 20 periods	Can identify Short-term Price Rebounds.
Average of the 50 period	Can be considered a Good Dynamic Resistance or Support
Average of the 200 period	Can Pinpoint the Boundary between Bull and Bear Markets

There are also many different types of moving averages, the construction of which depends on the different calculation methods and not exclusively on the number of periods.

The most used moving averages in technical analysis are the simple moving average, indicated by the acronym SMA - Simple Moving Average, and the exponential moving average, also indicated by the acronym EMA - Exponential Moving Average.

The simple moving average is calculated in a basic way, adding up all the closing values of the price candles falling within the reference period and dividing the result by the number of periods. With the appearance of a new candle, this will enter as the last closing value and the furthest, chronologically speaking, will be excluded from the calculation.

The exponential moving average is calculated in a more complex way. A specific weight is associated with each closing value of the prices falling within the period considered, therefore more recent values, chronologically speaking, will have greater prominence in determining the result than values more distant in time.

I will not go into the details of the formula as, for the purposes of this basic discussion, knowing the exact formula of an indicator, whatever it is, is not an essential fact, although it can be important cultural information for a Trader.

Just know that any Online Trading platform allows you to trace a moving average, calculating it in total discretion, quickly and effectively.

In *illustration #22* below, two moving averages that clearly cut the price chart have been constructed. The first moving average, with a sub-horizontal trend, is a simple moving average, while the second average, clearly more reactive, is an exponential moving average.

Both of these curves are calculated on the basis of the daily closing value and over a total of 200 periods.

The greater sensitivity to price changes can be a determining factor for the choice of the EMA over the SMA, the flip side of which is given by the greater vulnerability to volatility and market fluctuations.

In general, when doing longer-term trading, if you want to reduce the possibility of being kicked out of the market, it is advisable to use simple moving averages, moreover the latter are indicated for longer periods, such as 100 or 200 periods.

In carrying out our technical analysis of a financial instrument, moving averages can really offer a simple and effective help to identify the presence of a trend or the absence of the latter.

The confirmation of the market's uptrend can occur by observing the formation of price candles above a specific chosen moving average or, in the presence of multiple moving averages, with additional confirmation provided by the short-term moving average crossing above the long-term moving average.

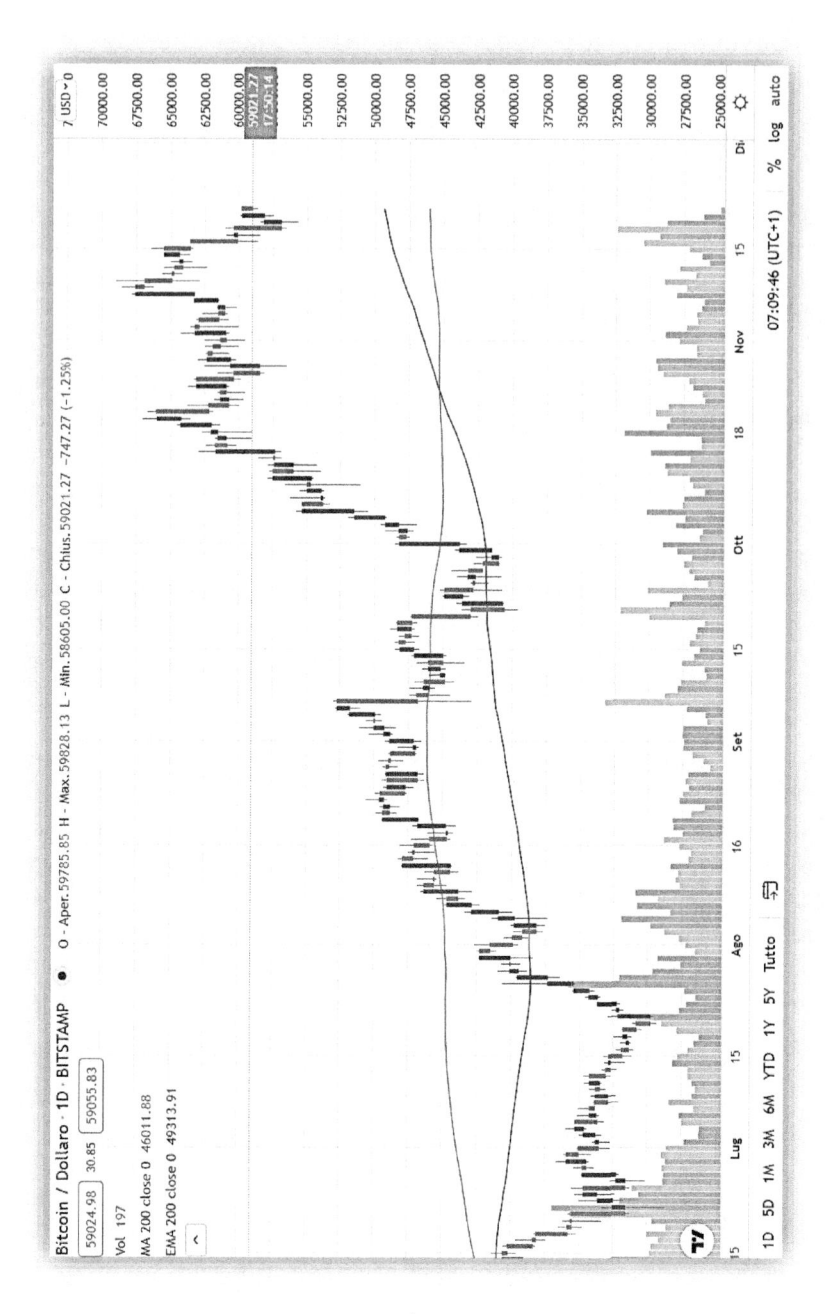

Illustration n.22– Bitcoin year 2021 chart with moving averages

The Bitcoin chart just reported already makes the idea of this characteristic remarkably good, but for greater clarity, I report a new chart of the S&P 500 index, as it is a markedly directional market.

In the chart of the S&P 500 index, which I report with a time window extended to the whole of 2021, albeit with a swinging motion, it is clearly seen that prices have always had an upward trend.

The first of the moving averages, built over 20 periods, is crossed several times by the price chart, both downwards and upwards, yet for most of its run, it lies below the price candles, maintaining an increasing trend.

The second average, built over 50 periods, has almost exclusively an increasing character and only occasionally sees prices violate it downwards. Note how it is much more frequent that the Price Action of the financial instrument finds in it a dynamic support to bounce upwards.

The third and final moving average was built over 100 periods. With a very regular conformation, this average confirms that the year 2021 was persistently in the bull market phase, and only in the last quarter did the price trend undergo an important retracement.

In October, the values of the 100-period average, acting as long-term dynamic support, gave a new upward push to the market, allowing us to observe new historical highs.

It is, therefore, easy to deduce, based on this simple reasoning, that in 2021 the market represented by the S&P 500 index was momentarily going through a phase of good health and sustainability.

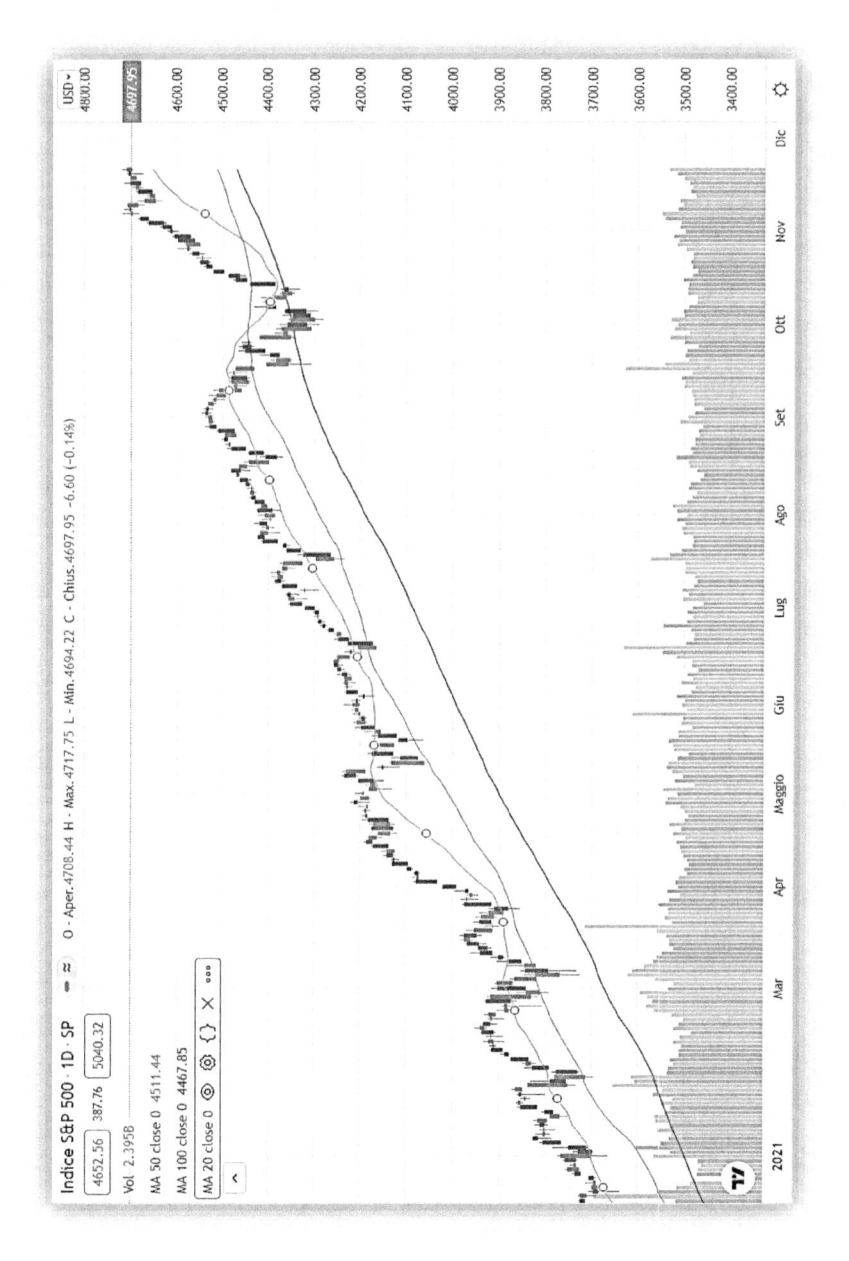

Illustration n.23– Standard & Poor's 500 Index chart for the year 2021 with moving averages

Obviously, these considerations can also be applied to identify a market's downward trend. To achieve this, you simply need to reverse the logic presented so far. Price candlesticks will settle below the moving averages, and generally, low-periodicity averages will often be below the long-term moving averages.

A case that I consider important from an educational point of view and extremely significant to represent a downward market is provided to us by the chart of the Chinese real estate giant EVERGRANDE, which in 2021 saw its total collapse.

On the chart, I applied the same moving averages observed in the previous example on the S&P 500 Index.

From around mid-March 2021 onwards, prices left a lateral phase to move below the averages. Crossing downwards in April, the averages gradually distanced themselves due to the downward acceleration of the quotation.

The lateral phase appears to have been reconquered in December, following the declarations of default by the rating agencies which, as an obvious consequence, caused the progressive blocking of trading on the stock.

Through the moving averages, as you may have guessed from the examples proposed, it is possible to search for levels of support and resistance in the market.

This particular feature of moving averages is applicable only and exclusively because they are among the tools most used by Traders, who use them daily and constantly, to obtain a Statistical Advantage.

Specific price levels will be identified with the help of the most common moving averages and the entry of a large number of orders will be based on them. If we observe the prices approaching the moving averages, we could find the massive execution of pending orders and therefore witness a new market imbalance.

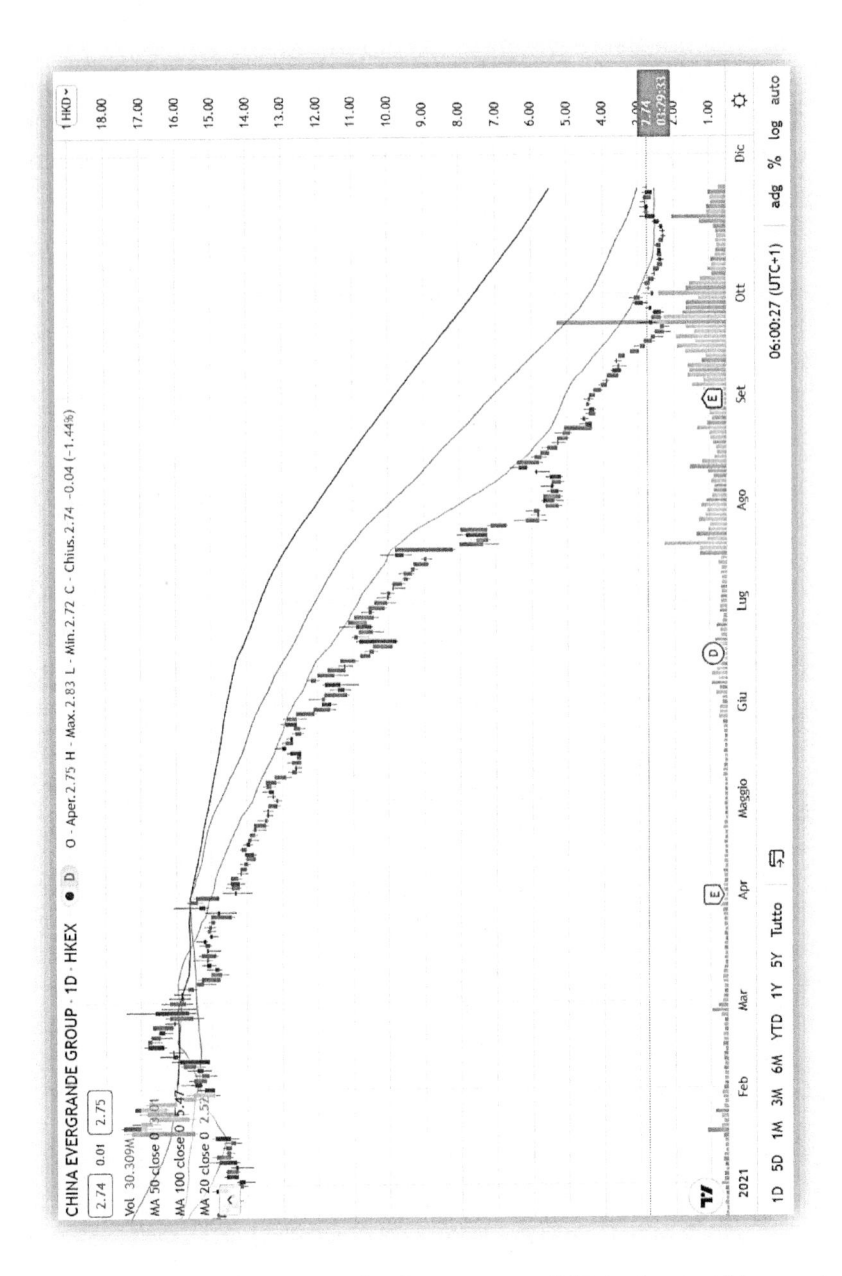

Illustration n.24– Evergrande Group year 2021 chart with moving averages

Remember that using the most common moving averages will give you a greater edge than using arbitrary averages. A moving average works best when many market participants observe it simultaneously, drawing the same information from it and reaching largely similar conclusions.

This type of instrument continues to be a favorite of Traders due to its simplicity of construction and use. For the reasons we have addressed so far, moving averages lend themselves well to inclusion in Trading Systems.

Signals deriving from the crossing of prices with the moving averages, the same crossing between different moving averages, or simply the indication of the current trend's direction are very simple elements to integrate into your trading strategies.

Thanks to suitable algorithmic trading programming software, such as the MQL5 Metaeditor of MetaQuotes or EasyLanguage, it is also possible to build fully automated systems. Unfortunately, this topic goes beyond the scope of this text, as it deserves a dedicated discussion. Surely, in the future, I will publish a didactic text on the basics of the programming of automated Trading Systems based on the MQL5 code.

If you were wondering how to choose the most suitable period for calculating a moving average, I want to underline that this choice depends on the specific trading strategy and your personal trading style. For these reasons, you will have to ask yourself about the number of operations you plan to carry out in a specific period of time, which ranges from day to week and so on based on your personal attitude.

We have seen that suitably combined, several moving averages can give us significant indications on the behavior of prices.

It is possible to categorize the most frequently applied averages according to the type of Trader:

- Day Traders use simple averages of 5 – 8 – 13 periods, applied on time frames of less than 4 hours;

- Swing Traders use exponential averages of 10 - 20 periods, as they are more reactive, together with further simple averages calculated over 50 - 100 - 200 periods, applying them on daily or weekly time frames;
- Position Traders generally limit themselves to the use of simple moving averages calculated over 50 and 200 periods, applied on a daily or weekly and, sometimes, even a monthly time frame.

Some Traders believe that, especially in the field of automated applications, which constitute the essence of Algorithmic Trading, it is advantageous to use the Fibonacci sequence numbers to choose the periods to represent the different moving averages.

They use simple, weighted or exponential averages based on this specific sequence of periods.

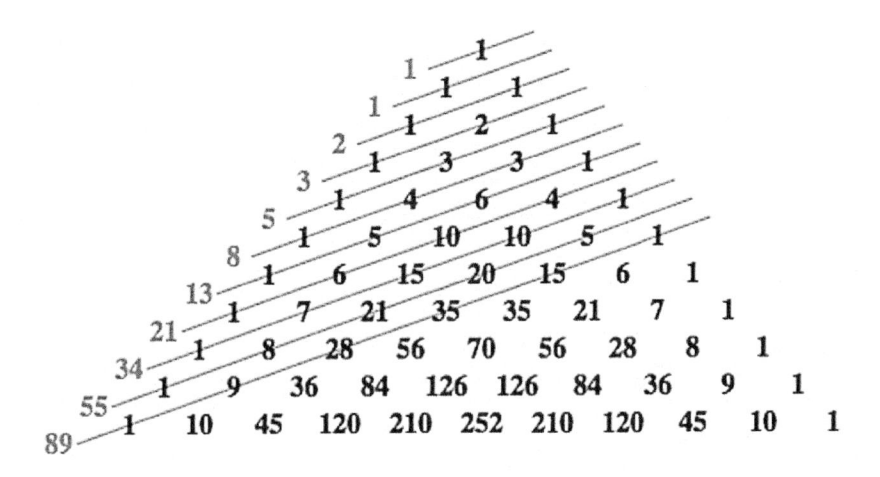

```
                          1   1
                        1   1   1
                      1   2   2   1
                    1   3   3   1
                  2   1   4   6   4   1
                3   1   5   10  10  5   1
              5   1   6   15  20  15  6   1
            8   1   7   21  35  35  21  7   1
         13   1   8   28  56  70  56  28  8   1
       21   1   9   36  84  126 126 84  36  9   1
     34   1   10  45  120 210 252 210 120 45  10  1
   55   1
 89
```

Illustration n.25– Tartaglia Triangle and determination of the Fibonacci sequence

Golden Cross e Death Cross

We have understood in detail what moving averages are, which are the most common and what advantages they can provide us, therefore, it is time to investigate the usefulness that derives from them, inserting them within our Trading strategy.

The most classic of all is the Golden Cross & Death Cross strategy. By cross, we refer exactly to the passage of an average, the fastest, through a second average, obviously slower.

When it comes to Golden Cross and Death Cross, the fast reference average is calculated over 50 periods, while the slow average is calculated over 200 periods. The crossing of these two specific moving averages is motivated by the frequency of application of these periodicities. They are moving averages widely used in the world of Trading and therefore are constantly observed by many operators in the market, both retail and institutional.

Naturally, the more Traders using an instrument, the greater the imbalance generated by a specific price setup.

A Golden Cross occurs when, on a daily candlestick chart, the fast 50-period average crosses the slower 200-period average from bottom to top. This kind of signal is always interpreted as a bullish signal and can confirm the start of a bull market.

Conversely, a Death Cross occurs when, on a daily candlestick chart, the 50-period rapid average crosses the 200-period average from top to bottom. As you may have already guessed, this signal is a bearish signal and can confirm the start of a bear market.

This kind of signal often acts more as a market filter than as an entry or exit operating signal.

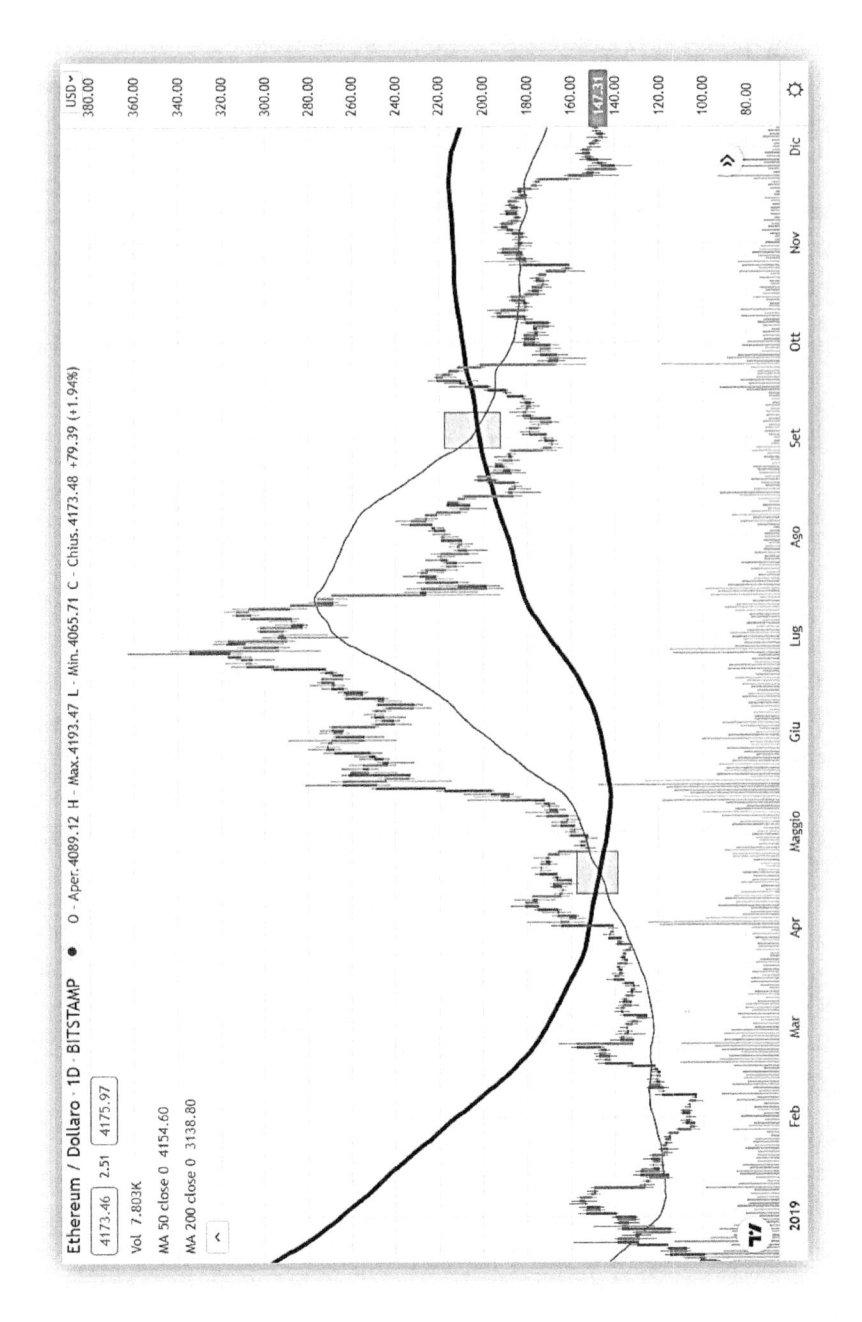

Illustration n.26– Ethereum chart year 2019

Looking at the chart of the second most capitalized Cryptocurrency in the world, Ethereum, we can see how a Golden Cross occurred in April 2019, which confirmed a clear bullish phase, which ended impulsively in July 2019.

With the continuous drop in prices, the formation of the Death Cross occurred in September 2019, which confirmed the onset of the bearish phase, which lasted until the beginning of 2020.

Among the best advice that can be given for this strategy, there are three that deserve specific mention:

- Never anticipate a Trade in the absence of the market entry signal;
- Never attempt to capture the high or low of the market in the hope of making a bigger profit;
- Inputs and outputs must always be defined by applying specific rules.

If it is true that entering a bullish market in advance could potentially give us a greater profit, the same operation, performed in the absence of any confirmation signal, could not find any technical feedback in the subsequent trend of market prices, invalidating the hypothesis of an imminent occurrence of the signal itself.

Let the bettors anticipate the market, instead you are a Trader, and before placing an order, you need confirmation. Financial markets will never do what we want so, for exactly this reason, we must build ourselves an appropriate evidence-based Statistical Advantage.

Further clarification should be made on the second suggestion. If it is true that exiting at the peak can provide us with greater profits, it is also true that, for a Trader who wants to be profitable over time, slavishly following the rules of his Trading System is enormously more important.

Hence the third piece of advice.

If you have built a Trading System based exclusively on moving average crossings, which identify your market entry and exit signals, in the absence of other rules that refine your decision-making process, you will have to force yourself to follow these rules. Any losing Trade is just a normal cost, as a normal cost would be to suffer a Stop Loss, even in the presence of an effective signal.

In this specific case, the strategy would be Stop and Reverse, i.e., buy when a Golden Cross occurs, hold the position until a Death Cross occurs, and, once the upward position is closed, regardless of the profit or loss obtained, open a new one now in the opposite direction.

It is obvious that, although sometimes very effective, this strategy is exclusively based on indicators of the Lagging type, i.e., delayed with respect to current market information because they are calculated on past prices, therefore it is subject to the generation of false signals.

False signals are nothing more than technically perfect signals from the point of view of the mere application, which fail to adequately filter anomalous price movements, especially if markets are not in trend and are in a consolidation/accumulation phase.

Despite the flaws, which will exist in any strategy regardless, the Golden Cross and the Death Cross remain reliable signals to define when a market is in a bull or a bear phase.

Now I would like to share with you some further suggestions of a more practical nature, which may be useful to you in trading based on moving average crossings. In order not to create confusion, I will continue to refer to the 50 and 200-period averages and will only report the bullish case.

- o When an uptrend begins, the 50-period moving average must cross the 200-period moving average upwards and stay above it;

- When a 50-period average crosses the 200-period average upwards, your trading must be oriented exclusively toward the purchase. Do not act against the trend;

- Watch out for side markets. The Golden Cross is an effective filter but, like any moving average, it does not work perfectly in sideways markets and can provide false signals. For sideways markets, trend-following operations are not indicated;

- After the bullish cross resulting from the Golden Cross, do not enter the position immediately. Wait until prices have first formed a higher high, a new growing high, and then a higher low, a new growing low, after which enter the bullish rebound in prices;

- As a type of Stop Loss, it is advisable to use the Trailing Stop technique, which consists in progressively moving the Stop Loss as the operation turns toward profit. If the market rises following the occurrence of a Golden Cross generating a small profit for you, you will have to raise the price level imposed for the Stop Loss up to the breakeven condition, the break-even point, so that, even if the operation returns down again, you will be protected from any loss. Applying this technique, in the case of particularly extensive bull runs, can potentially bring greater gains than a pre-set value of the risk/return ratio;

- Always remember that by applying the Trailing Stop in a long-type purchase operation, your exit point could be provided both by your dynamic Stop Loss and by the technical signal given by a Death Cross. The application of one or the other exit method will depend on the size of your Trailing Stop.

Backtesting

Although this strategy is technically complete and provides us with a good Statistical Advantage, I would like to clarify that, in trading on the financial markets, there are no guarantees of success, there are only probabilities supported by what has occurred in the past and the reasonable hypothesis that something very similar happens in the future.

For example, if we wanted to study the entire price history of a financial instrument, we would certainly have the ability to objectively evaluate how profitable this technique has been over time.

This kind of operation is called Back Testing, and it is used by the Trader to verify if and how much his Trading System is effective in the long run. In general, this strategy generates a probability of success of approximately 60%, and this percentage improves according to the length of stay of the operation on the market. Remember that, if managed as we have illustrated previously, juggling the risk/return ratio well, a technique with a 60% probability of success will certainly give us an adequate economic return.

Moving Average Defects

I would say that we have talked sufficiently about the advantages deriving from the use of moving averages and, for balance, we cannot overlook the defects, which are inevitably present in every technique and every indicator, moving averages included.

A moving average will always be the result of processing prices relating to a time interval, but its result will not always generate useful indications. The values of the moving averages, for example, cannot be of great help if there is a lot of volatility and speculation in the markets or when we observe markets extremely influenced by recent events and news that highlight their fragility.

When you calculate a moving average, or a combination of averages, on the basis of a specific time frame, for example, on the daily candlestick chart, you probably cannot expect that the calculation of the same averages on higher or lower periodicities will give signals of adequate effectiveness. The trend of a market can change significantly by changing periodicity. On shorter-term charts, the averages will have to elaborate a price trend characterized by greater volatility than in charts built on more high-level time frames.

It is not unusual for a moving average calculated over the same number of periods to indicate, in the short term, a bullish phase and, in the long term, a downward phase.

Another thing that can greatly influence the reliability of a signal given by the averages is the choice of using a simple moving average rather than an exponential one. The configuration resulting from the use of simple rather than exponential moving averages can vary quite a lot, therefore it can be confusing for a novice Trader.

Furthermore, in sideways markets, the effective use of moving averages is difficult. In some cases, for example, sudden price reversal movements are generated, called Whipsaws, which can cause significant Drawdowns in your account.

A Drawdown is the distance between the last maximum peak of your Equity Line, representative of the maximum price value that your account has reached during a Trading operation, and the last minimum. On an Equity Line chart, this phenomenon will typically show up as a sudden drop in the value of your account caused by a series of losing trades.

To be even more explicit about what an Equity Line is, imagine that you have placed $1,000 in the account and carried out 2 profit trades, with which you have earned $60 in total and 3 loss trades, for a value of $30. The Equity Line will be a line that, starting from the value of 1000, reaches 1060 and then drops to the final value of $1,030. The drawdown, in this case, will be $30.

In the case of using moving averages as the only operational entry and exit signal, you will have to expect your performance to collapse when the market lateralizes precisely because the moving averages have no filter function in these market phases.

For all these reasons it is appropriate that, as a Trader, you are able to make decisions based on multiple market characteristics, possibly adding further indicators of a different nature that can support and complete the analyzes resulting from the reading of the moving averages.

Remember that if, by your nature, you will become a trend follower Trader, moving averages will certainly play an important role in your strategies and in the respective operational decisions.

Chapter 6:
How to Use Technical Indicators

A technical indicator is a mathematical reworking of the prices and/or volumes expressed in a specific time interval and at a specific periodicity.

This definition assumes that historical price and volume data relating to a specific financial instrument or market can be translated into a derivative, graphical representation and that this can be clearly displayed on the screen, facilitating the Trader in his decision-making process.

Technical indicators are widely used in different markets, such as stock markets, currency markets, bond markets, and cryptocurrency markets.

Each technical indicator has one or more formulas that translate the original basic data into what will be graphed on the screen, therefore, it is very important to understand how it works, also by studying the formulas that make it up.

Before inserting any element in your Trading System, it is essential to fully understand its characteristics and functioning. Recklessly applying technical tools to the chart, unknowingly and without really understanding what you are looking at, is perhaps one of the best ways to lose money in the financial markets.

Furthermore, if you do not understand the risks and benefits of the indicator applied, you will be amazed to see that, even in the presence of impeccable technical signals and conditions with a high probability of success, your operations end up with a loss.

Professional Traders consistently use combinations of technical indicators in their Trading Systems, but this is not to be construed as an endorsement of the indiscriminate use of multiple random indicators on our charts.

Using more technical indicators does not reduce your chances of losing money at all, nor will it guarantee a more accurate signal. On the contrary, the simultaneous use of multiple indicators will create an increasingly stringent filter, such as generating conflicting signals, which will inexorably lead the novice Trader to paralysis.

Know that there is no perfect indicator, there is no perfect combination of indicators, and not even a perfect Trading System. You will never be able to create a custom indicator or system that detects 100% profitable trades; however, I want to reassure you that you can safely aim to increase your odds in a reasonable way.

Using algorithmic trading platforms, such as MetaTrader, allows a Trader who is sufficiently trained and able to program an algorithm, to create customized indicators.

In addition to exploiting the peculiarities of innovative systems and indicators of their own conception, these Trader programmers often sell their licenses to other Traders less accustomed to programming.

There are literally thousands of indicators, some famous and some less so, but in general, we can divide them into two large families: Momentum Indicators and Oscillators.

An important thing to keep in mind is that this categorization is not strict at all and some types of indicators can be included in both categories.

Momentum Indicators

Momentum Indicators are tools that help us identify the trend in its initial stages, i.e., they can help us grasp the transition from the lateral phase to the trend phase. What essentially happens following the break of a level of support or resistance.

In any case, and as already anticipated, blindly relying on this kind of indicator can cause the Trader to fall into a series of incorrect operations deriving from multiple false signals. Some notable examples of this type of indicator are the Bollinger Bands and the ADX-DMI.

Oscillators

The category of oscillators involves identifying specific areas where the market is considered overbought or oversold. Even this type of indicator can generate a large number of false signals before the trend strengthens in a specific direction and exits the lateral phase. It should be emphasized that, once the overbought and oversold levels have been reached, this will not automatically translate into a trend reversal, but this phase can last a very long time, especially when the current trend is particularly intense. Prominent examples are the Relative Strength Index and the Stochastic Oscillator.

Understanding the Indicator

Understanding the metrics behind each indicator, and how they themselves work, is certainly essential.

To better clarify this concept, I present a practical example relating to one of the most used indicators in Swing Trading operations: The Moving Average Convergence Divergence indicator, generally known by the acronym of MACD.

The MACD is a Momentum indicator made up of three main parts:

- MACD line
- Signal line
- Histogram

The basic settings of this indicator, regardless of the platform used, are:

- Fast period 12
- Slow period 26
- Signal damping value 9

Furthermore, some platforms allow you to refine the adjustment of the graph by choosing whether to calculate with a simple or exponential moving average and which price data to use as the basis of the calculation, whether closing, opening, etc.

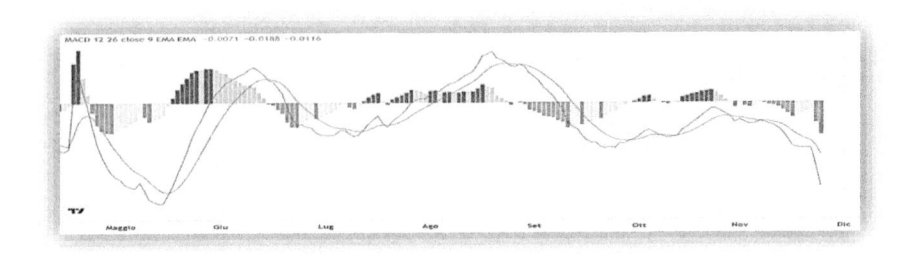

Illustration n.27- Representation of MACD

The MACD works as follows: the first line, more reactive, is the MACD line, and it is calculated by the difference between the EMA calculated on 12 periods and the EMA calculated on 26 periods. The second, less reactive line, called the signal line, is calculated by averaging historical MACD values based on the damping value, which we said is by default set to the value 9. The basic configuration values are generally suitable for the operation of Swing Trading. The third part is provided by the histogram, which basically represents the difference value between these first two lines. The greater the difference between them, the wider the corresponding histogram bar will be. I want to specify that, by default, the price value underlying the calculations is the closing value of the candle.

It is important to understand how the MACD is calculated as market conditions vary continuously and there are no values that adapt well to all conditions. Once you understand how the indicator changes when one of the parameters changes, you can configure it to best suit your trading style.

Let's now deal with the concept of Convergence and Divergence of the MACD. The two lines, of the MACD and of the Signal, can mutually distance themselves or approach and cross each other. Convergence is obtained when the difference between the values of the two lines progressively decreases, forming increasingly smaller histograms. Logically, we can observe the divergence when the difference between the values widens and the histograms increase.

Illustration n.28– Example of using the MACD

When the MACD line crosses the signal line, we have what is called the MACD crossing, a condition that can be used to measure the Momentum level of the market.

In a simplistic way it can be considered that, in the event of a bullish MACD crossing, we are in the presence of a Bullish-type Momentum, while if the MACD crossing is bearish, we have a Bearish-type Momentum.

Pay attention to one important thing, since the MACD is the result of the reworking of moving averages, its results will always have a physiological delay compared to the price values of the chart.

Indicators with this characteristic are called Lagging, while other types of indicators provide information that can anticipate price trends and are called Leading Indicators.

Lagging indicators are excellent tools for confirming short-term trends, however, they are not the best tools to rely on if you intend to catch the beginning of a trend.

Now, to better understand how the MACD can be useful in our Trading operations, let's go a little more into the operational sphere.

The very first phase of the study will involve the application of the MACD to a chart with extended periodicity, let's assume with daily candlesticks, to define and possibly confirm the current price trend.

The immediately following phase will be that of observing more detailed price movements, going down to lower-level time frames.

The purpose of the Trader when observing reduced periodicities, for example, with hourly candles, will be to exploit price movements in the early stages of the cycle, looking for optimal configurations for market entry such that they are always in agreement with the general trend identified.

The ideal relationship between the two observed charts, in terms of timing, gives good results when it is included in a multiplication factor of 3 to 5. If you want to make trades based on an existing setup on the daily candlestick chart, you will first observe a chart on a weekly basis. In this specific case, a total of 5 daily candlesticks will be equivalent to a weekly candlestick, therefore the multiplication factor will be equal to 5.

If you divide the 24-hour day by 5, you get a value of 4.8, so it will be appropriate to choose to display a 4-hour candlestick chart or the one immediately above.

On the higher level, weekly time frame, when the MACD line crosses the signal line upwards, we will know that the current market trend may be bullish. Taking advantage of this information, we observe the chart with short-term daily candlesticks, with the intention of grasping a bullish entry configuration that could be advantageous. In this second phase, we can use the patterns I have previously introduced and any other technique as long as it agrees with the bullish signal provided by the MACD on the weekly chart.

Similarly, if the MACD crosses downward the signal line on a weekly time frame, we will know that the current market trend could be bearish, and we will look on the daily chart for a configuration suitable for a short entry.

The graph below shows, with weekly candlesticks, the price trend of the FTSE MIB index until December 2021.

I have highlighted two crosses of the MACD. At the beginning of November 2020, we have a bullish signal, confirmed by a Bullish Engulfing Pattern. The second crossing, with a bearish signal, which will become the closing signal, is found towards the end of April 2021. Let's go down to a more accurate periodicity in search of a suitable entry point for a purchase transaction.

An excellent entry point occurs after the upward break of the resistance of $18,310.

For this purchase operation, the Stop Loss could be set below the minimum of the lowest candle of the immediately preceding days. The operation set up in this way must last until, on the weekly time frame, a new MACD crossing occurs.

For this specific example, the risk/reward ratio would have been approximately 1:7, an excellent operation even considering the overall duration of 5 months.

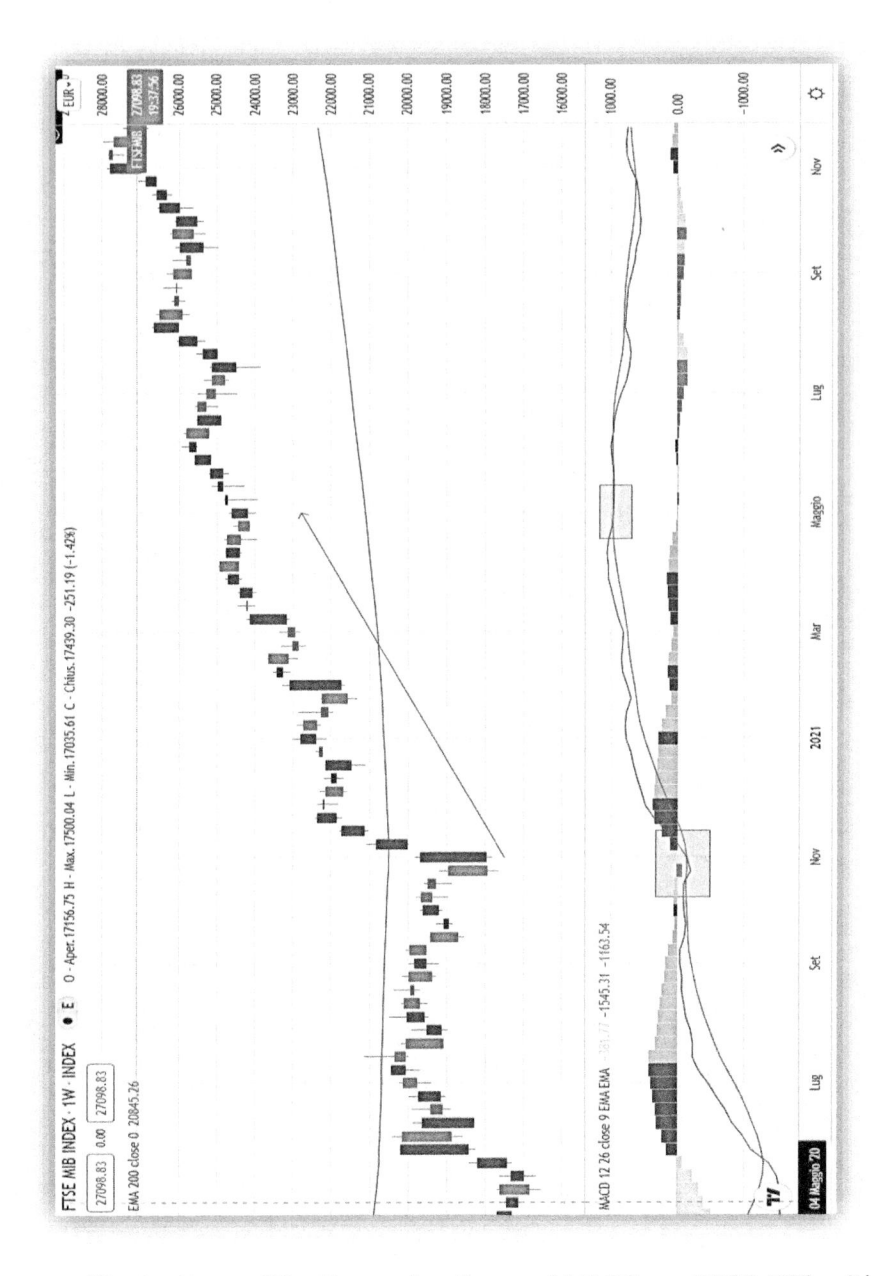

Illustration n.29– Example of use of MACD on FTSE MIB with weekly time frame

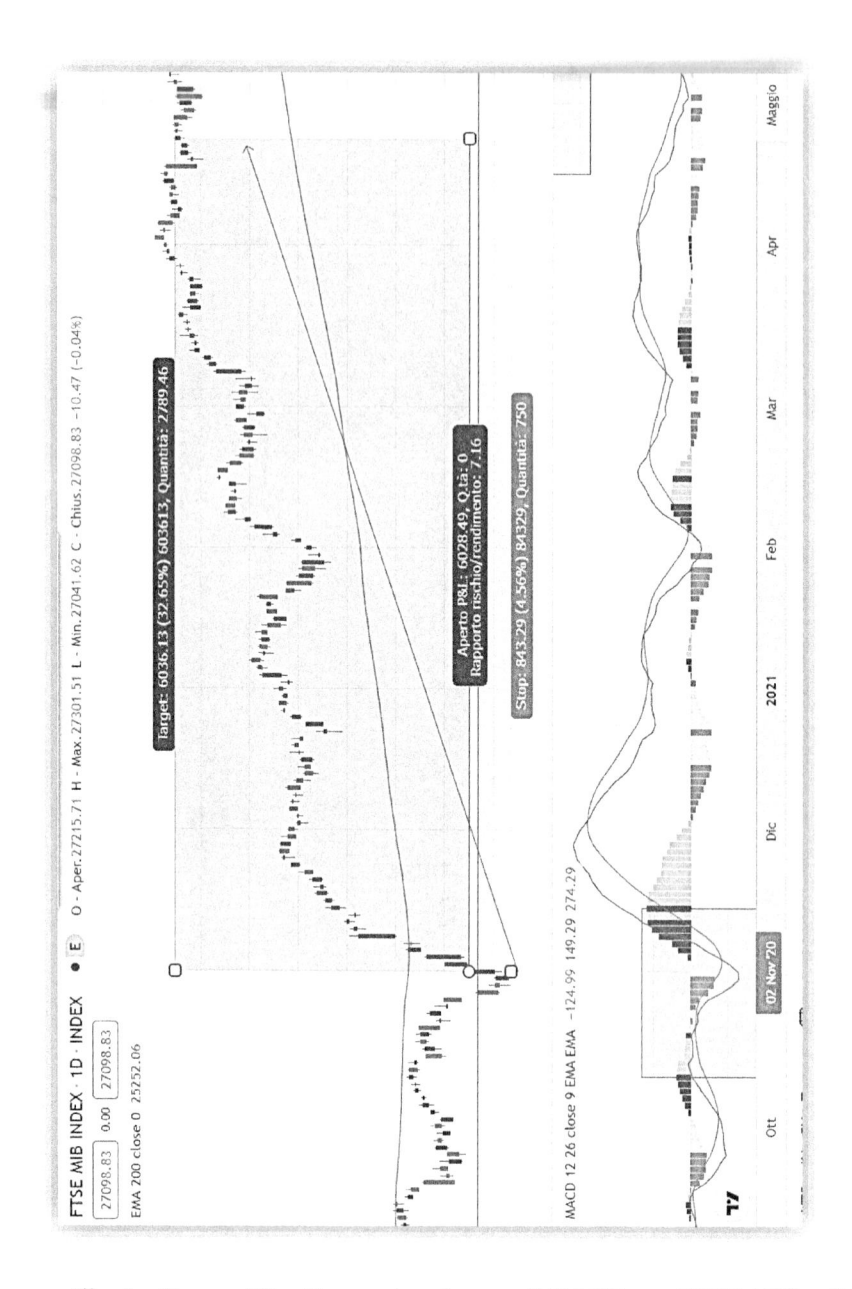

Illustration n.30– Example of use of MACD on FTSE MIB with daily time frame

It is also true that, for this strategy, it is always possible to apply predefined risk/reward ratios, but this could significantly limit your profit.

No strategy will ever be infallible, no strategy will ever be perfect, for this reason, I want to show an example of a transaction that didn't go as planned.

We observe that the MACD, albeit in an undecided way, generates a sell signal around the beginning of June.

In this case, if we based ourselves exclusively on the technical signals of the MACD, we would also look for a bearish signal on the daily time frame that would allow us to enter the market.

The bearish cross of the MACD on a daily time frame occurs on the 17th of June. The ideal Stop Loss for this sale operation would be positioned above the immediately preceding high. The Take Profit, as in the previous example, is not defined a priori.

Initially, the prices would have moved in the direction we imagined, only to then reverse the very short-term trend and lead us to a loss. Our intention to exit the market at the new bullish cross of the weekly MACD did not take due account of the dominant medium-term trend.

The operation would have been partially successful if we had applied a defined risk-return ratio of 1:1.5, or if we had applied the Trailing Stop technique, the break-even level would have easily been achieved once prices had moved in the direction we had chosen.

If you look closely at the chart, you will notice that I have always applied an additional indicator recently illustrated, a 200-period exponential moving average. With the help of this indicator, it was clearly at a glance that the market trend was essentially bullish.

We must always keep in mind the saying, *"The Trend is Your Friend Until it Ends,"* the Trend is your friend as long as it persists.

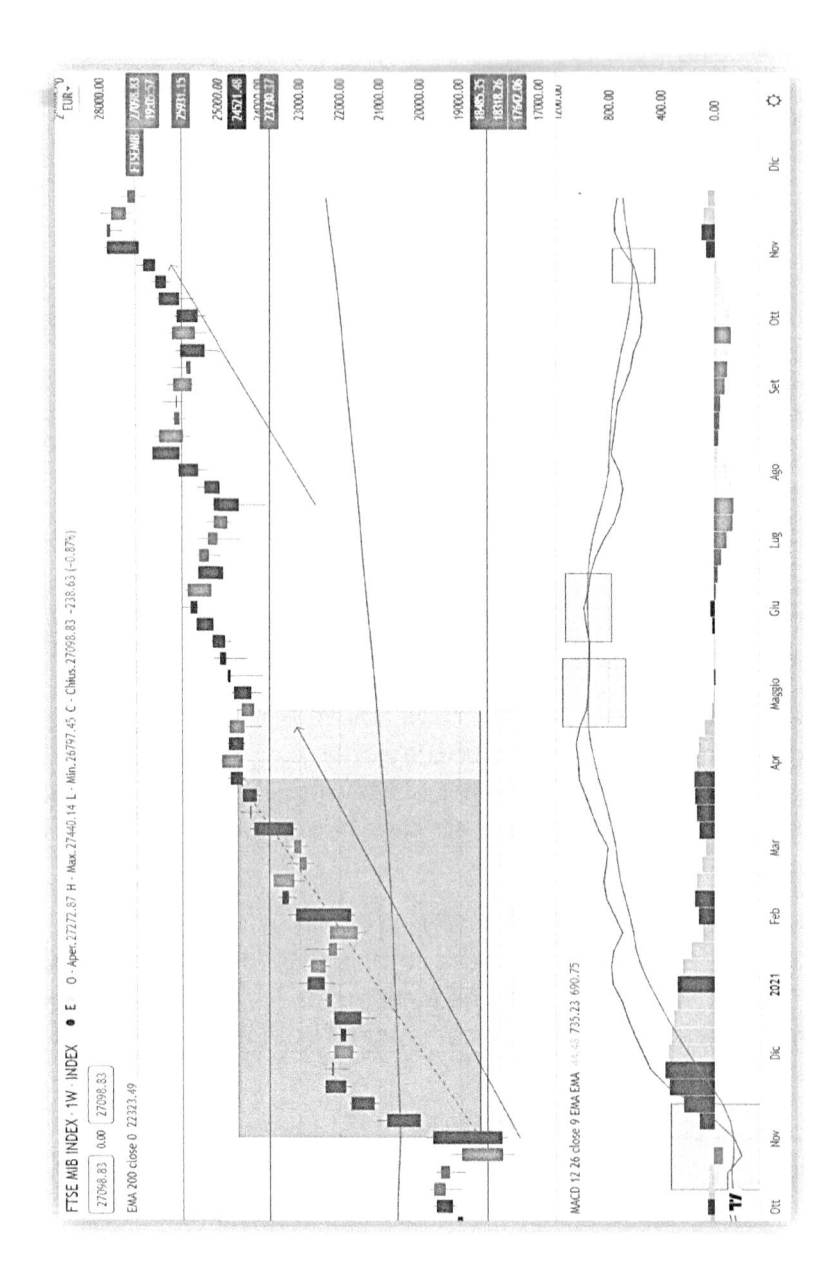

Illustration n.31– Example of use of MACD on FTSE MIB with weekly time frame

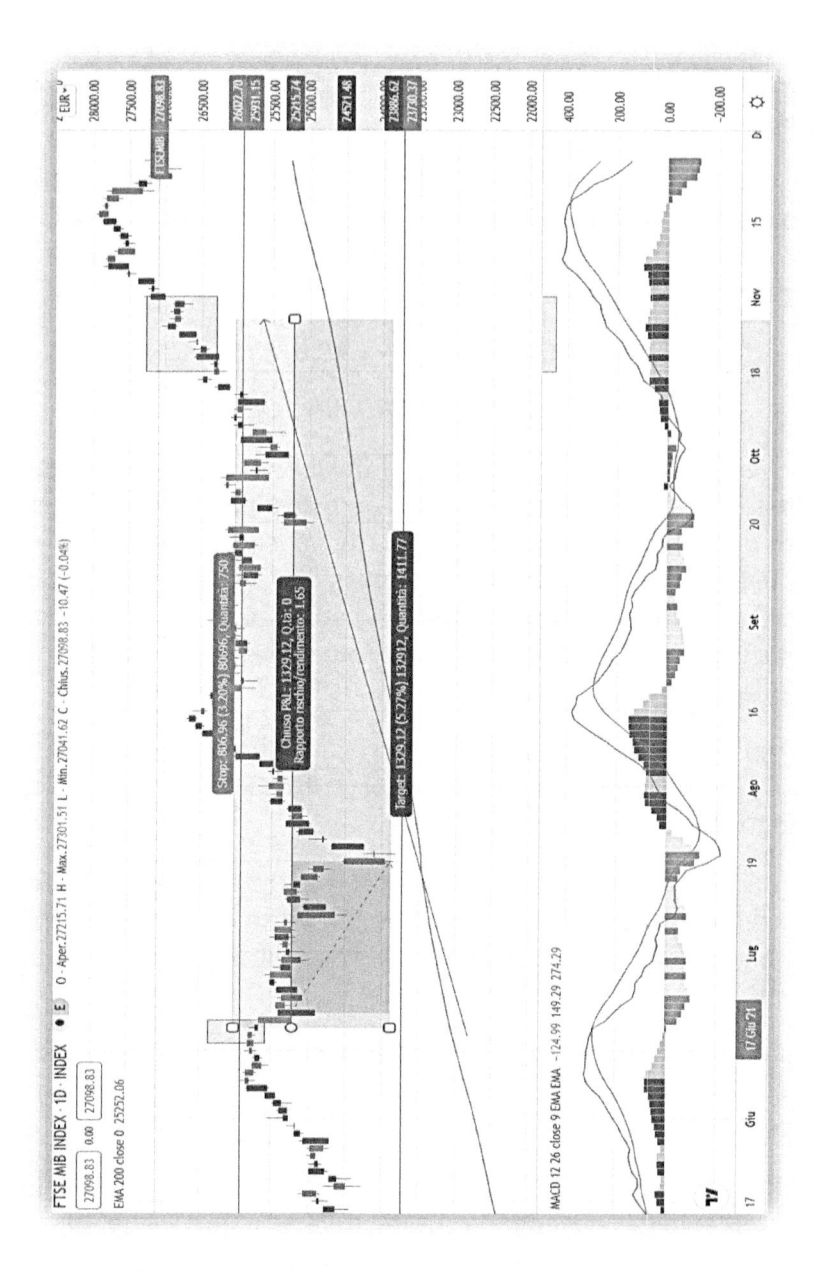

Illustration n.32– Example of use of MACD on FTSE MIB with daily time frame

This means that it is always better to look for market trades in accordance with the main trend rather than trade against it, as in the latter case.

Now you may wonder why I entered a wrong operation between the pages of this book. From my point of view, I cannot teach you what is correct if you cannot recognize and avoid trivial errors. Errors in the life of a Trader are a constant.

"GET USED TO FAILURE!

GET USED TO ABSORBING LOSSES!"

A professional Trader is not an infallible or perfect Trader. A professional Trader is methodical and applies his own rules for better or for worse, both when they give positive results and when they lead to negative results. A professional Trader has the ability to earn over the long term by carrying out a large number of trades thanks to his experience and ability to generate his own Statistical Advantage.

Now let's look at another very famous indicator, which we can classify as belonging to the category of oscillators, the Relative Strength Index, abbreviated RSI.

The RSI is, therefore, an oscillator that measures the ratio of ascending and descending movements, with variability from 0 to 100, and is useful for looking for overbought and oversold market indications.

A market is overbought when prices have risen excessively compared to expectations, conversely, a market is oversold when prices have fallen excessively compared to expectations.

The Relative Strength Index is built with a two-step formula. The first step involves calculating the relative strength value, obtained by making a ratio between the average gain value and the average loss value, both evaluated on the basis of a specific number of periods.

By average gain value, we mean the sum of the average of the price increases recorded compared to the closing of the previous candle. That is an average, calculated starting from the price differences recorded between the opening and closing of only positive candles, compared to the number of periods analyzed.

By average loss value, we mean the sum of the average of the price decreases recorded with respect to the closing of the previous candle. That is, an average calculated starting from the price differences recorded between the opening and closing of negative candles only, compared to the number of periods analyzed.

$$RS = Avg\text{-}G / Avg\text{-}L$$

Having understood what is meant by the average value of gain and the average value of loss, the second step involves a simple transposition of the RS value in relation to a reference scale whose limits are the value 0 and the value 100.

$$RSI = 100 - (100 / (1+RS))$$

Some professional Traders use the RSI as a momentum indicator, measuring the speed and strength of prices as they move in a specific direction or trend.

To better understand how this indicator works and the relative implications of the calculation that builds it, I will show you a chart of the Euro/Dollar market with the RSI applied.

In the lower part of the image, you can see a chart in which there is a broken line whose value varies between 0 and 100. This line is our RSI.

Above the value 70, the overbought area is universally defined, while below the value 30, it refers to the oversold area. When the line is within one of these areas, the market will be considered to be overbought or oversold, respectively.

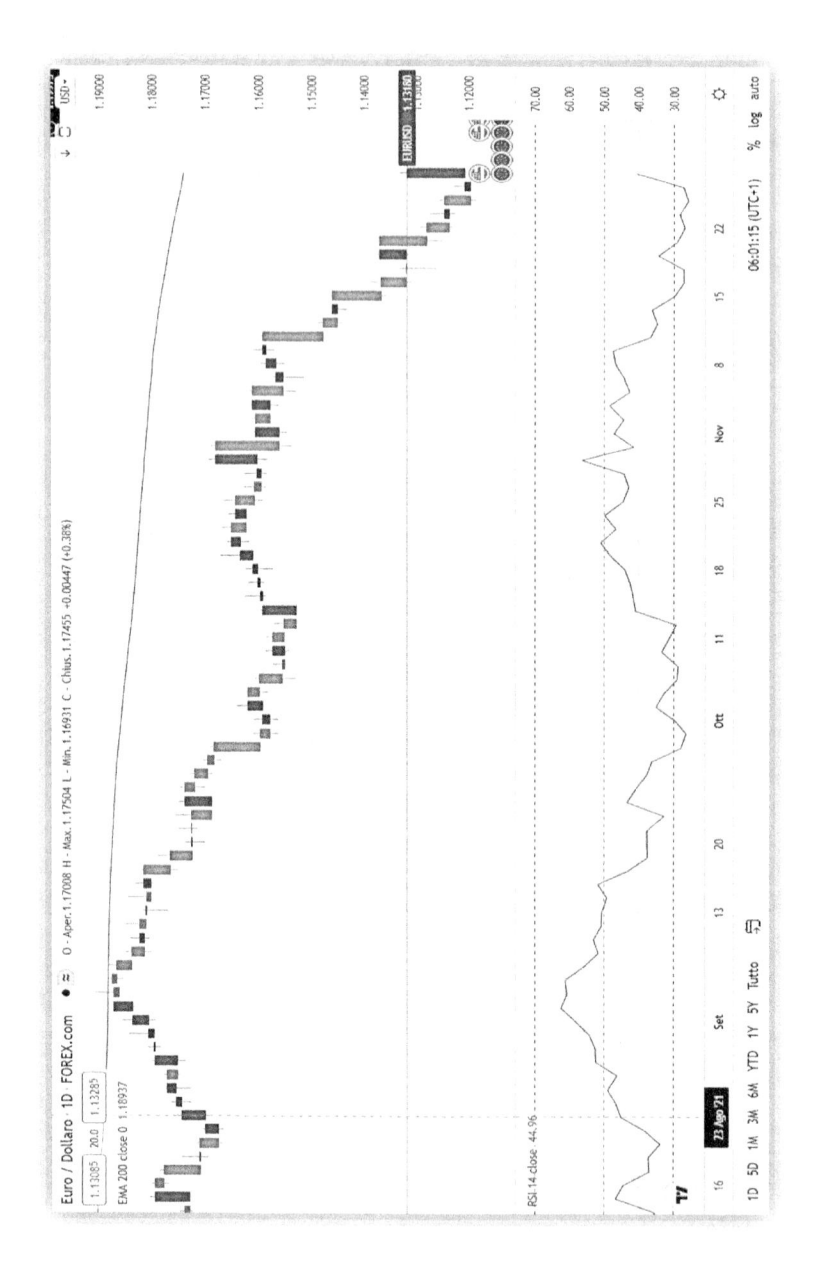

Illustration n.33– Example of RSI on EURUSD cross with daily time frame

These thresholds are obviously not strict. Each Trader can freely decide whether to expand or decrease their scope, for example, to bring them to 65 and 35 or 80 and 20.

A very important thing that I must clearly underline is that, in periods of strong trend, the condition of overbought or oversold can last for months.

I repeat it for clarity:

"THE OVERBOUGHT, OR OVERSOLD CONDITION OF A MARKET CAN LAST FOR MONTHS"

However, there is no doubt that the RSI indicator can be used to identify trend reversals. In general, a market will have a positive trend as long as the RSI maintains values between 55 and 100, and obviously, it can be deduced that a market has a negative trend as long as the RSI maintains values ranging from 45 to 0.

The area between the value 45 and the value 55 is a neutral area that acts, in some way, as a support or resistance area depending on the case in which we find ourselves. When the RSI crosses this neutral zone from top to bottom, we can expect a reversal of trend direction from up to down, and of course, the opposite is equally to hold.

Another method, divergence, is very effective in identifying a trend reversal. A divergence occurs when the RSI chart shows a different trend from the trend displayed in the price chart.

Let's imagine once again that we are observing the Euro/Dollar chart and that we are in a well-defined uptrend condition. In the lower part, however, we note that a new peak in prices does not correspond to a new peak in the RSI. It is also quite evident that the RSI is losing energy, defining a descending phase, this type of situation is called Bearish Divergence.

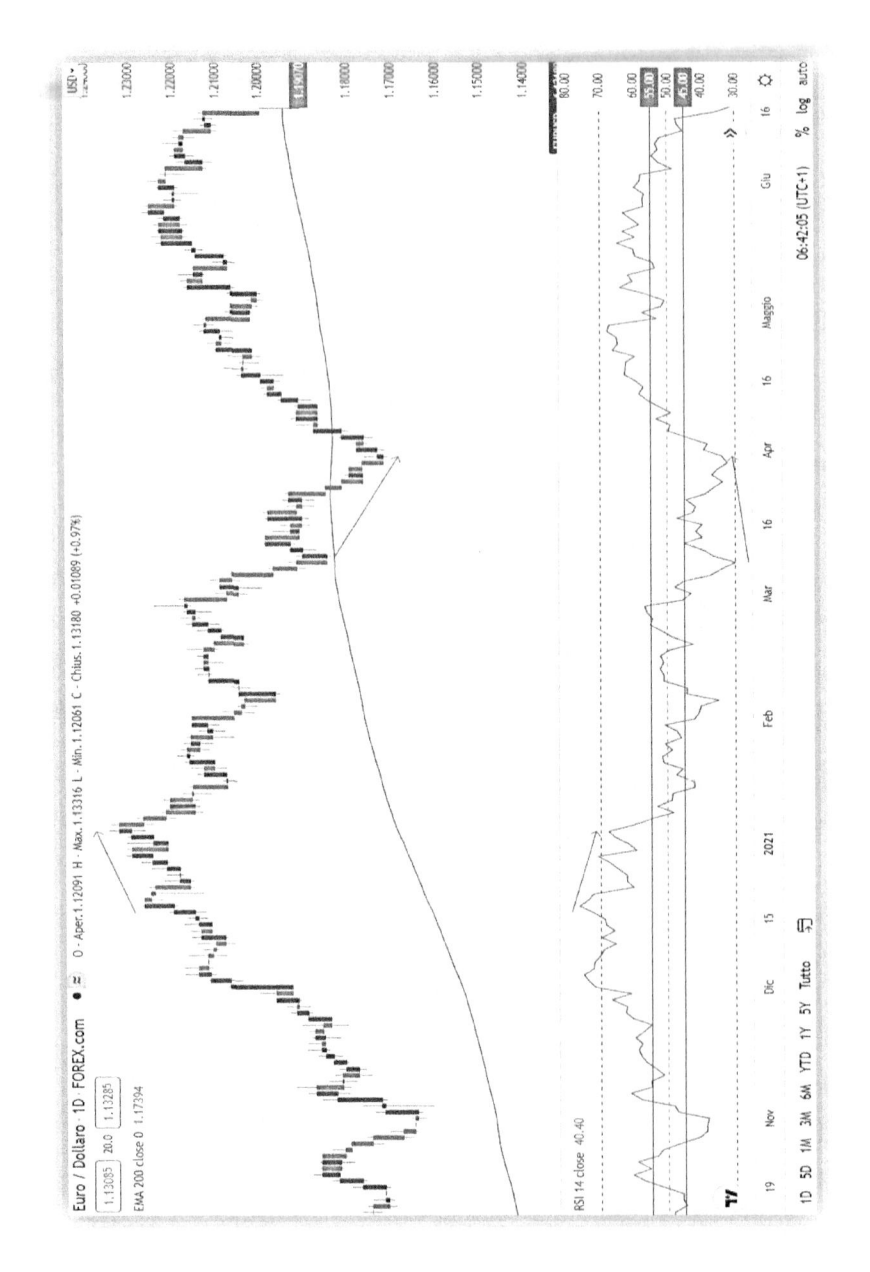

Illustration n.34– Example of RSI Divergences on EURUSD cross with daily time frame

The opposite case is the Bullish Divergence, where the price chart would create lower lows in a well-defined downtrend condition, while the RSI starts to turn up creating higher lows, therefore in disagreement with the lower trend chart prices. A new low in prices will not correspond to a new low in the RSI, which appears to be gaining strength.

Always remember that each indicator has its specific function for which it was designed and cannot be good in absolute and in all market conditions.

Creating combinations of indicators can increase your Statistical Advantage and increase your confidence factor in planning a market operation, but such combinations must be done wisely and conscientiously.

A common mistake is to think that, by increasing the number of indicators, our risk level in making an operational choice may decrease. Unfortunately, I have to warn you that this is absolutely not the case, you must always keep in mind that often, some indicators have similar functions and others instead provide conflicting information. The first indicator could tell you that the opportunity to go long in the market is perfect, while a second indicator could give you, at the same time and on the same time frame, a totally opposite indication.

Every time you decide to apply an indicator to your chart and, therefore, to your trading strategy, you must be fully aware of how it works, how it is built and what advantage it could give you on the market.

Another common mistake is to make an operational choice based exclusively on the indicators, feeling sure of their interpretation, only to then neglect the study of the Price Action and the supports and resistances.

The choice of indicators to use must be made consciously and by carefully assessing the risk associated with possible false signals generated by them.

Another thing to avoid is to buy ready-made and packaged strategies, perhaps automated in MQL or Powerlanguage, which promise miraculous earnings without effort. I want to emphasize that I am not saying that every auto strategy for sale is a scam. If you do not deeply understand the logic and functioning of the Trading System purchased, you will never be able to understand why your profits will be zeroed at some point.

In the near future, you could probably find a second book of mine that will explain exactly how to program such automated strategies in the MQL5 language yourself.

I have decided that, through this second book, you will have the opportunity to understand all the advantages and defects of your own trading ideas. This is possible when you learn how to perform numerous automatic tests of effectiveness and robustness using historical price data before letting your Trading Robots operate with real money.

Unfortunately or fortunately, there is a huge variety of technical indicators and the coverage of this chapter would be equally huge, so I hope I have given you some food for thought on how to approach the study and subsequent use of indicators.

I promise to write for you, perhaps later and subject to the interest that this first book will arouse, a distinctly practical text that illustrates the potential of the indicators most frequently used by Traders and the related application strategies.

Chapter 7:
Analyze the Market Cycle

In this new section of the book, we will deal with market structures and some recurring graphic formations that characterize the performance of financial markets. By recognizing these structures, we will determine optimal and effective points to successfully place a trade on the market.

As a beginner Trader, you will learn something that will really lead to a level-up in your trading.

There are two major groups of operators competing in the market, the retail operators and the institutional operators.

The group of retail operators is made up of small operators, people who generally carry out operations of modest size with reduced capital. A Trader falls within this first selection of individuals, despite the possible large size of his account.

The group of Institutional Traders consists of large Traders and large financial institutions such as banks, hedge funds, insurance companies, governments, etc. It is quite clear that the ability to establish itself on the market is practically exclusive to institutional operators.

Only the institutions can effectively influence the market trend, operating in such an important way that it is almost correct to say that they themselves constitute the market.

The aggregate capitalization of institutional players in a market is such that it considerably exceeds any contribution made by retail players. For this reason, every purchase or sale choice made by institutional operators can significantly impact the market.

In addition to having an important portion of the capitalization of a market, institutional operators can access privileged information and can count on an army of employees, often extremely capable and intelligent, to whom they entrust their trade decisions.

Very often, institutional operators are also referred to as SMART MONEY.

A retail Trader, who is adequately trained on these issues, must necessarily acquire the ability to observe the movement of money and pay more attention to where Smart Money is moving.

Institutional Traders generally move according to a repeatable cycle that involves four different phases:

- Accumulation phase;
- Growth phase or Markup, more commonly referred to as Uptrend or Bull Market;
- Distribution phase;
- Degrowth phase or Markdown, more commonly referred to as Downtrend or Bear Market.

The image below shows the construction of a market cycle according to Wyckoff's schematization. You can easily see how a lateral phase of accumulation generally follows a Markup phase, where the market gains strength and, with an almost defined trend, grows up to a plateau.

Translation: ACCUMULATION – MARKUP – DISTRIBUTION – MARKDOWN.

Illustration n.35– Wyckoff Market Cycle

After the bullish market phase follows a phase, generally reduced in extent, defined as the distribution phase which is followed by a phase of reversal of prices and a decisive contraction of the market.

Deepening our knowledge of the market cycle will help us understand the general picture, focus precisely on the psychology of the two large groups of operators, and will allow us to understand which of the four phases we are in. We will therefore have the opportunity to ride the wave for as long as possible, to exploit the various phases in our favor well in advance, and to be able to make plausible hypotheses on how the mass could behave.

You will understand why, far too often, retail operators tend to make mistakes, which inevitably favor institutional operators.

Knowing these notions will be necessary for you to take precautions to allow you to stay on the right side of the market for as long as possible.

You will learn the specific differences and configurations of each phase, observed from a purely technical perspective, which may be useful for carrying out profitable operations in each market phase.

From theory to reality, I show you a graph of the cyclical behavior of the FTSE MIB Index.

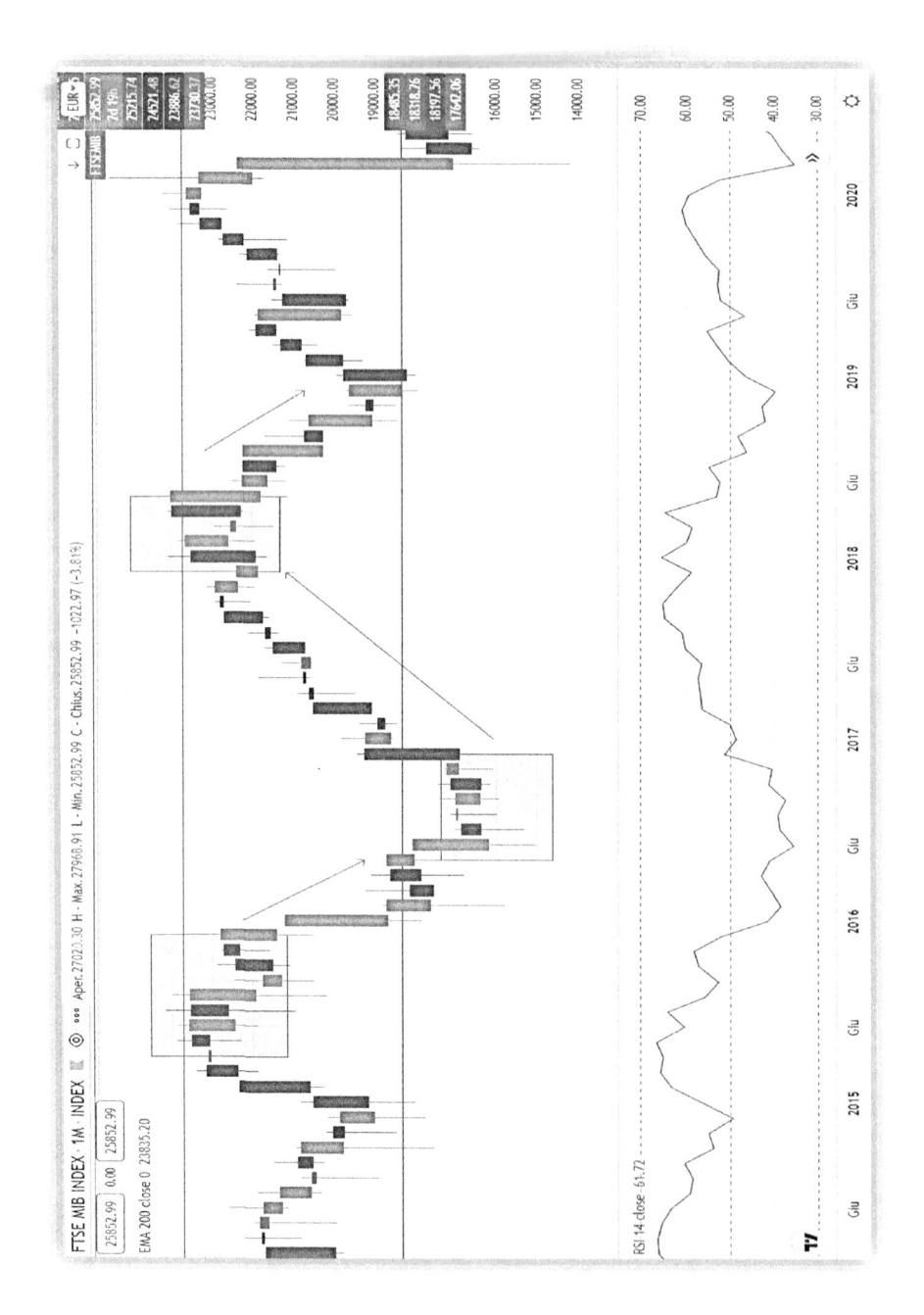

Illustration n.36– FTSE MIB chart from 2015 to 2020

Accumulation Phase

This first phase generally has a lateral trend characterized by very limited price movements and corresponding trading volumes. In this phase, precisely because of these characteristics, institutional operators begin to intervene in the market who progressively increase their market shares by carrying out their purchases with caution and accuracy.

They intervene at fairly regular intervals, in not too disproportionate quantities, so as to ensure the stability of prices in a certain range, a price which would suddenly increase if the same quotas were purchased in a single solution.

Generally in this phase, the attention of retail operators is low precisely because both the volatility of the market and the price levels do not arouse particular suspicions.

This phase ends when the large institutional operators, already strong in a good slice of the market, decide to make sudden important purchases, moving large volumes of capital and pushing the market beyond the upper resistance of the lateral phase, generating an upward break.

Markup Phase

At this moment, we are entering phase number two, the bull market, where both institutional operators and retail operators enthusiastically participate in the bullish momentum. Buying pressure is growing, as are the prices of financial instruments.

This phase is characterized by consecutive increasing highs alternating with consecutive increasing lows. Institutional operators, who have long ago made purchases in the previous accumulation phase, see their profits grow and therefore tend not to sell their shares, increasing the feeling of scarcity of the asset traded in the market.

It is also possible that institutional operators acquire additional market shares to give a greater upward push to the trend and attract the less aware retail crowd by generating in them the F.O.M.O., Fear of Missing Out. No one would want to miss out on an opportunity as tempting as an obvious bull run. As a technical Trader who makes more use of technical rather than fundamental analysis, in this phase, the signals provided by the indicators are often quite reliable, therefore, it is easier to generate profitable trades.

Insight into the Markup Phase

For a novice Trader, the best way to start trading is to take advantage of the second phase of the cycle, the markup, which in my opinion, and for the purposes of this treatise, deserves further study.

A bull market often begins when the majority of market participants do not pay attention to it, and therefore, when some retail operators begin to operate, they do so in an uncertain way and imagining the possibility that prices will return downwards. In this immature start of the bull market, the opinions of market participants are typically mixed.

Once institutional Traders push the market up and past resistance, even those with a bearish view will be forced to buy back their losing positions. Furthermore, all the people who were waiting for an entry signal will start buying with good enthusiasm.

Purchasing power grows, also aided by the amplification provided by media outlets, which begin to provide positive information and give reasons after reasons that attempt to explain the cause of so much momentum.

At the same time, market volumes start to increase, and some institutional Traders start taking their first profits, partially giving up their shares to the crowd in F.O.M.O. at the last moment. All the retailers who missed the second bullish wave enter the market, giving impetus to a third bullish wave and participating in the delicious opportunity.

At this point, Smart Money starts selling their shares to the last retail operators and, at the same time, increasingly optimistic, excessively optimistic news arrives from the media channels, such as to convince even our grandmother that maybe investing in BITCOIN is a good thing.

The upward thrust shows no sign of diminishing, but volumes, insidiously and almost veiled, are becoming increasingly reduced, and the market is starting to show the first signs of weakness.

"Aware" Traders realize that indicators differ from the price and follow the institutional sales, which at this point of the cycle are now safe and have sold all their shares to the Dumb Money, the "Stupid Money," the last and most naive retail operators.

Distribution Phase

The distribution phase typically constitutes the market peak and is characterized by a substantial slowdown in growth, followed by a lateral phase.

In this case, the balance between supply and demand is generated because institutional operators cautiously begin to sell all their market shares to the last naive retail operators who have entered the market, the ones I introduced earlier as DUMB MONEY. These latter retailers believe that, since the market has been growing strongly for a fair amount of time, it will continue to do so for a long time.

In any market, if someone is willing to sell his shares, he will have to find someone else willing to buy them. This happens in this phase, where all sales orders placed by SMART MONEY are promptly purchased by DUMB MONEY.

This transfer phase will last until the balance between supply and demand is broken again, but this time it will be characterized by high selling pressure.

Markdown Phase

Also referred to as bear market or downtrend, markdown is characterized by large selling volume caused by institutional Traders, which results from huge sell orders or short selling operations, further increasing the selling pressure in the market. Volatility is typically higher than in the bull market. Volatility is typically higher than in the bull market.

In fact, it is said that, in the financial markets, prices go up with the stairs and down with the elevator, a metaphor that gives a good idea of the two different speeds and durations.

In this phase, most retail operators suffer huge losses, which gives rise to the notorious panic selling, the sale at an extreme loss to get rid of the stock in a nosedive.

Often when retail operators start selling their positions under the pressure of panic, we are very close to the end of the markdown phase. Exactly at this moment, realizing the changed market conditions, institutional operators begin again to cautiously make purchases from sellers, who are now completely disheartened, effectively starting a new process of accumulation of market shares and causing the cycle to repeat itself.

Fake Breakouts

Remember that, in the accumulation phase and in the distribution phase, before actually entering the trend phase, false breakouts can very often occur, therefore it is at least recommended to carefully study the volumes, which during this phase passage will increase supporting and strengthening movement.

In the markup phase, some intermediate accumulation phases could alternate with bullish impulses and small retracements. It is by no means a foregone conclusion that there are no major downward movements in a bull market.

Since the downward speed of the markets is generally faster than the growth speed, everything will be more evident and defined in the bear market phase. In the bull market, growth typically occurs with smaller volumes and less volatility.

You might think that trading in an uptrend or downtrend phase is the same thing but in different directions, but in reality, it is not. Unfortunately, most Traders master only one of the two directions because each phase of the cycle requires specific skills of specific personalities, which, combined, create the suitability to operate in a market phase.

The four categories of Trade

Every trade we are about to place on the market, based on technical analysis reasoning, can be enclosed in one of the four main categories.

1. Trending market with Trend Following operations;
2. Trending market with Trend Termination operations;
3. Sideways market with price rebound operations on Support or Resistance;
4. Sideways market with operations on breaking of Support or Resistance.

Professional and expert Traders improve their overall performance by creating complementary strategies that counterbalance each other, exceeding the limit of the single preferred category. Imagine that you have developed a strategy that is specific to trading in the sideways market. When there is a break of the limits defined by support and resistance, you would suffer losses in normal conditions, and the strategy would become temporarily ineffective. It is, therefore, useful to think ahead of the occurrence of this option, in this case, to suspend the first strategy and use one developed to be effective in this second scenario.

Many novice Traders focus exclusively on one strategy, but when it fails, they are forced to wait for further opportunities, which may be late in presenting themselves, or they despair because their beloved strategy, in which they have placed a thousand hopes, no longer pays as before.

It is extremely important to always be prepared for the opposite eventuality to the one we hoped for so as to be able to react with an already foreseen strategy, in this way, we will force ourselves to ask ourselves, before every single Trade, what could go wrong.

Having more than one strategy will help prevent unwise entry. Trading can be really boring at times and while waiting to observe your coveted entry signal, you may feel tempted to force your rules just to fit a particular configuration into your strategy and finally be able to operate.

Remember that the strategy is given by a set of SELF-IMPOSED rules, which you have carefully checked and trusted well before operating on the market, therefore, it is not wise to change any parameter of the strategy rashly.

Even if you make conscious decisions, your subconscious mind, under pressure, will attempt to seek out additional information to support your decision, whether or not it is correct.

I would like to underline that this is not at all a suggestion of the type *"Open two positions in opposite directions at the same time and then see what happens,"* but it is simply an advice to be very careful before intervening, to ask targeted questions and to always carry out a careful assessment of the specific risk related to each operation.

Trending market with Trend Following operations

In trend-following operations, Traders look for markets that are already trending, observe their price configurations and, on the basis of their own strategies, analyze them with the aim of obtaining the maximum advantage from the prevailing direction.

Trend trading will clearly adapt better to bull market or bear market phases, as they are purely directional.

In these phases, even the beginner Trader will be able to identify, with fairly simple, valid configurations and will have less difficulty in understanding the market, executing his Trade, and managing the respective risk.

In this type of category, managing the risk/reward ratio is vastly more important than the number of trades. Taking profits early and cutting losses too late are the two conditions that lead to the systematic loss of your capital in any trend following system.

An example of trend following operations is the strategy of crossing moving averages, illustrated by way of example when we talked about Golden Crosses and Death Crosses.

Trending market with Trend Termination operations

In this type of category the Trader looks for opportunities for very short-term counter-trend trades and, for this reason, will be looking for hyper-extended trending markets, which are reducing their strength and therefore preparing to retrace.

This is counter-trend trading, significantly more challenging than a simple trend following strategy. Examples of this type of operation can be found more easily in the directional market phases of markup and markdown.

This category of Trade can be very attractive for those who do not want to lose even a moment in their operations, as they are operations, as already mentioned, very fast and which go against the trend of the mass. The reverse of the medal consists in the fact that they are operations with a greater degree of complexity, which require excellent skills, both from a technical point of view and from a mental point of view.

Accurately entering the market and knowing how to suddenly cut losses are the two most important things in this type of category, again due to the limited time frame of the action.

You will agree with me that, for all these reasons, counter-trend trading is certainly not advisable for a novice Trader.

Lateral market with operations on price rebound on Support or Resistance

In this category, the Trader is able to clearly and reasonably accurately identify the levels of support and resistance that delimit the boundaries of the lateralized market. It then exploits these boundaries by waiting for configurations in which the price approaches support levels, at the base of the channel, or resistance levels, at the top of the channel.

The technique is most effective when the lateral market is well-defined, typically when going through an accumulation or distribution phase.

Learning how to manage lateral phases is an important quality for a Trader who wants to operate professionally and, in general, for a Trader who wants to reach non-trivial levels of trading. The reason is that in terms of duration, the lateral market, for most financial instruments, develops for a significantly longer period than the trending market.

In this phase, the volatility of prices generally decreases, consequently causing the reduction of the risk/reward ratio.

This reduction is compensated by the greater probability of success, combined with the reduced risk and the greater time extension of this type of market.

The most common configuration, other than the simple reversal pattern, is that of the false breakout. In a false breakout, prices go beyond the limits of the lateral market, but this push, not being accompanied by significant volumes, tends to end in the short term, bringing prices back to the ranging phase, lateralization within the channel.

Sideways market with operations on breaking of Support or Resistance

Just like in the previous category, the Trader has previously identified support and resistance levels that define the market structure and is simply waiting to observe an upward or downward breaking configuration of these important limits.

Once the downward or upward break has occurred, if this break is accompanied by important volumes, two main situations can occur:

- A decisive trend phase may begin.
- A retracement of the price, called pullback, can occur, characterized by the return to the level of support or resistance just violated. A bearish pullback will occur when the price breaks a support and then pulls back from the bottom with a sharp retracement, turning it into resistance. A bullish pullback will occur when the price breaks a resistance and then returns from above with a sharp retracement, turning it into support.

This kind of configuration is noticeable:

- At the end of an accumulation or distribution phase can lead to the start of a new trend.
- After an intermediate phase of accumulation/distribution formed during the run of a trend already in progress.

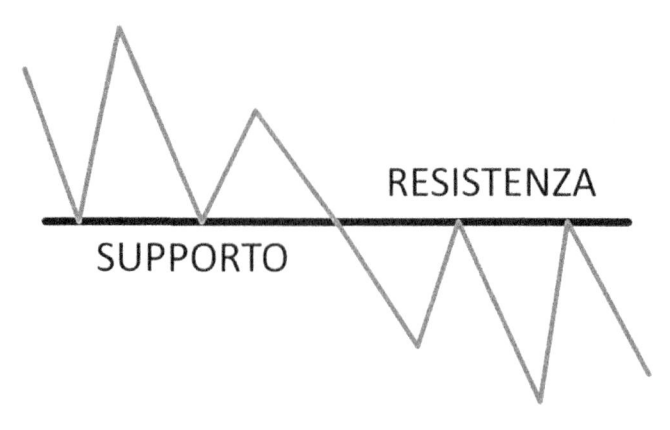

Translation: SUPPORT – RESISTANCE.

Illustration n.37– Schematization of the pullback.

The latter case, in which the continuation of a trend occurs following a breakout, offers an exceptional risk/return ratio, which makes it one of the most awaited configurations by Traders.

In order not to give you false hopes, I anticipate right now that many breakouts will fail, therefore, it is not easy to capture this kind of movement.

A Trader who wants to apply this type of operation will have to deepen the study of the formation and representation of trading volumes.

During a breakout of a level, the market tends to have an unusually high level of volatility associated with low liquidity.

Given the complexity of the topic, which likewise deserves a much more extensive discussion, I will have to ask you to elaborate on the topic, as it goes beyond the scope of this text.

I would like to emphasize that the proposed categorization is only an approximate and non-exhaustive picture of the possibilities that the market offers us. The subdivision into these macro-categories will be useful for identifying some peculiarities of the market phases. I have made them more understandable for a novice Trader so that you have the possibility to evaluate which of these trades is the most fitting for you, therefore do not take this classification as definitive, rather see it as a dynamic classification that can help you understand the behavior that is behind the price action.

Some Traders are comfortable in more than one category, especially if they use multiple time frames or interfaces on different types of markets.

I could feel comfortable with strategies that favor lateralization in FOREX and then, through other reasoning, use purely directional strategies on INDEXES, and no one could object.

A novice Trader will always have to continue to deepen the study of market configurations, and therefore, every time he observes a price configuration, he should ask himself which category it falls into, identify the elements of support and resistance that determine its movements, and finally, how it can be invalidated.

Chapter 8:

How to Trade Trends

In the following pages, we will analyze and deepen the ideal market phase for a Beginner Trader, the trending market, and we will do it with the same perspective as a professional Trader.

I will try to explain some of the most important secrets of trend following Trading, secrets that you will understand well now that you have learned how to recognize an uptrend and a downtrend.

Recalling that both an uptrend and a downtrend are made up of the alternation of swing high and swing low, produced in turn by the alternation of impulse movements and retracement movements, there are three main notions, which must be paid attention to in order to evaluate the health of an uptrend or downtrend.

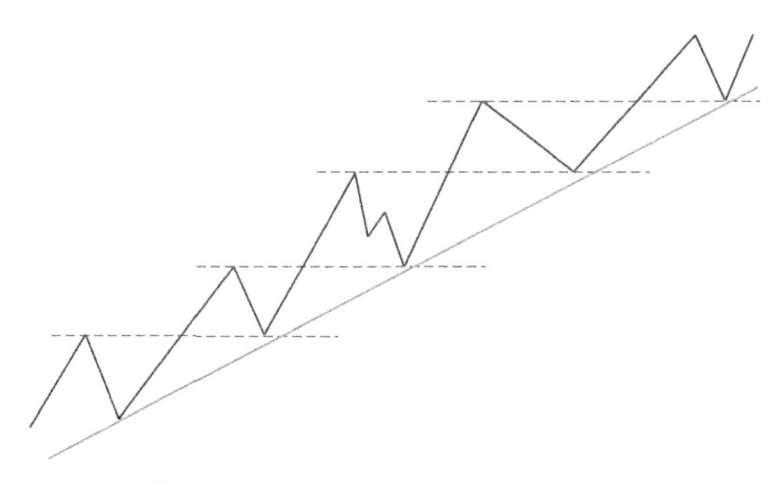

Illustration n.38– Schematization of a Bullish Market.

First of all, in an uptrend, both the maximums and the consecutive minimums must always be increasing with respect to the previous ones.

Each leg of the trend, defined as a price movement from its minimum to its maximum and vice versa, and even better if only the impulses, should be similar in extension or even greater than the previous one. Finally, any retracement will have weak momentum, thus generating minor counter-trend moves. This becomes clearer by looking at the following illustration.

Extending the view, we observe that the bullish movement is much broader but characterized by less impulsive phases. These phases show less agreement between RSI and price movements, but always constantly above the 200-day moving average.

Illustration n.39– Europe 50 Index chart

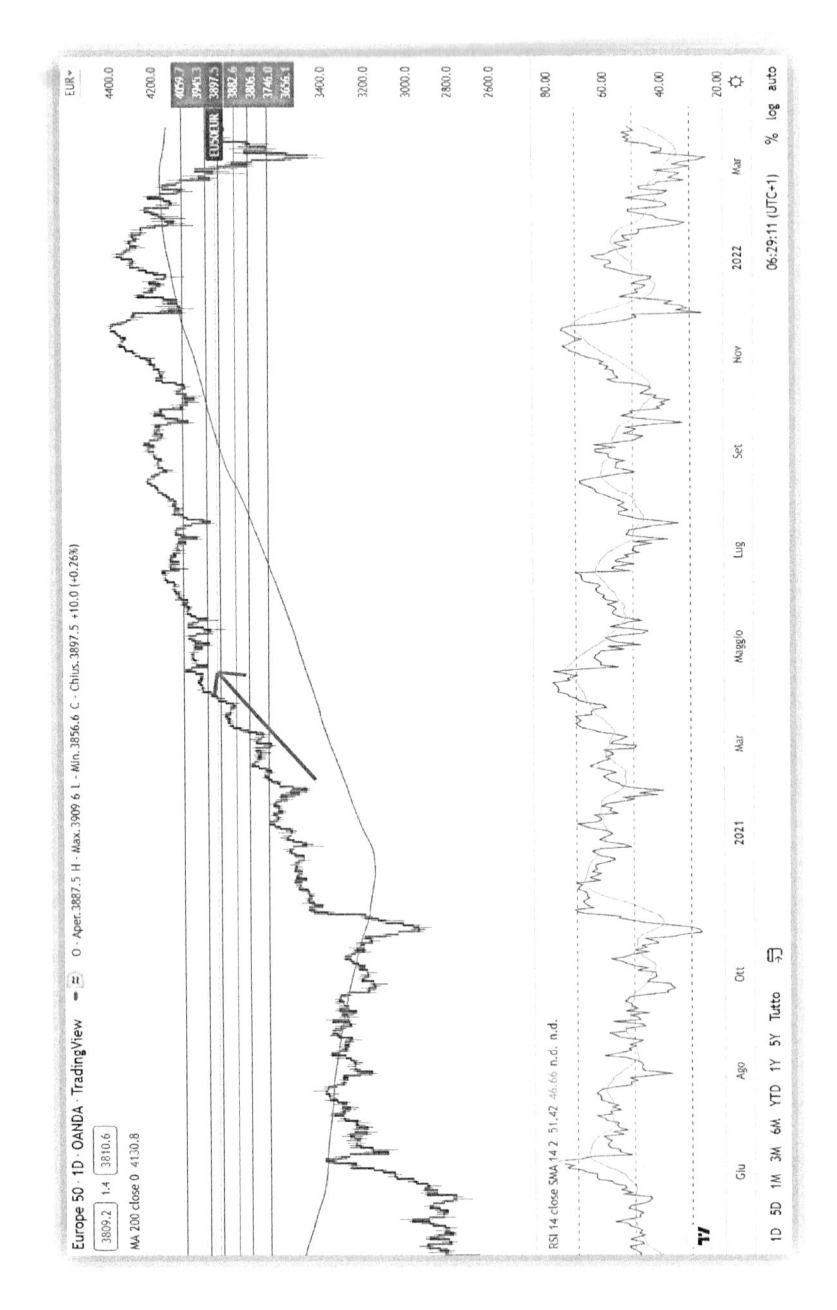

Illustration n.40– Europe 50 Index chart

In a downtrend, the situation is the same but reversed. We observe progressively decreasing highs and lows, each leg has an extension more or less similar to the previous one and, in countertrend retracements, we observe low Momentum.

On the following page, on the Euro/Dollar currency cross chart, we note that, between September and December, prices break a support downwards, giving rise to a trend phase. Progressively decreasing maxima and minima are found. The Price Action is located below the 200-period moving average and, as a reconfirmation of the downtrend, we see a succession of progressively decreasing maximums of the RSI and the passage of the last maximum below the 45 value, which we have previously seen to be a limit threshold between neutral trend and bearish trend.

Observing this configuration, the ideal operation would have envisaged entry into the market when the support was broken in mid-September, the positioning of the Stop Loss beyond the resistance value immediately above the violated support and a take profit with a risk/return ratio default of 1:2 or 1:3.

Another thing to look at in a classic bear market is the amount of volume and volatility, which will typically be higher when the price moves down and less when prices move up. Simply put, prices will tend to have faster movements and increasing rates of change in bear markets.

Obviously, prices will never move linearly from top to bottom and vice versa, and in every bear market and bull market, we will always have more or less marked countertrend retracements.

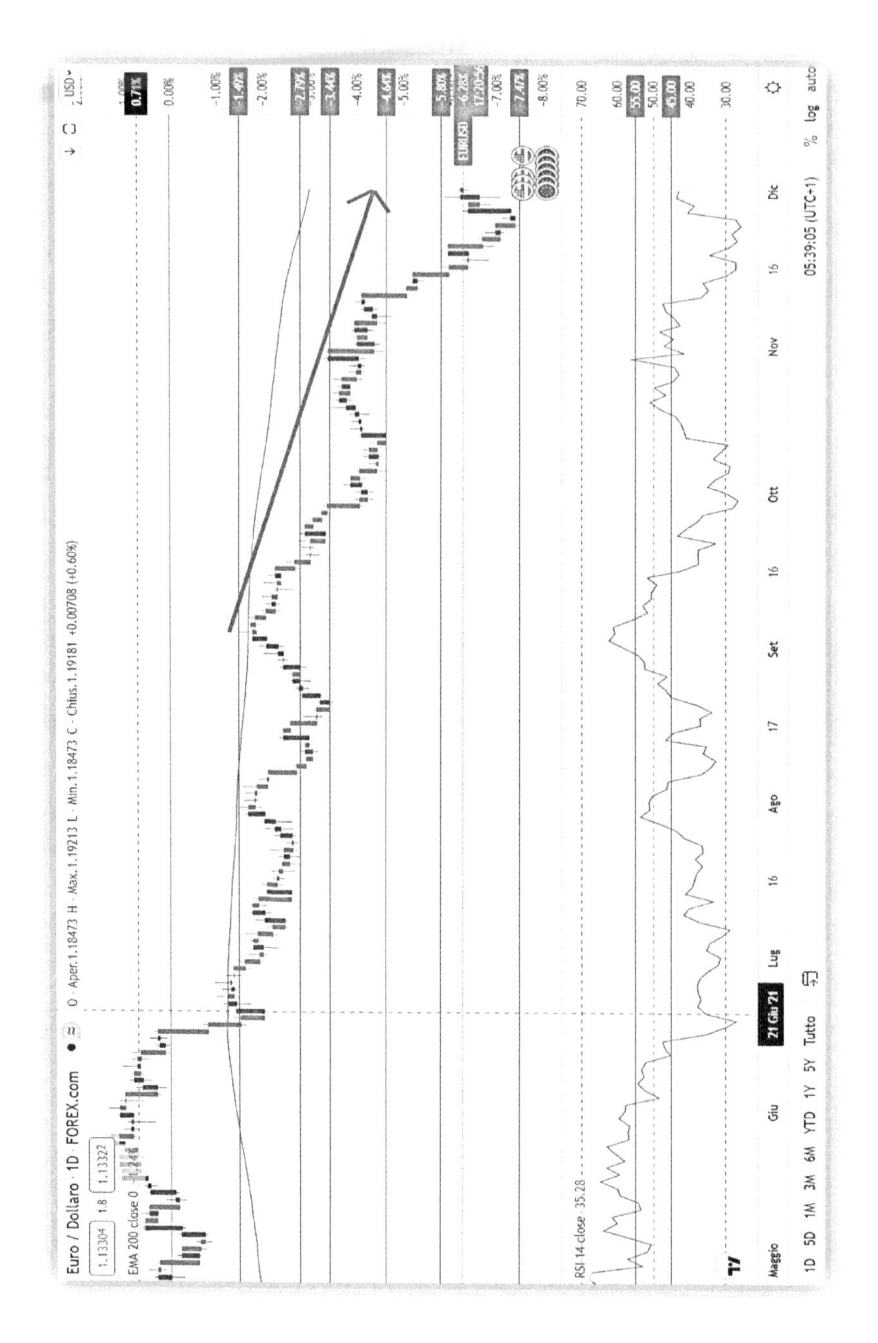

Illustration n.41– Chart of the Euro/US Dollar currency cross

Retracements

Retracements are very important and are often ignored by novice and sometimes even experienced Traders. Some retracements can offer good market entry setups in the direction of the main trend, giving us the opportunity to buy more shares to increase our current market positions or enter at a lower price while reducing the risk of execution in Stop Loss. They also provide us with some important information about the potential continuation or conclusion of the current trend.

A retracement is a counter-trend move that anticipates a new, vigorous leg in the original direction of the trend. When a retracement occurs within a bullish phase, it often generates a pause to consolidate the conquered price level and accumulate energy for the next impulsive movement.

One of the potential causes of a retracement is partial profit-taking by market participants. The trading volume in these phases is generally lower than in impulsive movements. There are two types of retracements, simple retracement and complex retracement.

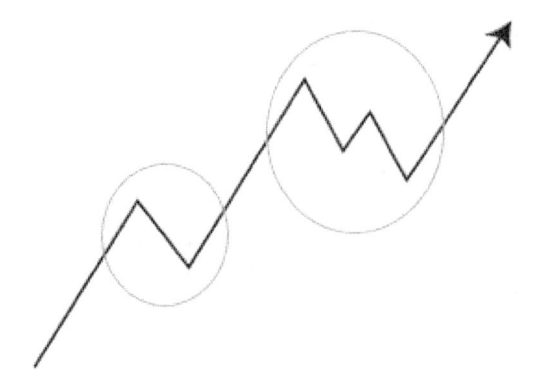

Illustration n.42– Schematization of the type of retracement

There is a rule on retracements regarding alternation. This rule of thumb tells us that it is quite difficult to observe a trend with 5 well-defined impulses alternating with 4 simple retracements. It is quite frequent to observe a trend with 5 impulses alternating with 2 simple and 2 complex retracements.

Below I show an example of the euro / US dollar chart in which the birth of a first impulse in mid-May is evident, followed by a simple retracement in June. Subsequently, we observe a second impulse, which extends until the first days of September, followed by a new retracement and subsequent movements, so weak that they cannot be considered as impulses. Finally, in November, we can observe the development of a third impulse which, in December, will break upward the level of the previous swing high reached in September.

It is important to know how to recognize an impulse with a peculiar characteristic. An impulse can be classified as such when its extension is such as to exceed the maximum or minimum price level defined by the impulse that preceded it, and its extension must be comparable with the previous impulses.

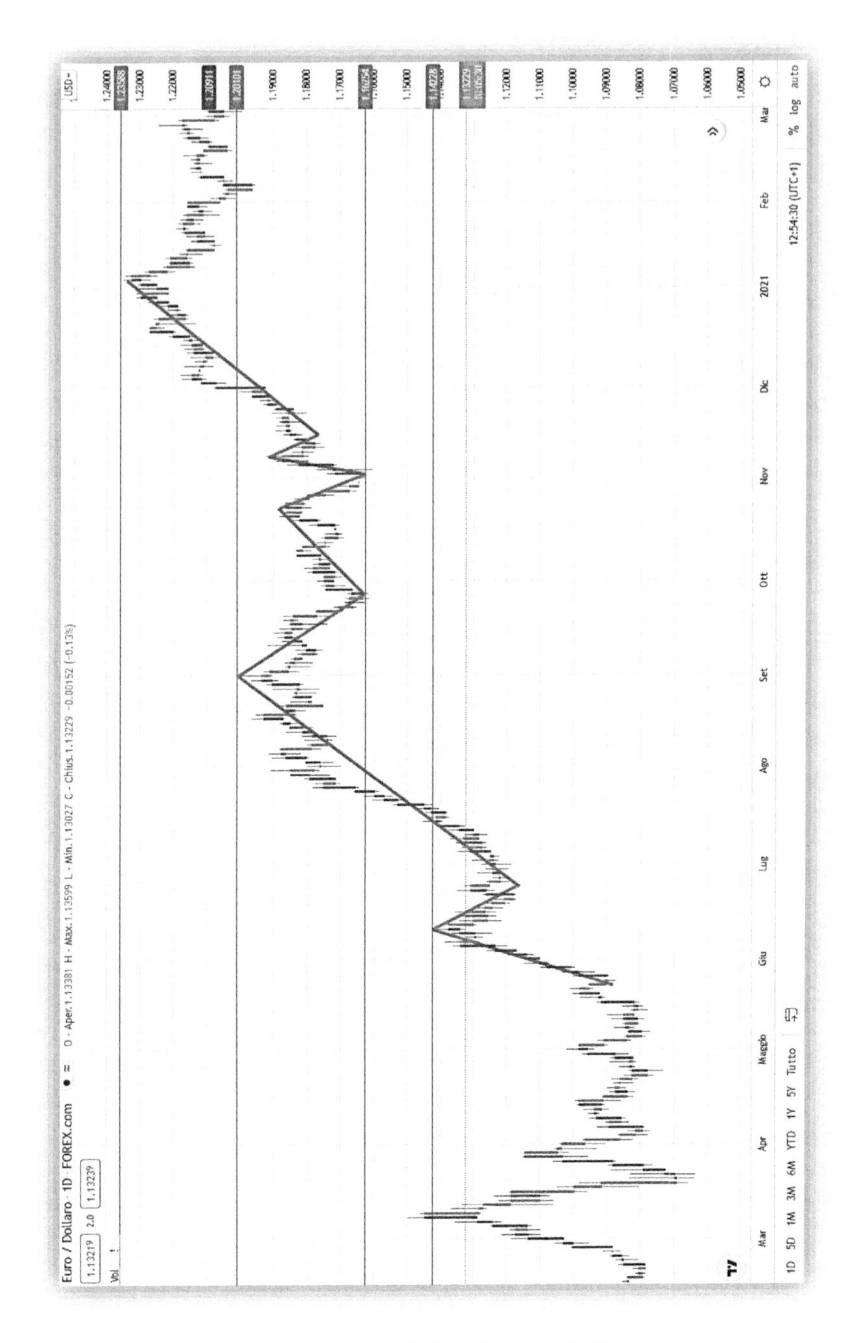

Illustration n.43– Chart of the Euro/US Dollar currency cross

Trend Lines

Knowing how to trace and identify a trendline is one of the basic skills that a technical Trader must learn and master if he wants to operate according to trend following strategies.

Identifying trend lines becomes possible, and even trivial, when you understand the imbalance between purchasing power and selling pressure inherent in a market at a given moment.

In bull markets, we will pay more attention to the consecutive growing lows which, suitably connected with a line that collides at least three of them, define a trendline acting as dynamic support for the prices.

This line can also be defined as a demand line in which the selling pressure is reduced in favor of purchasing power.

We will look for the opposite in bear markets, where we will pay more attention to consecutive lower highs. Like the previous example, if we find the possibility of connecting at least three consecutive highs with a line, we will identify a bearish trend line, which has a dynamic resistance function.

This line can also be defined as a supply line in which demand collapses under the vigorous push of supply.

Using trend lines we can obtain a great deal of visual information, which enhances the current trend state of the market, of which three, in particular, deserve attention.

The first information we find is the slope of the trend line, which can provide a Trader with information relating to the intensity and speed with which the trend is developing.

The second important information concerns the extension of the legs, information that gives us the sensitivity to understand how strong and how sustainable the current trend is.

The third piece of information concerns the position of the next potential, Rebound/Retracement, which becomes more probable the closer prices get to the trendline.

The four essential capabilities in trend following

There are four skills necessary to operate effectively with trend following strategies which, as the aptitudes of a professional, determine the success of a Trader.

Regardless of how trivial they may seem, I invite you not to underestimate them since their acquisition is anything but obvious.

1 - Knowing how to buy when the market is strong and knowing how to sell when the market is weak

This sentence contains the essence of trend following operations:

"KNOWING HOW TO BUY WHEN THE MARKET IS STRONG AND KNOWING HOW TO SELL WHEN THE MARKET IS WEAK"

Essentially, in a trend following strategy, we will buy when prices rise and sell when prices fall.

You might imagine that this is nonsense because you may have always heard that you buy at low prices and sell at higher prices on the stock exchange.

I anticipate that, if one really wanted to operate by buying at low prices to resell at high prices, one would adopt an operation of little effectiveness, mainly characterized by very long waits, protracted in the hope of reaching the bottom of the market and finally finding the opportunity at a discount.

Remember that a healthy business grows, so seemingly high current prices may not be all that high in the future. Regarding the Tesla company, in 2020 the title appeared very overvalued and many were certainly scared of it. Nonetheless, the quotation continued to grow in the following years. If we had waited for a reversal of the price to buy shares, hoping for a return to the values of 2020, we could have remained on the sidelines for years.

The first thing to do when approaching the market with a trend following mentality is to immediately stop thinking that the price is "Too High" or "Too Low." The word too much is superfluous in this type of operation.

In any market, even if you think the price is excessively high, there is always a chance to see a breakout, and at the same time, when you think the price has bottomed out, there is always a chance to call—Further meltdowns.

For these reasons, the price will never be so excessive as to prevent you from opening a long trade if the market configuration and your analysis are showing you an adequate Statistical Advantage, and obviously, the same goes for the opposite case.

As a trend follower Trader, your decisions will have to be made on the basis of objective data representative of the strength and weakness of the market, avoiding making the mistake of focusing on the mere price value of the financial instrument.

2 - Know how to operate in every market

Knowing how to operate in each market is exactly the skill that the Trader acquires in the continuous diversification of his exposure. By diversification, I mean the intentional allocation of one of our capital shares, well defined on the basis of our risk attitude, on markets that are clearly uncorrelated.

In this way, the possibilities of carrying out operations are increased since the panorama of financial instruments is broadened, and at the same time, the overall risk of our account is reduced.

I would like to delve into the concept of decorrelation for a moment. Two markets are defined as decorrelated when the dynamics that influence the first market do not influence the second in any way. Conversely, two markets will be defined as correlated when the same dynamics influence them. Furthermore, two markets will never be linearly correlated but could be subject to various degrees of correlation based on whether the same dynamics can more or less influence them. For example, with the beginning of the war in Ukraine in 2022, the prices of natural gas underwent a strong surge, at the same time, all the energy markets, with different degrees of magnitude, also showed increases, demonstrating precisely a strong correlation.

Trend following operations should never focus on a single market for some essential reasons. A market will be attractive to a Trader as long as there is enough Momentum and enough liquidity.

Since markets move sideways most of the time, the only way to maximize the number of trades will be to move from one market to another or to be in multiple markets at the same time that do not correlate with each other.

The trend following approach does not provide for the creation of balanced and risk-free portfolios. Comparing them with the operations of investors and position Traders, typically trend following operations are short-lived and envisage that one enters the market in the birth phase of the trend and that a decision is made to exit completely from the market when the trend, now mature, begins to show obvious signs of weakness.

As already mentioned, the markets move sideways most of the time, therefore the choice to operate in trend must necessarily include a watchlist, a list of securities, and financial instruments such as the one I initially suggested you to prepare.

This list of favorites should include instruments belonging to different markets and chosen so as not to be correlated. By making this simple list, you will greatly reduce the time needed to search for an interesting financial instrument and significantly increase the chances of identifying the emergence of new trends on instruments that are familiar to you.

I would like to dwell again on the concept of correlation to dispel any doubts about its interpretation. Imagine you want to operate on the currency market, and you decide to enter the Euro/US Dollar market, the operation has a configuration that gives you a good Statistical Advantage, and you are confident that you have the possibility of making a profit. Scrolling through other markets, known as the Pound / US Dollar market is also healthy, you also observe a very promising configuration here, similar to the previous one, which again gives you a Statistical Advantage.

I'm sure you've already figured out what the deal is with these two financial instruments.

The reason for this "luck" is inherent in the fact that both currency crosses predict that the quoted currency is the US dollar, therefore, as the dollar moves, the graphs will have more or less similar trends. Carrying out operations on two markets so intimately linked generates the overlapping of the specific risk. When the first operation goes well, the second one will also do it with a very high probability, and obviously, when it loses, you will lose twice as much.

Let's go back to a very strong correlation, the one linked to the energy raw materials sector. Let's imagine I want to short oil, once again, I look at the chart, and I notice an ideal configuration to go down. I open the position and move to the other energy instruments, I am captured by the trend of the petrol graph, it too goes downwards and it too is configured to offer a Statistical Advantage for a short operation.

Knowing the concept of risk well, I will know that I don't have to open a sale transaction on this second market as petrol is a derivative of oil and depends on it in an important way.

The correlation, in this case, will be direct, if the first market is bearish then the second market is also bearish and so are all other oil-related instruments, including oil companies, petrochemical companies, currencies that base their economy on oil, and other sectors heavily influenced by the cost of this raw material. Before trading on multiple markets, always check which instruments you are exposing yourself to and their possible interconnection.

Remember that I have already anticipated the existence of different degrees of correlation, and for this reason, it is not unusual to find financial instruments with inverse correlation. This particular kind of correlation provides that the two financial instruments are subject to corresponding movements in terms of time or also in terms of price volatility but with inverse directionality.

Returning to the subject of currency crosses, if I find a bearish setup in the first instrument, Euro / US Dollar, I can expect a chart with an upward trend of the US Dollar / Swiss Franc cross.

This occurs because, in the first case, the US dollar is the quoted currency, while in the second case, the dollar assumes the role of the base currency; furthermore, the Swiss franc undergoes macroeconomic influences very similar to those affecting the euro, a situation which is by no means negligible and which further strengthens the correlation.

3 - Knowing how to be patient and wait for the closing of a winning Trade

Knowing how to patiently wait for the closing of a winning Trade, and being sudden in closing losing Trades, is the third ability of a trend follower Trader.

At the end of the year, a trend follower will notice that a large part of his profits derives from very few positive Trades characterized by an excellent risk/return ratio. On the other hand, he will notice that he has performed a large number of losing trades but of a very modest size compared to the winning trades.

Among the main causes of the failure of trend following strategies is taking profits too early. Failure to be patient will cause emotional and impulsive actions which, in the long run, will devastate the overall performance of the strategy.

You will need to be prepared to take a large amount of small losses waiting to catch the correct move to ride, therefore, learning how to close losing trades quickly is essential.

You will have understood that it will not be enough for you to undertake the Trade operation correctly and enter the trending market to be an effective Trader. You must always be prepared to see your operations fluctuate between positive and negative.

There are several retracements during a trend, some of them even deep and important. Precisely in these cases, the use of a well-studied strategy is essential. If your Trading System expects you to exit following a certain event, and it is not currently providing any exit signals, you must keep the trade open.

Remember that a single operation will make no difference, even if it is an exceptional trade. While the robustness of the strategy over time, deriving from the Statistical Advantage resulting from having made your considerations well in advance, will be the real generator of your profits and will make you a winner.

I'm not a fan of the Pareto principle, according to which 80% of the results are generated by 20% of the actions we take, but I have to admit that in the trend following approach, this relationship fits quite well. So expect to see that only 20% of your trades will be profitable, and 80% of your single strategy earnings will be generated from it.

4 - Stop predicting market highs and lows

Finally, the last skill to develop is to stop trying to predict the achievement of the market highs and lows. This kind of focus will subconsciously put you in the mind of being able to anticipate market movements and will cause a growing sense of satisfaction and omnipotence, should you happen to be actually right. Unfortunately, I have to bring you back to earth and warn you that no market will ever fulfill our predictions. No matter how technical, in-depth, and detailed, based on historical data or on the stars they are, the market will never be 100% responsive to our hypothesis. Convincing yourself that you are always right will only cause harm.

A conscientious Trader knows well that his operation could go wrong, even if all the indicators, all the assumptions made, and the entire macroeconomic and microeconomic panorama fall within the parameters of his strategy. The reason is simple, a professional Trader knows to operate according to probabilities and never according to certainties.

Put your ego aside and rely on the facts, he accepts that he's not perfect, that he doesn't have to be perfect, and that he can't be a winner 100% of the time.

In trend following operations, forecasts are not made, conditions are sought that demonstrate the existence of a trend already in progress and are followed for as long as they are valid, and there is no maximum time. The trade can end in one day or six months, and your strategy will dictate when you should exit the market. The mere fact that you are tired of waiting and want to cash out your prize is not a valid reason to close the deal.

Trading is not an activity that must generate tension, it must be boring and predictable within the limits of statistics. Obviously, if you prefer scalping and need emotions, the trend following approach is not for you, although the considerations made so far are easily applicable to this type of operation as well.

Analyzing the market highs and lows is one of the most important skills to develop if you want to become a professional and profitable Trader, but the total profit does not come from having bought at the lows and having resold at the highs or vice versa, but from knowing how to identify with discrete precision the interval between them and knowing how to make the most of it.

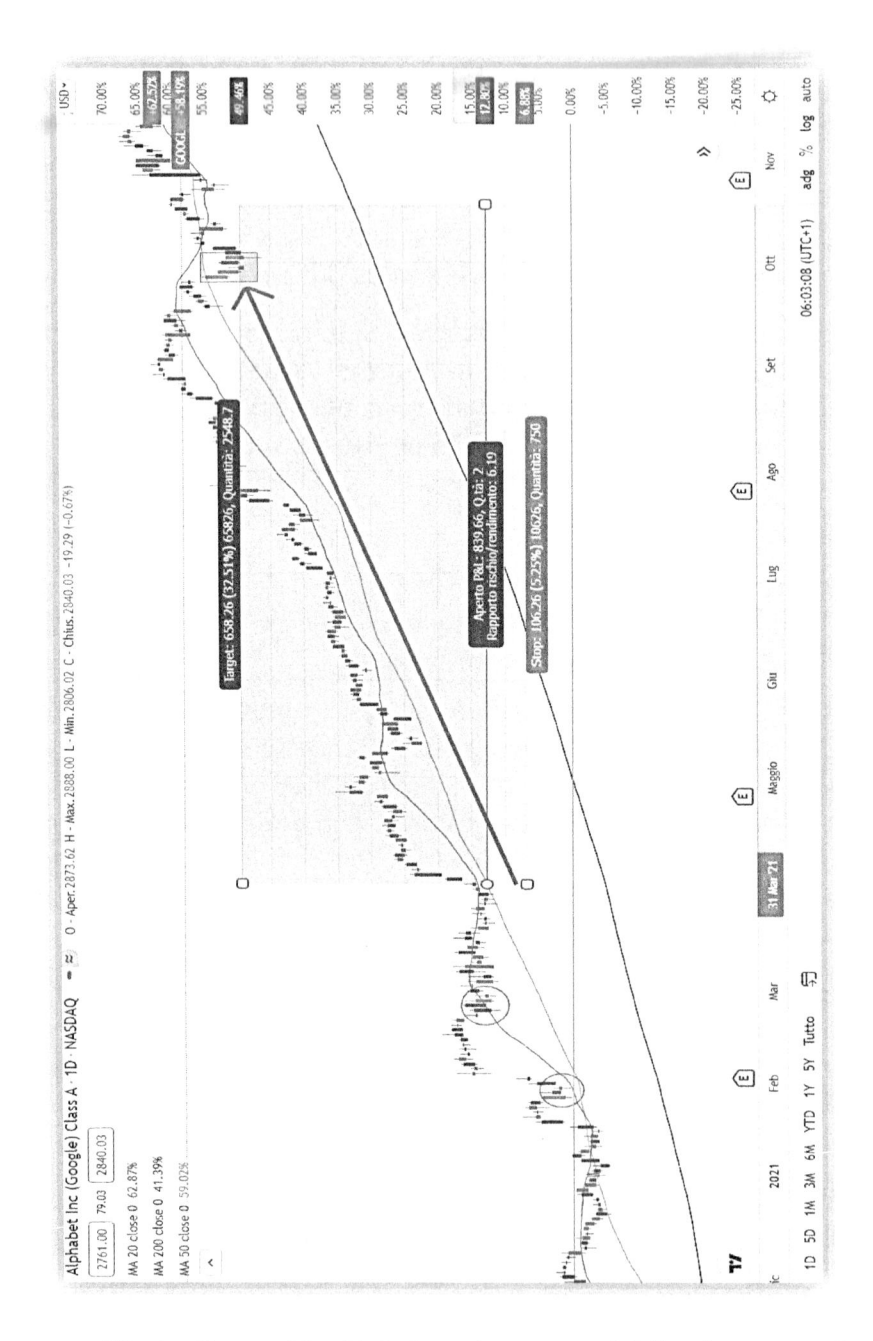

Illustration n.44– Alphabet chart, trend following operation

Now I show you an example of trend following trading based on the use of moving averages.

On the daily chart of Alphabet, the company that owns Google, you can see three lines, and three moving averages, respectively, at 20-periods, 50-periods and 200-periods.

The 200-period average informs us of an ongoing trend, so we know we are observing a bull market. The first signal comes from the bullish crossing between the 20-period moving average and the 50-period moving average. Let's start paying attention to the development of the graph and wait for prices to rebound for the first time on the 20-period average and then a second time. Based on these observations, we would have a fair chance of success if we bought this stock.

We wait for a further signal, which can be a new bounce on the 20-period average or on the 50-period average, and we buy. Finally, we set the Stop Loss that makes sense, perhaps with reference to a nearby support or based on the current volatility value, which can be determined through the Average True Range.

The operation must remain open until it goes into Stop Loss or until the prices break down the 50-period moving average, generating a succession of two daily candles below it.

For Alphabet this operation, which lasted from approximately March 31st to October 15th, would have generated a risk-return ratio of approximately 1 to 6. It is also obvious that if we were accustomed to the use of the Trailing Stop, the risk would have been progressively canceled.

Now ask yourself, could this extensive operation be right for you, or do you need something more dynamic? An impatient person will hardly be able to apply these kinds of strategies.

Obviously, the same considerations can be made in the case of short operations, where the 200-period average will indicate a clear bearish trend, and the prices will meet resistance in correspondence with the 20- and 50-period moving averages, bouncing downwards.

Success requires study

Before trading in the financial markets, you will need to build a solid foundation of knowledge about position sizing and capital management. Deprived of the knowledge of these notions, even the best Trader would go broke in a short time.

If you want to become a successful Trader by applying trend following strategies, you cannot avoid learning when a trend is potentially exhausting or about to reverse.

To help you start this study path, I propose three of the main methods of evaluating a trend among the various existing methodologies and signals.

The first method consists in carefully observing the graph with the aim of finding in it a configuration that suggests the weakening of the current trend, which we can intuit by reading the current strength and momentum of the graph.

The weakening of the thrust occurs when two consecutive bullish impulses show a principle of weakening, characterized by progressively more contained extension of the legs than the previous one.

These bullish impulses considered weak are usually confirmed in the respective retracements/rebounds of substantial importance and extension similar to the impulse itself, if not greater. All of this happens due to the reduction in the presence of buyers in the market, with a consequent reduction in the purchasing drive.

In the Bitcoin/US Dollar graph it is evident how the current trend is gradually weakening, although we continue to observe ever-increasing consecutive highs and lows. The break-down of the last low further confirms this weakness, which could lead to a subsequent reversal.

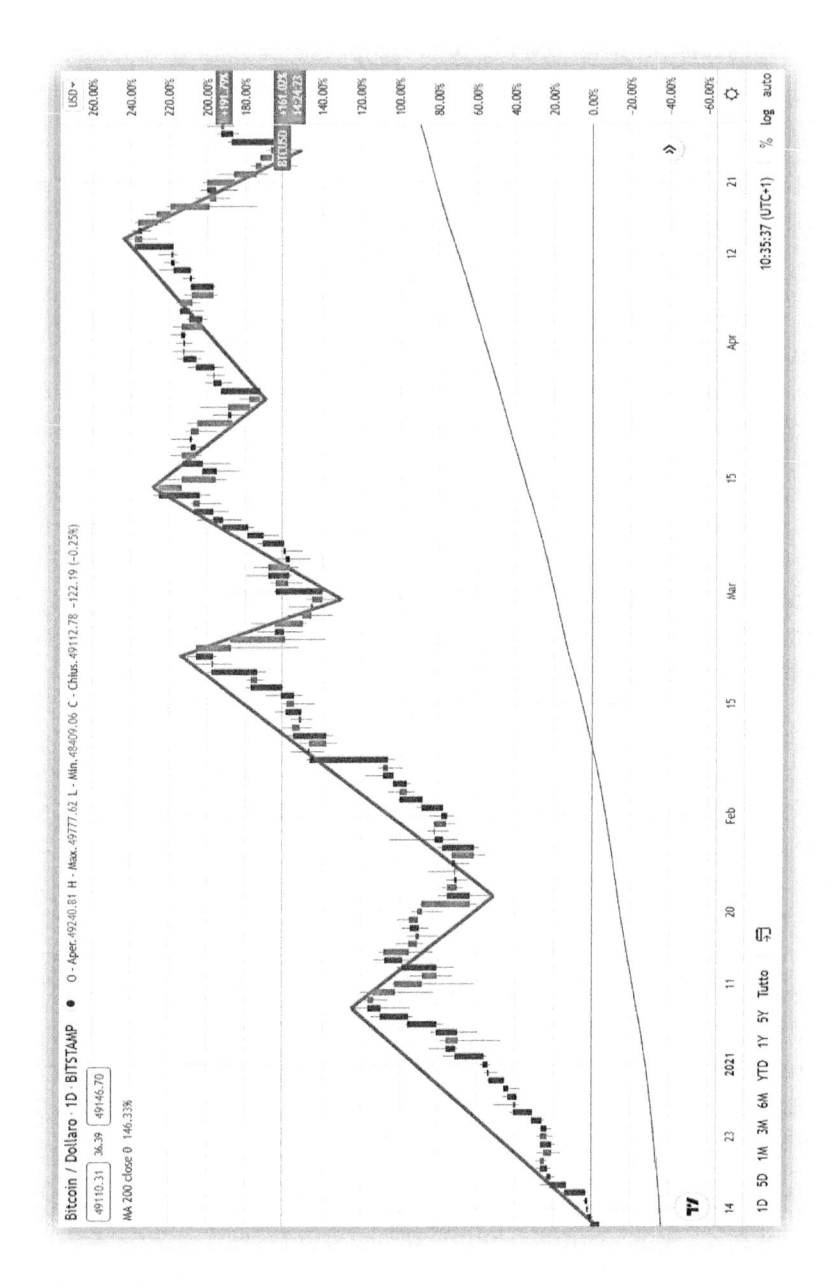

Illustration n.45– Bitcoin / US Dollar chart, progressive weakening

In fact, after another last bullish impulse, starting from May 10 2021, the price saw an important reversal on this financial instrument.

Obviously, when this configuration occurs, a prudent Trader must start paying close attention to the market or, if even more prudent, look for a good exit point from the operation.

This kind of signal is not necessarily a trend reversal prophecy. It could simply be a moment of lateralization of the market which is followed by the recovery of the price movement in the direction of the main trend, a bit like stopping during a run to catch your breath and then starting running again.

The second noteworthy signal is called *"Parabolic Impulse."* It occurs when we notice a series of increasingly marked slope impulses in the graph, which are a clear sign of excess interest. The higher and steeper the slope, the more abrupt the retracement will be. Such sudden movements in the market create weakness and uncertainty, therefore, knowing how to identify them can avoid even significant losses.

One way to identify these situations is to use band indicators, such as Keltner channels or Envelopes. We will have a first sign of excess strength when a trend will take on enough energy to push beyond the limits of these bands, creating three or more candles outside of them. In the immediate future, a clear retracement usually follows, bringing prices back at least to the return of the moving average values. In terms of probabilities, we most often observe the beginning of a lateralization phase and, more rarely, a market reversal. Below is an example on the Litecoin/US Dollar chart.

The third sign of exhaustion of a trend is given by the formation of a minimum and a maximum decreasing with respect to the previous ones, which even beginners will know as head-shoulders formation.

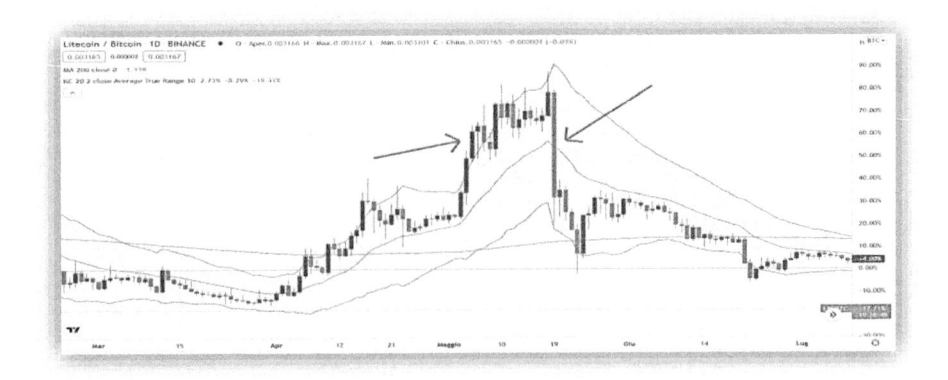

Illustration n.46– Litecoin / Bitcoin chart, price excess detected through Keltner channels

This pattern appears on the chart when the price retracement is deep enough to reach price levels similar to the previous swing low. In the immediate future, prices try to rebound in the direction of the main trend but, no longer having enough strength to reach the previous maximum, they create a decreasing maximum.

Following the formation of this last important piece of information, the market becomes aware of the weakness that is being generated, and a new deep retracement occurs, similar or greater in extension to the previous one and which pushes prices below the neckline. The neckline of the head and shoulders pattern is identified by tracing a straight line passing through the two previous low swings.

When we realize we are in this situation, we must be ready to exit the market and possibly open a transaction in the opposite direction to the one previously executed. An image from the EUR/AUD chart will best clarify this example.

Look at the chart of the cross Euro/Australian Dollar, the market in this window has an evident moment of a bullish trend that from April until July did not see particular moments of rest.

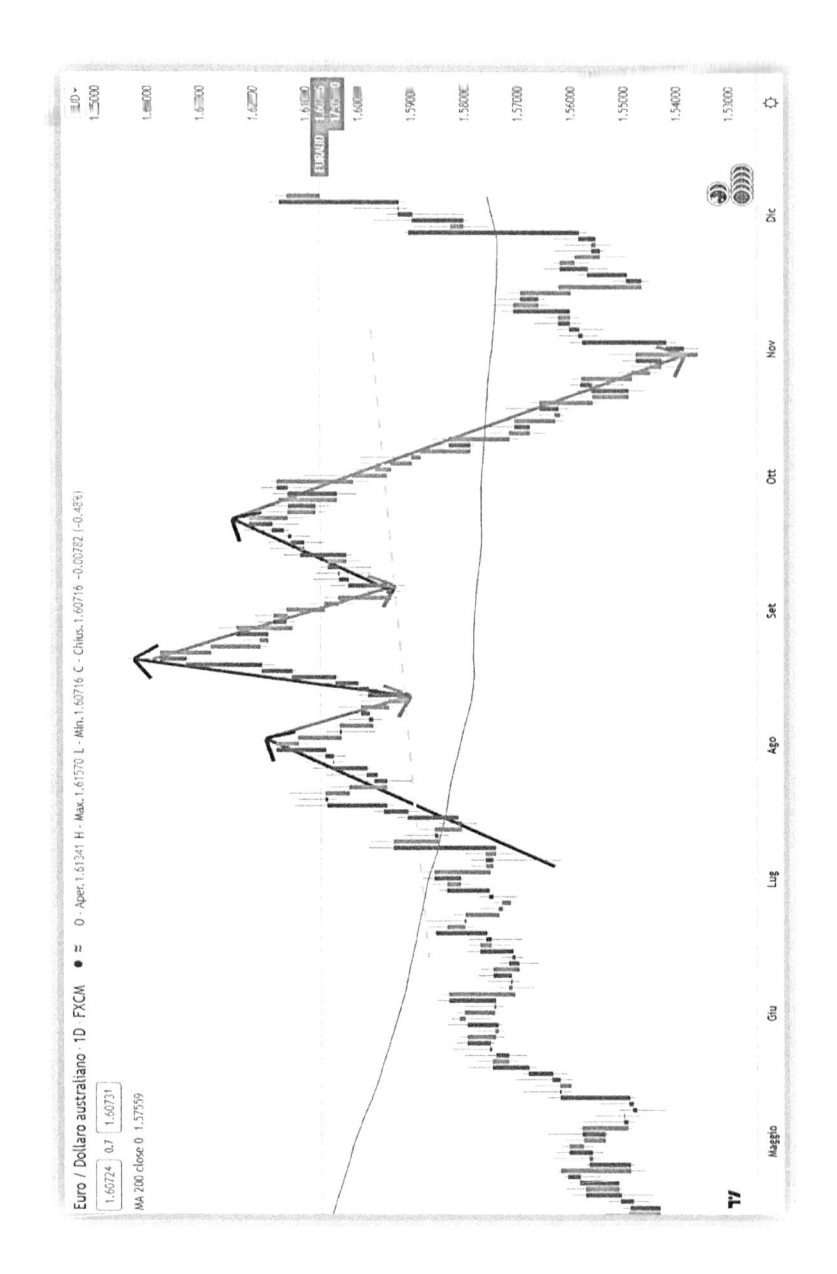

Illustration n.47– Chart Euro / Australian Dollar, Bearish Head-Shoulders

From July to August there is an increase in the slope of the price graph, followed by a first retracement. In mid-August we notice a new impulse that culminates in a new relative high, immediately followed by a deep retracement, such as to reach price levels similar to the previous low.

From September we note that there is a new impulse, less extensive and characterized by a lower slope, which generates a new relative maximum, lower than the previous one and comparable in price level with the maximum of early August.

The definitive signal will come with the break in October of the neckline, drawn with a dotted line, caused by a deep retracement, which lasted until the beginning of November.

Keep in Mind

Remember that if you wish to trade trend following strategies, the leg length of each impulse should always be longer in the direction of the trend and shorter in retracements, as this demonstrates the strength of the dominant trend.

The candles at the beginning of each trend must be long, while in retracements and lateralizations, they must be smaller than the candles of the dominant trend.

A consolidation formed during the trend phase, when conforming with modest-sized candlesticks accompanied by modest volumes, provides us with an excellent continuation signal.

Always look at the higher level, broader time frame chart to remove any market noise and get a clear view of the trend.

Chapter 9:
Exploit Breakouts in Sideways Markets

In this chapter, we will study the correct way to approach the market when it is in a lateral phase. I will also show you some techniques to operate successfully in these conditions.

The sideways market is characterized by the alternating movement of prices with a frequent bounce between a support and a resistance. It can also form, as already indicated in the previous chapter, in the form of an intermediate phase of a trend.

To better understand the difference between the two market situations, let's make a timely comparison.

Trending market	Sideways market
The price is moved by a strong non-arbitrary component, which unbalances the balance of supply and demand.	The price is moved by substantially very similar relationships between supply and demand. Therefore the balance does not undergo obvious imbalances.
Prices move in a specific direction and are more predictable.	Prices are more random and much less predictable.
The risk is clearly definable.	The risk is difficult to define.
It is a market more suitable for beginner Traders.	It is a market that requires a greater ability to analyze supply and demand.

Knowing how to understand the moments of transition between a trend phase and a lateralization phase can give us a significant Statistical Advantage in the market in terms of entry and exit timing.

The sideways market can conform in three different structures:

1. Parallel movement;
2. Movement in contraction;
3. Expanding movement.

The direction taken by the support and resistance lines delimiting the lateralization interval distinguishes one type of structure from the other.

Structure with parallel movement

In the first case, a market with a parallel structure, the support line, and the resistance line are parallel to each other. This feature makes this kind of lateralization the simplest and most frequent.

This structure shows generally constant volatility within the range.

The support and resistance lines can be both horizontal and oblique, a peculiarity that does not affect the validity of lateralization. There will therefore be two most frequent configurations in the market: the sloping sideways range and the sideways range with consolidating prices.

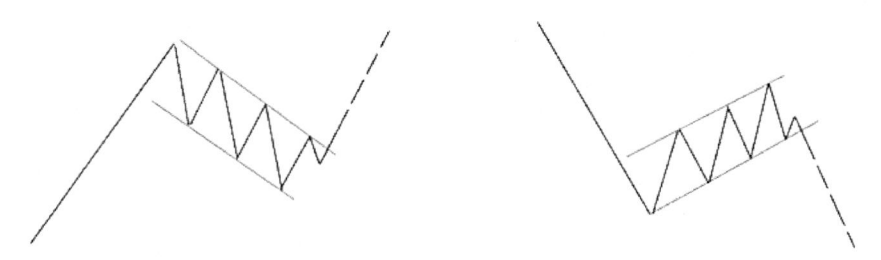

Illustration n.48– Schematization of a lateral market with a parallel sloping structure

In the first case, following a trend phase, the market begins to accumulate, generating a channel with parallel lines, which usually leads to an accumulation phase in the opposite direction to the main trend, implemented by a complex type retracement.

The accumulation will have a regular shape, it generally suggests that there is the possibility of a new push aimed at continuing in accordance with the main trend.

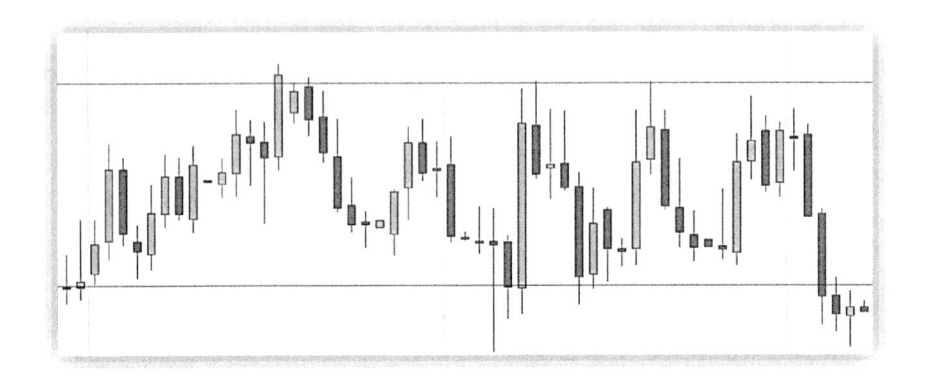

Illustration n.49– Example of a sideways market with a parallel structure in consolidation

In the second case, a lateralizing market begins to implement a contraction of movements near a support or a resistance, as if to indicate the intention to move in a precise direction. This kind of configuration is, in effect, a signal that anticipates the occurrence of a breakout.

When we are faced with a market that shows price contraction close to a support or resistance, the price range narrows, creating a new channel that further strengthens this contraction.

When this situation occurs, it is not rare to observe that the secondary channel is approximately 25-30% of the original range.

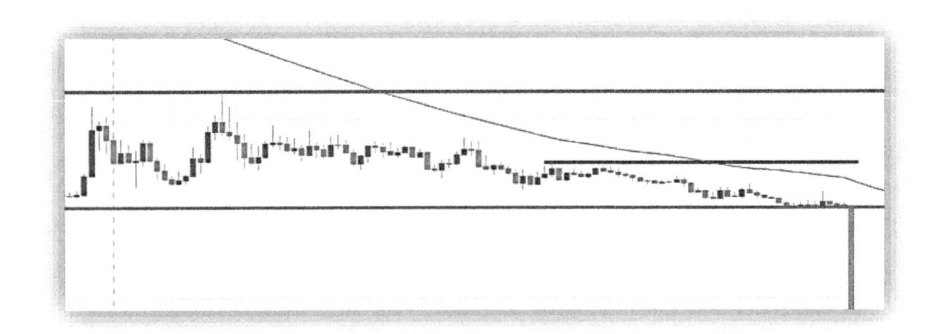

Illustration n.50– Example of sideways market with parallel structure in consolidation with breakout

This characteristic of the prices highlights how there is, respectively, a greater interest of the buyers when the contraction occurs near the resistance or of the sellers when the contraction occurs near the support.

A typical example that determines exactly this behavior can be observed in the formation of cup and handle patterns, in which prices roughly form two arcs, the second of which is smaller.

It should be emphasized that the pattern can be formed in different ways, especially the handle can be formed later:

- At the narrowing of one of the two lines that define the lateral movement;
- The formation of two new parallel lines but with a different inclination compared to the original limits;
- A retracement that takes prices to a dynamic support line belonging to a more extensive converging and contracting formation.

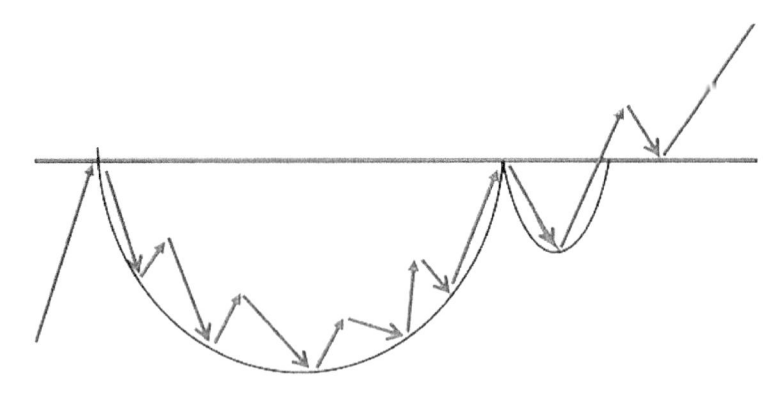

Illustration n.51– Schematization of a Cup and Handle Pattern

Structure with contraction movement

In the case of a contracting movement structure, the support and resistance lines, not being parallel, appear to cross at an ideal point in the near future.

Among the best-known configurations of this type are triangles.

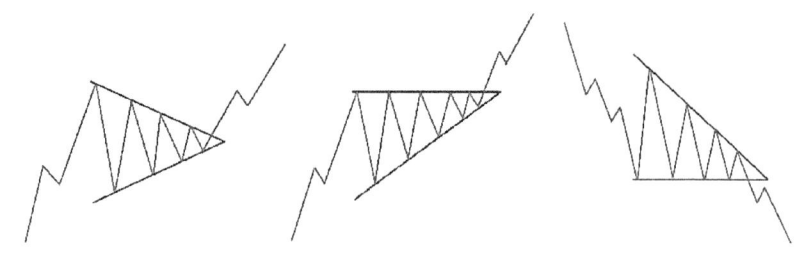

Illustration n.52– Schematization of converging structures

In symmetrical triangles, both support and resistance lines are inclined and slope with a similar angle of incidence. Due to their peculiar conformation, symmetrical triangles absolutely do not lend themselves to any type of directional forecast, therefore the technical analyst who identifies this pattern will simply have to take note of the contraction in volatility and then complete his own analysis through the use of further tools, which will be expressly devoted to identifying the probable direction.

In ascending triangles, support tends to slope upwards, while resistance is horizontal. This configuration suggests that the purchasing power of buyers begins to predominate over the selling pressure.

Conversely, in descending triangles, support is horizontal, while resistance tends to go downwards. This latter configuration of the triangle suggests that selling pressure is building and more and more buyers are walking away from the market. Ascending and descending triangles generally provide excellent indications of the next occurrence of a break in the direction of the trend.

Structure with expanding movement

Each bounce tends to be larger than the previous one in expanding lateralizations, or expanding triangles. The support and resistance lines have such a direction that they diverge and move away from each other.

This type of configuration underlines the uncertainty and confusion present in the market at a given historical moment. There are significant difficulties in identifying a possible direction, assessing market volatility, and also assessing risk.

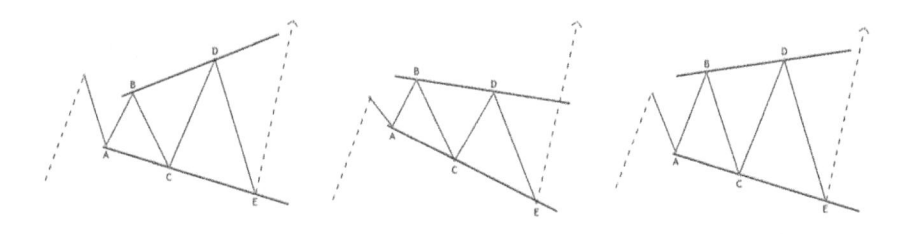

Illustration n.53– Schematization of divergent structures

Normally nothing happens beyond the limits defined by supports and resistance until the next break, but considering the peculiarity of these configurations, they are not easy to apply for beginner Traders.

Including the various possible situations in which you could find yourself, it is always advisable to ask yourself how to take advantage, and therefore how to operate successfully from the specific scenario that presents itself ahead.

Level Breakouts

In a breakout, a Trader does nothing but place a buy or sell order, depending on whether there is an upward breakout of a resistance or a downward breakout of a support, only when he finds that these breakouts are supported by a visible increase in trading volumes.

The best breakout trades that you can aspire to join will be those in which, due to the interest of institutional Traders, an important movement is observed.

Breakout trading often fails, as there are such deep retracements that they suddenly bring prices into the lateralization range. Nonetheless, a trained Trader who knows how to best manage the risk/return ratio will be able to manage losses serenely while waiting for the winning operation.

To clearly illustrate breakout trading, I recall the ascending triangle formation.

In the following illustration, it is possible to notice how the Price Action forms increasing lows, useful for the construction of an increasing dynamic resistance line. The resulting information is an increase in buyer interest, expressed precisely through the consequent increase in demand.

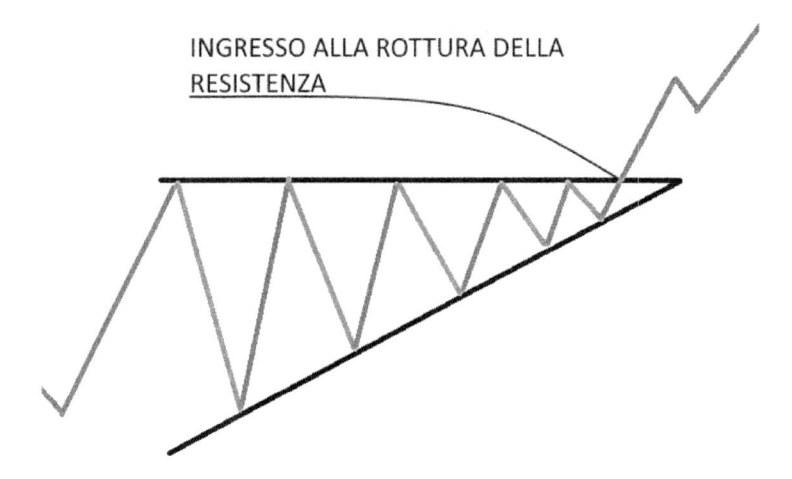

Translation: entrance to the resistance break.

Illustration n.54– Schematization of a bullish breakout.

Buyers in this situation decide to make purchases at progressively higher prices, causing the extension of each retracement to decrease, as if to make clear their intention to accumulate positions.

All this indicates a great potential for prices to break upward, as the imbalance of market interest in favor of buyers is evident.

Operations in breakout

Knowing how to recognize these configurations with a high probability of occurrence and potentially profitable, we will have to enter the market by applying precise methodologies.

There are three common types of market entry when it comes to breakouts:

- A. Enter immediately when the price breaks its support or resistance line, which will give us the advantage of having a better entry price while increasing the risk of taking a loss in case of a false breakout.

B. Entry following the formation of the first confirmation candle above the resistance or support line just breached. In this case, we reduce the risk associated with false breakouts, but we also reduce our risk-return ratio.
C. Wait for a pullback to form, which confirms the reversal of the nature of the support or resistance line just breached. Since the retracement does not always occur, in this case, the greatest risk will consist in the probable loss of the impulsive movement given by the increase in volumes, repaid by a greater probability of success of the operation and by an excellent risk/reward ratio if the pullback actually occurred.

There is no right and wrong method, the choice of how to deal with these configurations will have to be made by you based on your attitudes and abilities.

As regards the Stop Loss, once again, we can indicate two major possibilities of definition:

A. Setting the Stop Loss on the price level constituting resistance or support just breached will present the advantage of having a small stop and possible minimal losses, which positively influence the risk-return ratio to our advantage. However, this choice will expose us more to the risk of execution at a loss if the price were to retrace.
B. Set the Stop Loss at the previous swing low, thereby increasing the breadth of our trade at the expense of our potential return.

When trading on these breakout configurations, determining an exit point from the market will essentially depend on your personal trading style and strategies. Even more generally, a specific target cannot be defined a priori, and given a large number of possible false breakouts, it will be advisable not to set a fixed take profit but to let the operations run to recover possible consecutive losses.

Important in this type of operation is the ability to resist successive and constant small losses, consequently a risk/return ratio very oriented in our favor could make the difference in the final calculation of the Trading System's performance.

A sideways market break usually results in a new trend, so you should ride this new opportunity for as long as possible to maximize your profits.

Keep in mind that an increase in volumes of at least 25% from the average volumes of the last five days will add further value to the break and increase our Statistical Advantage.

The breakout level must be clearly visible in the market structure, i.e., it must be easily identifiable through simple trendlines or horizontal lines.

Avoid using market orders on the breakout level. Generally, they are levels in which the price is very volatile and with less liquidity, therefore, slippage of the order could be generated.

Slippage is the shifting of the purchase or sale price of the shares of the financial instrument that you are about to trade to a different value from what you had observed and evaluated. Given its random nature, depending on the availability of shares of the financial instrument at that particular moment, the broker will assign the first available price to your position and closest to your request. This automation of the trading process can take the form of both a more advantageous price and a more disadvantageous price, therefore it can improve or worsen our risk/return ratio and, in the long term, can significantly influence the performance of the strategy.

At the beginning of this path, it is always advisable to operate in a simple way, aiming to become skilled in identifying a specific configuration and then learning how to manage it. Once this is done, when you are able to master the specific technical configuration, well aware of all that can derive from it, you can add further complexity to it.

Another important situation, which should not be underestimated, concerns the formation of price gaps. They are nothing more than price ranges not filled during the trading phases. On the chart, they are exactly price gaps that make it more difficult to enter the market in the breaking phase and can give us the feeling of having missed a good profit opportunity. Nonetheless, a price GAP highlights the extreme will of a group of Traders to take a certain direction, a signal that actually confirms the choice to operate in a breakout.

To complete a strategy, it is extremely important to investigate how to carry out the correct determination of the shares of the financial instrument to be traded, a choice to be made on the basis of your specific starting conditions, through notions of Position Sizing, which I will deal with in the following chapters.

Chapter 10:
Price Chart Configurations

A price chart pattern is a specific pattern generated by the pattern of price movements; it is identifiable using lines, curves, supports, and resistances that highlight the structure of the market. The main feature of a price configuration is recognizability.

Price configurations, when recognized, provide some of the most effective indications in technical analysis, and a Trader absolutely cannot ignore their knowledge and usefulness.

The configurations allow us to:

- Observe the market structure and its current conditions, having a bigger picture view.
- Find possible operations that have a high probability of success.
- Accurately identify entry and exit points of the operation;
- Better manage the risk of the operation.

There are multiple price configurations, but most can be enclosed in two specific categories: reversal configurations and continuation configurations.

In reversal configurations, the charts take on a shape that suggests a potential reversal from the current market direction and essentially define the end of a trend phase. Among the best-known examples we have the Head and Shoulders chart, the Double Top and Double Bottom, the Triple Top and Triple Bottom.

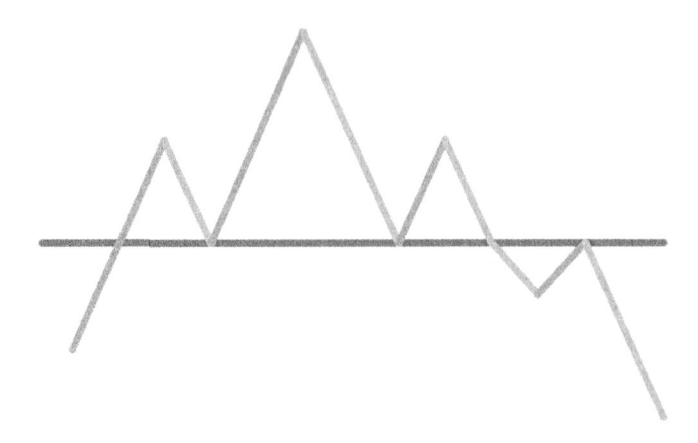

Illustration n.55– Bearish Reversal Head and Shoulders schematic.

A setup is considered bullish when prices have potentially bottomed out and entered an uptrend phase. Conversely, it is considered bearish when prices have reached the potential maximum price level and begin a downtrend phase.

The second category of configurations is that relating to the continuation of an ongoing trend and indicates, when present on the graph, that the current trend phase is healthy.

When we observe this kind of configuration, it is evident to us how prices undergo a momentary phase of rest, an accumulation aimed at recovering new potential thrust energy. We expect that, despite a momentary outage, the Traders moving the market will maintain good control over it.

Among the most significant examples, we find the Cup and Handle and the Bullish or Bearish Flags.

The Cup and Handle configuration, already introduced in the previous chapter, is considered a continuation configuration and is among the best known. A Trader who recognizes it will get excellent entry signals linked to operations of breaking the support or resistance identified by it.

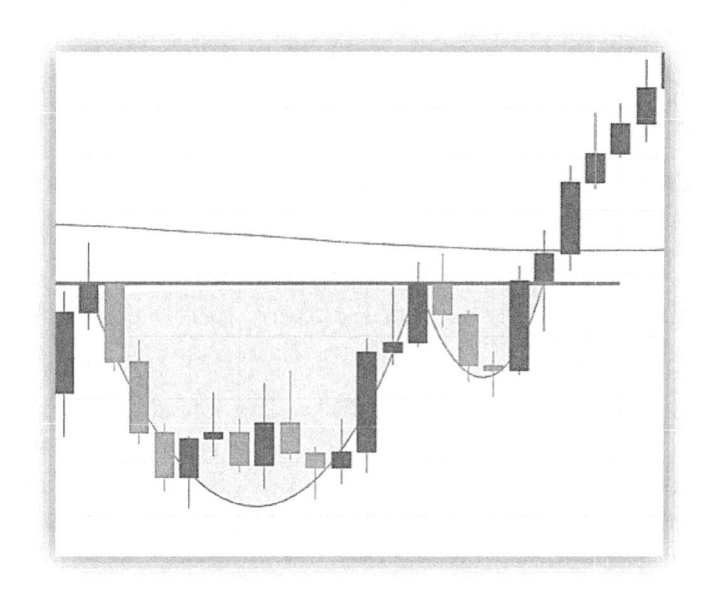

Illustration n.56– Example of Cup and Handle

On the other hand, a flag configuration envisages, following a trend phase, a lateralization phase, i.e., a minimum and temporary inversion within a channel with parallel limits, which will be followed by a break in the direction of the main trend.

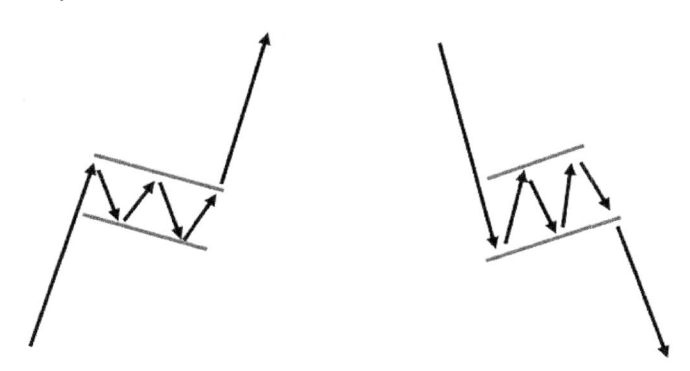

Illustration n.57– Schematization of flags

Head and Shoulders

The head and shoulders configuration should always be easily recognized by any Trader approaching the market professionally.

As anticipated, the reversal figures can be both bullish and bearish, in this case, the example of a bearish head and shoulders will be treated.

A bearish head and shoulders pattern forms in a four-phase sequence:

1. At the end of a markup phase, the left shoulder is formed following a first retracement. The retracement will have depth such as to often reach a price level acting as support, thus giving space to the first interpretation of physiological retracement of the market.
2. Head formation, consequence of a new bullish impulse ending with the achievement of a new high, followed by a major retracement. The latter ends approximately at the price level identified by the low of the first retracement and has an extension comparable to the size of the bullish impulse. The line of resistance identified by joining the two low swings is called the Neckline.
3. Formation of the right shoulder, driven by the buying push caused by the last buyers of the market, who entered with the desire to profit from a new price high. Unfortunately for them, a new high will not be made in this formation and the drive will end at approximately left shoulder high.
4. The price range identified by the conjunction of the two highs of the shoulders and the two lows of the previous retracements forms the neckline area. When the price fails to push beyond the maximum line and breaks the neckline downwards, the signal generated is a potential trend reversal and the beginning of a bearish phase.

In defining the limits of a head and shoulders, it is always important to pay attention to the market structure that existed before its formation.

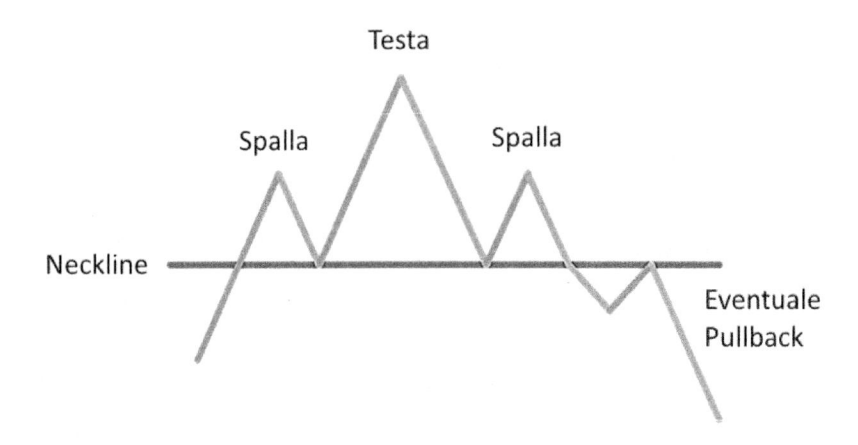

Translation: Neckline - Shoulder - Head - Shoulder - Possible Pullback.

Illustration n.58– Schematization of Bearish Head and Shoulders.

It is important to anticipate that a head and shoulders formation is not a foolproof signal, like nothing in trading. For example, if we observe an intermediate phase of a stock in a strong upward trend, supported by higher than normal volumes, even if we find the formation of a head and shoulders, the probability of a trend reversal would be minimal.

The duration of the head and shoulders formation is also important, a configuration that took a few months to complete is certainly much more significant than a head and shoulders that developed over a few days. A head and shoulders formation developed within a quarter is often a good compromise.

In the Bitcoin futures chart, you can see how a first retracement is formed in March 2021 and follows an uptrend phase. Subsequently, the price resumes its run, reaching a new price high around the middle of the month of April.

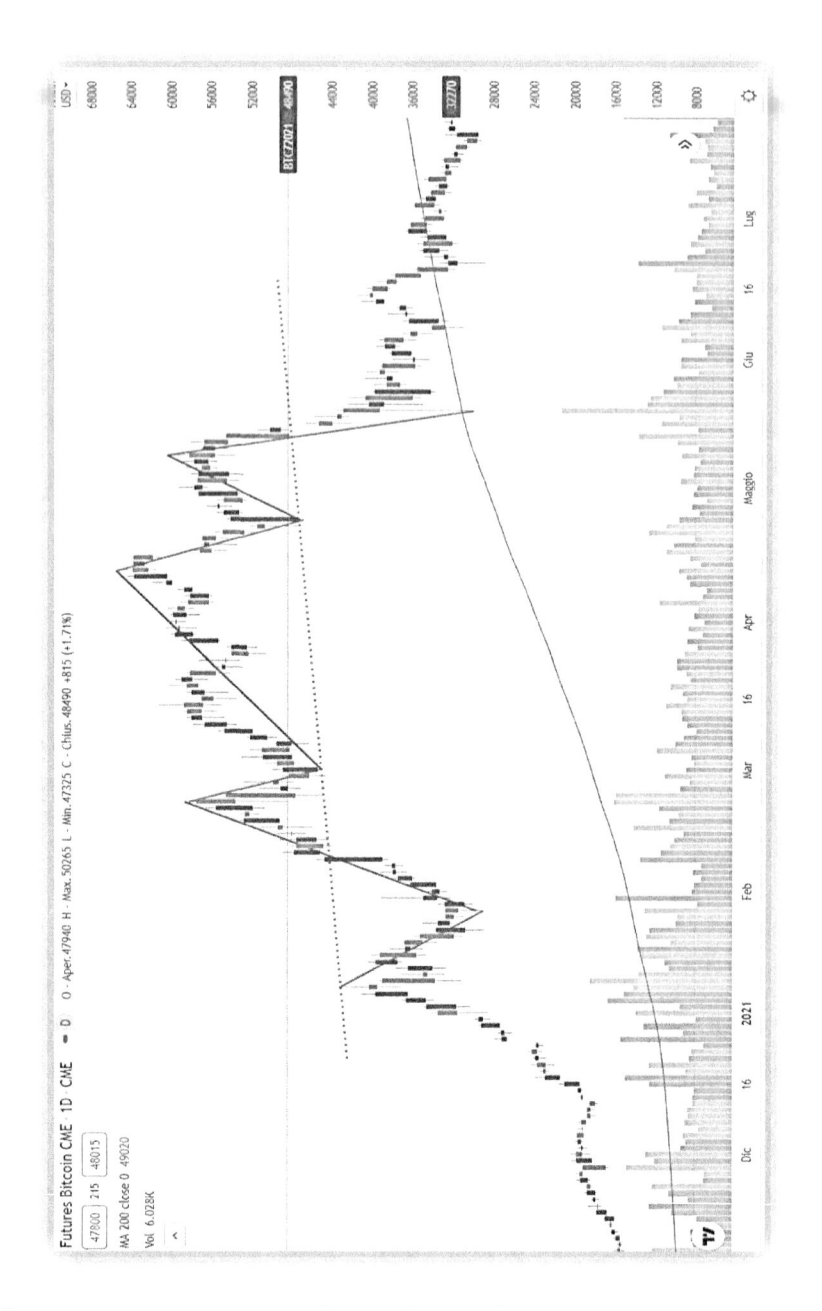

Illustration No.59– Bearish Head and Shoulders on Bitcoin Future

From the high, you can see a deep reversal of prices, which defines the shape of the head and identifies the second swing low necessary to trace the neckline.

At the end of April, we have a further bullish push, which ended in mid-May, the peak of which reaches values similar to the maximum of the left shoulder.

By now, the idea has formed in the market that this is a bearish head and shoulders, let's see how prices fall decisively back towards the neckline, even breaking downwards with a gap.

The extent of this bearish leg is comparable to the distance between the high of the head and the neckline, and this measure is usually used to define our price objective.

It should be noted that prices stopped at the 200-period daily moving average and that the formation of the head and shoulders occupied a time interval of approximately three months.

In a head and shoulders, there are three possible entry points, increasingly cautious in terms of the risk/return ratio, each of which provides for a specific Stop Loss level.

1. We could enter the market at the right shoulder peak, our head and shoulders formation would not be fully defined therefore, having not seen the actual conclusion, we cannot be reasonably sure that prices break down the neckline. The Stop Loss could be determined using the value of the Average True Range, useful for defining a possible loss exit point based on volatility. For example, we will use the ATR value measured from the peak of the right shoulder as the stop level. This decidedly aggressive entry has the advantage of having a very interesting risk/return ratio;
2. We could enter after the bearish breakout of the neckline, in this case, we would be sure of the completion of the formation, but we would expose ourselves to a potential, albeit unlikely, false breakout. The Stop Loss could be determined in this case using the value of the ATR measured from the neckline. This entry, more prudent, has

the advantage of generating an operation with a reduced risk/return ratio but with a high probability of success;
3. We may enter the market following a neckline retest. This kind of occasion may not necessarily be a first operational choice since it represents an exception that does not always occur. Consequently, it is much more useful if you want to increase market positions already open in the other two methods or enter into an operation that we have failed to seize at the right time. The Stop Loss could be determined in the same way as in the previous point. This last entry, considerably more prudent, maintains the same risk/return ratio as in point 2, further increasing the chances of success.

It is clear, but not obvious for trading beginners that we cannot place our stops exactly on the price structures formed by the market, as they are excessively predictable by institutional operators who could sometimes, with their ability to influence the market, make prices move just enough for us to run at a loss.

When the head and shoulders configuration has formed and we have confirmed the chart, it is reasonable to expect an important reversal of the current trend.

In this type of occasion, the optimal decision would see the use of the Trailing Stop as a useful ally, i.e., a progressive variation of the Stop Loss level aimed at first reducing and then canceling the risk associated with the operation as the prices move in our favor.

The use of the Trailing Stop technique depends a lot on the character of the Trader. Some will prefer to manually move the Stop Loss to a break-even condition and then subsequently to a profit, while others will prefer to have the system manage everything automatically, setting a certain percentage of decline from the last peak. Still others will prefer to base the movement of their Trailing Stop on the change of an indicator such as the Supertrend, Donchian Channels, Moving Averages, or Parabolic SAR.

To maximize the chances of success, when this is possible, it is advisable to combine your trend following strategies with the interpretation of this specific configuration.

Cup and Handle

You can observe that on ENI's daily candlestick chart, following a false bullish breakout in June 2021, the price has dropped below the resistance line again.

In the lateralization band, the price repeatedly insisted on the resistance line from below, first at the end of June and then in the first ten days of July.

Rejected to the downside, it met support in mid-July, convincing waiting buyers. The new participants provided the energy needed to reach resistance once again in mid-August, only to see prices rejected downwards again.

Only after the last push at the end of August ENI will see an upward break in prices, and we will witness the birth of an uptrend.

It should be noted that, towards the end of September and before the actual start of the trend, there was a retest of the resistance value, which validated the reversal of its nature into support.

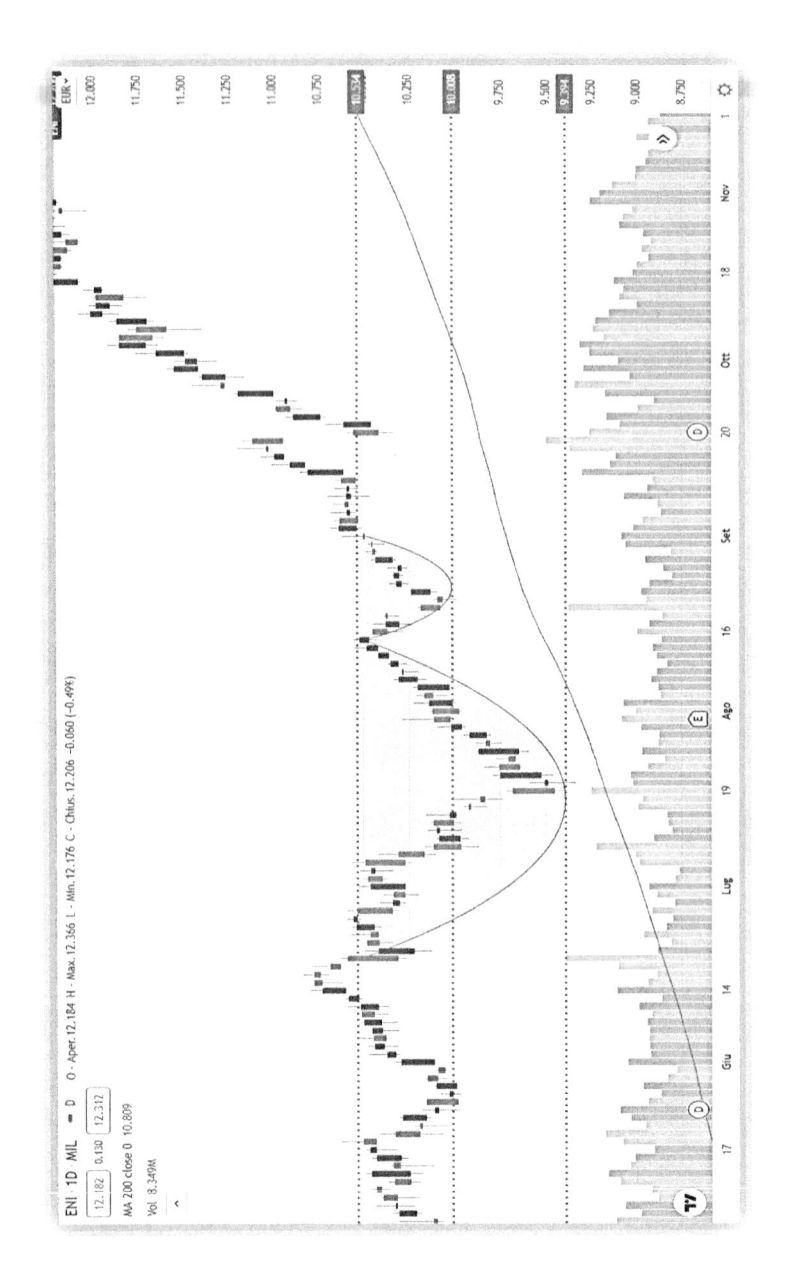

Illustration no.60– Bullish Cup and Handle on ENI

The stages of the formation of the Cup & Handle configuration include a series of steps that are driven mostly by psychological reasons:

- o Sellers enter the market with the intent to push the price down.
- o Falling prices attract the attention of buyers, who observe the Price Action with growing interest.
- o Once the minimum price level has been reached, the buyers will begin to operate, entering the market with increasingly important quotas, causing a rise in prices towards the resistance value.
- o This time, the sellers will wait for the price level they consider interesting to be reached, which we have seen to be set close to the resistance because they know they can sell their market shares at a better price.
- o However, the new downward thrust is unable to satisfy all the demand from buyers, who will no longer want to wait for the previous support to be reached again. They will not want to risk missing out on an opportunity that is starting to be even more interesting, so they will enter forcefully, causing a second push of prices upward.
- o All eyes in the market are now turned to the resistance value that defined the upper limit of this pattern, and we see a slight rebound in prices before seeing the resistance breached.
- o All Traders who operate on the breakout will only wait for the confirmation of the definitive upward breakout to join the market with long-type purchase positions and start the trend recovery.

The reason why all price setups work, with a good level of confidence and reliability, is that they are a graphical representation of the supply and demand levels of a specific market.

A Trader, who applies technical analysis, carries out operations based on the imbalance between buying power and selling pressure existing in a given moment in the market. The levels of supply and demand, shown in the price configurations, can be of great help in identifying this imbalance and give us a Statistical Advantage that supports our decision.

It is often said that history does not repeat itself, but it often rhymes, and the market is nothing more than the accumulation of psychological, rational, irrational and emotional reactions that have influenced a given financial instrument.

In the price charts, we assume that every event has now been absorbed, and every information present at the moment is assimilated in real-time and therefore is presented before our eyes in a readable form. From this assumption arises the idea that similar events and circumstances generate similar price trends on the chart, therefore, they offer us a kind of path to follow when we try to operate in the same market after some time.

Chapter 11:
Position Sizing

Position Sizing is one of the most important aspects to consider if you intend to become a capable and consistent Trader over time. Each Trading System must have an adequate definition of the position size, which essentially consists in deciding how many market shares/shares/contracts to acquire for a given market operation.

Position sizing is something planned, as well as necessary, that serves the purpose:

- o To define the level of specific risk deriving from each single Trade in case the operation goes in loss.
- o Eliminate, or at least limit as much as possible, the risk of excessive losses compared to what was estimated.
- o Limit the aggregate amount resulting from a series of losing trades.
- o Limit the total risk in the case of trading on multiple financial instruments that are correlated to each other.
- o Define the maximum level of risk with which we can feel sufficiently comfortable in relation to the size of our account.

Therefore it is clear that the sizing of the position has the absolute purpose of limiting the risk to which we expose ourselves, it has nothing to do with maximizing profits.

As anticipated in the principles of this book, we must be able to accuse even a large number of loss-making operations as long as, in the long run, the Statistical Advantage proves us right. To achieve this result and to survive for a long time in the financial markets, the only viable way is precisely that of limiting the risks.

Without adequate sizing of positions, a Trader would be at the mercy of large market fluctuations, with the consequent risk of

Drawdown of his Equity, therefore he would face great difficulties in recovering capital.

Imagine if you lose half of the money deposited in your Trading account, you will have lost 50% of the total value that can be used to place trades.

To recover 50% of the capital now lost, you will therefore have to use the 50% of the remaining money, i.e., generate an increase in the present value of your account equal to 100%.

To give you a yardstick, and make you understand the difficulty associated with this kind of recovery, know that a good professional and capable Trader can make an average of 30% - 35% profit per year, and a great Trader can generate up to 60% on average, with sporadic peak years exceeding 100%.

These numbers should therefore have definitively removed from your mind the idea that, through Trading, wealth can be generated quickly and easily.

I want to be more specific and accurate in this regard, demonstrating one of the mathematical realities that concern the asymmetrical relationship between the Drawdown percentage and the percentage required for recovery.

Assuming that you have suffered a loss of X% on your capital, to determine the percentage of profit necessary to fully recover the loss, we should use the formula:

$$R\% = X\% / (1 - X\%)$$

Applying this formula to the numerical example with a loss of 50%, I get:

$$R\% = 50\% / (1 - 50\%) =$$

$$50\% / 50\% = 1 = 100\%$$

Instead, assume now that you suffer a reduced loss compared to the previous case, let's say a loss of 10% on the total capital, our formula will give us back:

$$R\% = 10\ \%\ /\ (1 - 10\ \%) =$$

$$10\ \%\ /\ 90\ \% = 0,11 = 11,11\ \%$$

In the light of this numerical example, it seems extremely obvious that, in order to be durable in the market, you will have to be able to reduce the depth of the Drawdown as much as possible so that the effort required to recover its value is reasonable.

A strategy that provides for an adequate sizing of the position, and the relative risk management, will help the Trader to focus above all on containing the extent of the losses and consequently also the overall Drawdown, naturally leading him to accept the unavoidability of the same in this type of business.

After placing an operation on the market, the Trader's job is reduced to checking and managing the risk associated with the open positions, carefully observing the negative possibilities, and letting the side of the positive possibilities run.

Given the importance of this fundamental skill, you will need to be able to calculate the exact size of the position you intend to place on the market.

Three steps to correct sizing

The very first thing to do is to define the specific risk for each operation, to which I will give the abbreviation RS for convenience. Specific risk is a predetermined percentage of the capital in your account at any given time.

To put it simply, on an account of $15,000, if we decided to allocate an RS of 1% for each individual transaction, the corresponding value would be equal to $150.

Professional Traders use specific risks in managing their trades on an ongoing basis. They adjust the sizing of the position following the evolution of their account, carrying out the operation that we can define as a rebalancing.

Let's assume for a moment that our Trading operations have allowed us to obtain a capital gain of 20% on the $15,000, bringing the current value of the account to $18,000. In these conditions, our RS at 1% would give us back an economic value of $180 rather than the initial $150.

At this point, we could use this increase in value to buy further market shares on the instruments still open, which however, must not already have undergone an increase in valuation such as to have exceeded the respective risk.

If a security has grown in such a way as to bring the corresponding risk to $160, we can evaluate buying a further $20 of shares, but this purchase must be made only if the market conditions have not changed in such a way as to compromise our initial hypothesis.

It is also possible to use this rule to decrease the risk associated with a share that has grown excessively by liquidating a portion of shares in order to bring the value of the specific risk back to what resulted from our calculation.

Simplifying as much as possible, if your Equity grows, you will be able to afford to be more aggressive, vice versa, if your Equity decreases, you will necessarily have to become more conservative.

Empirically, it is possible to categorize the risk attitude of a Trader precisely on the basis of the specific type of risk to which he is exposed:

- A Trader who wants to operate cautiously on the markets will necessarily have to expose himself little for every single operation, therefore it will be advisable to apply an RS lower than or equal to 1% of his own capital;

- A Trader who wants to operate aggressively on the market will take greater risks and opt for an RS that settles between approximately 1% and 3% of his capital.

Going beyond this limit would expose you, as seen previously, to a greater Drawdown, therefore, to a possible future inability to recover.

To provide a benchmark, imagine yourself losing five or six trades in a row or suffering a loss equivalent to your RS multiplied by 5 or 6 times. If, from this brief mental calculation, you believe that you are still in a position to absorb particular moments of market instability and volatility or that you are capable of dealing with catastrophic news such as, for example, the collapse in oil prices following the lockdowns caused by the COVID-19 in 2020, then the specific risk you adopt can be considered adequate.

The second necessary step to do, before entering the market, is to correctly set the Stop Loss of an operation.

The Stop Loss that we must set must have a precise meaning to clear the level of risk to which we expose ourselves. Without a clear definition of the construction of the Stop Loss, we would always act by exposing ourselves to chance, even in the presence of a possibly profitable Trade.

In every trade you place on the market, you'll need to be able to answer in advance the question, *"If things didn't go the way I imagine, at what price level would it be appropriate to exit the market?."*

Many rules in Trading can be flexible, each Trading System can have different ways of defining a Stop Loss level, but there is one rule not to be broken:

"BEFORE ENTERING THE MARKET, BEFORE EVEN THINKING ABOUT PROFIT, FIX IN ADVANCE THE MAXIMUM LEVEL OF LOSS THAT YOU WILL HAVE TO ACCEPT IN CASE YOU ARE WRONG"

This means that the Stop Loss is admittedly more important than the entry point into the market and, ultimately, much more important than the profit target.

The third step involves calculating the risk associated with a single share, called risk per share, which I will abbreviate below to RPS.

To correctly determine RPS, we need to do a simple subtraction:

$$\text{Risk per Unit} = \text{Entry Price} - \text{Stop Loss Price}$$

For short operations, we invert the terms:

$$\text{Risk per Unit} = \text{Stop Loss Price} - \text{Entry Price}$$

Let's take a practical example if the current price of a single Poste Italiane Spa share is $11,050, and I wanted to sell, I could think of setting the Stop Loss at $11,500, the result of my risk per share would be:

$$\text{Risk per Unit} = 11{,}500 - 11{,}050 = 0{,}45\ \$$$

In the next step, we should carry out the sizing of the position of the single Trade, the number of shares to be acquired in a single market operation will result from the ratio of the Specific Risk compared to the Risk per Share:

$$\text{Number of Units} = \text{Specific Risk} / \text{Risk per Unit}$$

I remind you that we assumed a capital of $15,000, for which, at 1% risk, we calculated the specific risk at $150. Knowing that each share of Poste Italiane has a risk per share relating to our specific transaction of $0.45, we will have:

$$\text{Number of Units} = 150\ \text{USD} / 0{,}45\ \text{USD} = 333{.}33\ \text{units}$$

As an added caution, we round down to the nearest value and then imagine the short sale of 333 Poste Italiane shares.

Therefore, selling 333 Poste Italiane shares is equivalent to multiplying the price value currently sold by this number.

Necessary capital = 11,050 USD x 333 quotas = 3,679.65 USD

The last thing necessary to operate according to this logic is the ability to think in multiples of the risk value. When you think of a loss, you will associate a multiple of the risk value, as well as when you think of the possible profit.

By reasoning in this way, the Stop Loss value will become your R risk parameter, and the possible profit will become a multiple of this value.

$$Risk = 0{,}45 \text{ USD} \times 333 \text{ quotas} = 149{,}85 \text{ USD}$$

Our take profit will therefore be n times the value of the Risk, i.e., if we imagine a risk/return ratio equal to 3, our Take Profit will be:

$$3 \times Risk = 3 \times 149.85 \text{ USD} = 449.55 \text{ USD}$$

The price target to be reached on the Poste Italiane Spa instrument will consequently be:

Price Target = Entry Price - Take Profit Value / Number of Quotes

$$= 11.050 \text{ USD} - (449.55 \text{ USD} / 333) =$$

$$= 11.050 \text{ USD} - 1.35 \text{ USD} = 9.70 \text{ USD}$$

It should be emphasized that in this calculation, I am not considering the cost relating to the market commissions made by the broker for each execution.

Thinking in terms of risk multiples will make you do a mental change in which you will no longer think of the operation in monetary terms but in terms of risk, therefore, you will see the mental pressure associated with the possibility of losing money lightened.

Also, remember never to associate the losses of a Trade operation with something real that affects you personally. If you are losing $1,000, for example, you will never have to compare this loss to the value of your salary. This way of reasoning would only generate further tension in you, leading you to want to close your positions early when you are in the profit phase and make you erroneously hope to recover when you are obviously losing, things that we have seen to be totally wrong.

A professional Trader approaches the economic value of Trades almost as if they were the score of a game where the Risk is the unit value.

Chapter 12:
Risk Management and Trade Management

In the pages of this chapter, you will learn the most common techniques concerning the management of your Trading operations. So far, you have learned the correct way to identify operations with a high Statistical Advantage, interpreting the price graphs of financial instruments, and evaluating, based on the size of your capital, the correct size of the position to place on the market. Trade management, in addition to position sizing, is another very important part of risk management.

When we talk about Trade Management, we first have to deal with how to correctly place the Stop Loss. If you think you have already learned everything you need to know about this subject in the previous chapter, I must inform you that this is not the case. In these pages, we will go into much more detail, we will define which are the most common mechanics and approaches which you should pay attention to when setting a Stop Loss.

You already know that the Stop Loss must be defined before placing an operation on the market as a fundamental action for a professional approach to Trading that protects your capital. The moment you have clearly defined the maximum risk associated with a single Trade, removing the emotional influences linked to loss, you will know a priori what can go wrong, therefore, you will have already absorbed the shock in case of a wrong operation. You will have understood that the definition of the Stop Loss has a lot to do with the removal of emotion and, for this very reason, it will be an essential phase in determining the size of the position. If the Stop Loss is too close, you will have the advantage of having a potential greater profit but a greater probability of exiting at a loss, and vice versa; if the Stop Loss is wider, you will most likely encounter less important profits with the advantage of having less risk of execution at a loss.

When we talk about Stop Loss, in fact, we are talking about a specific condition deriving from the Price Action, a condition that can be determined both through a predefined percentage, as already seen above, and with an approach based on the volatility of the specific market, and on the basis to the structure of the market itself.

The predefined percentage approach is the simplest to understand and apply, it is based on nothing but your ability to bear any losses by determining the maximum risk to which we are exposed. This is exactly what we did in the previous chapter, and it is certainly an approach that has demonstrated its effectiveness over time, despite being the most dated. The advantage associated with this first type of Stop Loss is precisely its clarity and simplicity, and although it is not perfect, it is still useful compared to not having any type of protection.

We cannot consider this approach among the best for reasons related to the different intrinsic characteristics of the various markets. If I used a fixed loss percentage on a volatile market like Bitcoin and similarly applied the same percentage on a sideways market like FOREX, I would be reasonably confident that I could not expect the absolute best performance.

Stop losses determined on the basis of volatility are a more advanced approach, however simple. The breadth of their scope will depend precisely on the volatility of a market at a given moment, exceeding the limit imposed by the fixed percentage approach.

Among the most common indicators used to evaluate market volatility, we mention the Average True Range, ATR, calculated on the basis of 20 daily periods, which is suitable for application in short-term trend following strategies or for Swing applications Trading.

The general indication provides that the Stop Loss level is set at about one and a half or two times the value indicated by the 20-period ATR, determined starting from the market entry price.

Therefore, in the case of markets subject to high volatility, the ATR will determine a more extensive Stop Loss, and therefore, the risk/return ratio will be reduced. Volatility-based stops are ideal for Traders who prefer trend following trading.

Stop Loss determined on the basis of the market structure require, as the name suggests, to correctly identify supports, resistances, trend lines, dynamic trend lines and, in general, all the elements of the market structure useful for suggesting where to correctly position our Stop Loss.

It is completely normal that, even if you had the same entry point to the market, different Trading Systems would suggest different points of application of the Stop Loss.

The Stop Loss determined on the basis of the market structure is widely used by expert Traders, who apply some steps to better define the positioning of our lifesaver.

- It is advisable to set the Stop Loss near the most robust level of resistance or support in the short term;
- Avoid getting too close or too far away, therefore let the ATR suggest you, multiplying its value from 1.5 to 3 times;
- If you are buying near weak support, with many lower wicks below it, the only stop that makes sense will be the one placed beyond the lower point of these same wicks. The reverse is valid for sale transactions;
- Never increase the risk associated with a specific transaction by changing the size of the Stop Loss. You can reduce it but not increase it. If you made certain reasoning at the beginning of the operation, that same reasoning must give you the serenity to proceed forward until the conclusion of the Trade, even if it loses. Rather, if you believe that the risk is too high and you no longer feel safe with the initial exposure, consider partially closing it until you reach a specific risk that is such that you feel more comfortable.

I also want to emphasize one thing, it is never wise to increase the position of a losing trade in the hope that it will recover more value and go in the direction we choose. Adding positions to Trade at a Loss is the quickest way to zero your checking account.

Finally, there is a further type of Stop Loss, which is determined not by the Price Action but by its prolonged absence over time. Let's talk about the TIME STOP.

Generally, in the case of trading on traditional and non-derivative financial instruments, one enters the market expecting a certain price movement in a given direction which arises from an imbalance between supply and demand.

Sometimes it happens that this imbalance is late in showing itself, that the markets move sideways for so long as to invalidate the reasoning underlying the operation itself. If what prompted us to make a certain operational choice is no longer valid, our Statistical Advantage on the market is reduced or disappears.

When the expected movement does not take place, it is advisable to make a decision regarding the open position, leaving money stationary on an instrument that is late in showing its action is just a waste of time and opportunity. Since our capital is limited, we should always try to make the most of it.

Therefore, to define a stop linked to time, we can operate in two ways: define in advance the maximum time of an operation or progressively move your Stop Loss towards the entry price at regular intervals, like a Trailing Stop, but regardless of the movement's price in our favor.

When a trade has made a significant move into the profit zone, it is good practice to protect part of these profits by raising the Stop Loss bar. We will initially move it towards the break-even point, after which we will continue the adjustment in the profit zone. In this way, if the operation closes as initially expected, we will have an excellent risk/return ratio. Conversely, if the operation turns against us, we will have reduced the level of risk and possibly obtained a small profit.

A Trader who wants to apply this type of rule, when he sees the operation turn in the expected direction, will dynamically move his Stop Loss level, executing this operation at regular intervals of one risk unit at a time.

Let's take a numerical example if I entered the market by taking a short position, with the current value of the security at $12 per share, hypothetically setting the Stop Loss at $14, my unit of risk would be equal to $2. When the market drops to $10, I will feel comfortable moving the Stop Loss level to breakeven at the opening price of the position. From this moment on, in the worst conditions, I will close the Trade in balance, in the best conditions, the operation will go up by further units, offering me the possibility to further and progressively move my stop in the profit area.

Approaching the markets by applying this operating technique means being able to resist the temptation, when the market turns against us, to bring the Stop Loss value back to the previous level of risk. When you close a Trade with a loss, you must be aware that nothing has happened other than the occurrence of one of the situations initially foreseen, therefore, you will take note of it with serenity and think about the next operation.

It is clear that the Trailing Stop is much more performing in trending markets, therefore, it will give greater satisfaction when combined with trend following strategies.

The risk of correlations

Something very often underestimated, and sometimes even ignored, is the correlation between different financial instruments of the same market or from the same financial instruments on different markets. I am well aware that I have already abundantly illustrated this concept, but in my opinion, a further reminder is necessary.

Let's imagine that we have observed the price dynamics and the structure that has formed on the oil future, having ascertained that it is in an uptrend phase, we will be able to take a long position in complete serenity, aware that we have done everything we deem necessary. Then we move on to diesel, and we notice a very similar price structure, we do our studies which further confirm what we have seen and we enter the market again.

We still observe petrol, it surprises us with its spectacular similarity of the graph with the previous financial instruments, we think it is an exceptional, wonderful and exciting day, we repeat our technical analysis and proceed with the operation. After a few hours, OPEC announces its intention to increase oil production substantially and almost immediately, all our financial instruments, which are impeccable in terms of technical analysis, turn downwards and make us close at a loss.

Similar securities or companies or raw materials that have a more or less evident correlation between them will have very similar behaviors on the market, and operating on them at the same time is equivalent to acquiring more shares of just one of them, increasing our specific risk beyond the threshold of acceptability that we had calculated so meticulously in the previous chapters.

When you find yourself in these conditions, it is still possible to operate on the various correlated instruments, but obviously, you must be careful to determine the specific risk taking into account all the instruments on which you intend to operate.

We define X as the maximum amount to risk on a single sector, with X being a multiple of RS. In the example of oil, it could be X equal to 3RS. If we hypothetically associate the value of 1% of the total capital with the specific risk, the total amount of capital to risk in this particular industrial sector will categorically correspond to 3% of my account.

For these reasons, imposing a certain maximum risk on the entire portfolio becomes an essential requirement, especially when we use brokers that allow us to operate with financial leverage.

A rule of thumb is that you never risk more than a total of 20% of your entire capital at any one time. A more conservative rule suggests dividing the capital into 10 equal parts and totally diversifying the sectors in which these shares are used.

The rules protect us in the very unlikely but devastating case in which all our operations are simultaneously executed in Stop Loss.

My dispassionate advice is to further reduce this percentage. You will have fewer market operations, and your progress will be slower, but the first rule of Trading is "Don't Lose Money," and the second rule is "Remember the First Rule," Warren Buffet Docet.

Chapter 13:
Design Your Own Trading System

In this chapter, we will explore the logic and method necessary to design a Trading System with potential profitability on the market, and I will give you the opportunity to understand what the key elements that make it up are.

So far, you have learned that there are, and must be respected, three cornerstones to be a successful Trader:

1. Knowing how to generate a Statistical Advantage.
2. Apply a risk/return ratio unbalanced in one's favor.
3. Possess the psychological aptitude necessary to consistently apply the rules set by the Trading System.

You learned what it takes to understand price charts, recognize market structures, and take advantage of different configurations. You have understood the fundamental skill of knowing how to manage risk in a technical and professional way, and now you have all the necessary tools in hand to be able to operate adequately on the market.

What you still lack now is a set of rules that define exactly what to do from start to finish. You will have to transpose all the theoretical knowledge learned so far into a clear path, which acts as a map of the market you want to operate on. Without a path to guide you, you would still be at the mercy of a series of unforeseen or predictable situations that could cause you quite a few problems.

Learning how to trade is like going on a boat, if you have a very powerful motorboat, but your sailing skills are poor, you will not be a good captain and may even get blown off course and run out of fuel in the middle of nowhere. As painful as it is, all the theoretical knowledge, even those contained in this book, regardless of their validity and undeniable usefulness, will be worth nothing if you don't start to experience the joys and sufferings of trading, typical of the real experience of the financial markets.

So now I ask you to take a new step forward, treasure what you have learned, and humbly admit that you still need to learn.

A profitable and consistent Trader must possess an important cultural baggage regarding the markets, financial instruments, technical analysis, and fundamental analysis, with which he will build his own Trading System to derive a Statistical Advantage on the market. Let me be clear, the best Trading System, without constant application, will be useless. It is essential to develop a psychological attitude that allows you to constantly apply the Trading System itself.

Placing it in a hierarchical way:

- From theory, we learn the necessary rules;
- By mastering the theory we can gain direct experience of the markets;
- With this experience, we develop the sensitivity necessary to build our operational plan expressed through a Trading System;
- With the development of the Psychological Attitude, we will finally be able to apply the Trading System without deviating from the path it provides.

A Trading System suitable for our purposes must be mainly mechanical, i.e., it must consist of a sequence of predefined actions that can always be performed in the exact same way.

Expert Advisor programmers understand this concept and literally write their code with all the necessary instructions, the computer will work autonomously for them, and they will be relieved of the psychological pressure of having to do everything perfectly every time.

If you wonder what it is, an Expert Advisor is nothing more than an algorithm developed for the MetaTrader platform in MQL code with the aim of automating Trading operations.

From mechanization, you get the double advantage of the perfect execution of the rules of the Trading System and the possibility of filling any gap concerning the psychological attitude.

Therefore a good mechanical Trading System will include a closed system designed in such a way as to automate the various steps of our operations. Regardless of the starting conditions, we define what we will have to do if the various foreseeable scenarios occur and, therefore, which decisions to take in terms of position sizing, financial instrument, market, type of stop, risk/return ratio, etc.

Through a Trading System, equipped with simple, clear and, above all, defined rules for each circumstance, it will be easier for you to generate a profit.

Obviously, the attention linked to the creation of our system will be limited to everything we can control, being able only to hypothesize possible scenarios regarding what will be uncontrollable for us. For example, I certainly cannot control the size of the trading volumes of a financial instrument, but I can give myself a rule that tells me what to do if the volumes increase or decrease within a certain pre-set limit.

A good Trading System will help the Trader to eliminate the emotional component from his operations in favor of an operation as objective as possible.

A mechanical Trading System, which is effective, should make the decision-making process simple to allow you to apply it easily, and since the rules do not vary, it will have to be boring and repetitive.

A complete Trading System is based on six main elements, already fully addressed in the previous chapters, which must be adequately considered in the design phase:

- o The reference market;
- o The sizing of positions;
- o Market entry rules;
- o Stop rules;
- o The market exit rules;

- The rules that define the Trading System.

Every Trader on earth, who wants to be profitable in the long term, will have to properly manage each of these aspects. From this comes my desire to deepen its content.

Reference market

The market is the component that defines a priori what to buy and what to sell, therefore, it is absolutely the first of the decisions that the Trader must make in defining his system.

Remember that different markets, and different financial instruments, have very different trends. In addition to what has just been stated, you must take into account that there are different ways to identify and categorize markets.

You may want to classify the markets by Asset Class, i.e., define whether they fall into the category of currencies, commodities, and so on, or you could perform a market structure-based discretization, thus defining whether they are typically trending or typically sideways markets, and again, you may find subcategories based on geography, religion, or market capitalization.

For example, we could decide to focus exclusively on cryptocurrencies, so much attention in this period, and in this sector, we would find further sub-categories such as oracles, securities, tokens, NFTs, or stablecoins.

It doesn't matter how you make this categorization, the important thing is that it is clear and defined so that you know specifically what you are working on.

You will have to find the happy medium between observing too many markets and observing too few. If you observed too many markets, it would be difficult to produce and manage Trading Systems for each of these because you would be more prone to careless errors.

If, on the other hand, you limit yourself too much, the latency between one operation and the next could be excessive. Latency could extend to the point of leading you to operate almost blindly on other, apparently favorable markets without providing adequate Trading Systems to apply to them.

It is also advisable to focus on moving markets, avoiding markets with low trading volumes. This choice is mainly linked to the ease of manipulation of markets with low market capitalization rather than those with large capitalization.

For novice Traders, it is certainly advantageous to start from markets that are more interesting and familiar. If I were interested in Bitcoin, the Crypto market could be a sensible choice to start trading. Obviously, and as already mentioned, it is much easier for a beginner to operate in trending markets rather than in sideways markets.

> Didactic example:
>
> The Trading System will have to be based on a stock market index because, typically, indices of this type move in trend, and I find this information useful for my purposes. I will look at the indices of a country based on the performance of a group of shares geographically located in it.
>
> For this reason, I choose the S&P 500 Index, representative of the 500 best companies on the American Stock Market. Considering my need to operate with reduced capital, I choose an ETF that tracks this index and whose unit quota is lower, AMUNDI ETF SP500 B whose ticker is I550U. I will use a 4-hour periodicity chart.

Position Sizing

The second component is the sizing of the position which, as we have already observed, defines the size of the market share that we are going to trade.

Since we are talking about the QUANTUM, this second element of the Trading System is extremely important and often ignored by many novice Traders.

To keep this essential aspect under control, we must master it, know exactly how much risk to take in our operations, how to manage it, and how to diversify positions.

In the previous chapters, we defined the amount of our specific risk using the value of our capital as a basis. You know well by now that operating with too large a percentage of our capital can lead us to bankruptcy in a short time, while with too small percentages, we risk not seeing consistent results or even physically not being able to place an order on the market.

The sizing of positions must always be done considering their diversification, which can be obtained by operating both on similar markets but in opposite directions, on poorly correlated markets, on traditional financial markets, and simultaneously on markets for derivative instruments in the same sector.

For the latter type, imagine you want to operate on oil futures, you have observed an increase, and you want to open a long-type operation, after which the economic context begins to make you suspect that a trend reversal could occur, perhaps in following possible decisions on the production of the raw material. In order to reduce your risk, you place a second trade, this time on the derivative options market, structuring it so that if the price does indeed rotate against you, you will be adequately protected.

Remember that it is not important that the market goes up or down or even lateralize, the important thing is to have the ability to recognize the opportunity that presents itself.

Here too, the suggestion for novice Traders is not to risk more than 1% of their capital on a single Trade and avoid opening too many operations at the same time.

Even if you decide to focus on just one financial instrument for two years, I can assure you that you would certainly get better results than if you traded on several instruments at the same time.

> Didactic example:
>
> I assume the management of limited capital, 10,000 US dollars. My exposure should not be more than 1% on any market trade. To date, the I550U beats a price of $82.78 against a real price of the SP500 Index of $4373.95.
>
> My specific risk per assumed Trade will be 1%, equivalent to a maximum exposure of 100 dollars per single operation.

Market Entry Rules

The entry rules have the function of defining the moment of entry into the market. To do this, specific market weaknesses, specific configurations or price events are identified, which constitute an opportunity for us.

Although important, defining the entry rules is a less relevant element than the first two. With well-managed risk and a carefully chosen market, entering at an exact moment, or shortly after or shortly before, will only minimally influence the final result of the operation.

Some Traders mainly exploit the Price Action to define an entry into the market, while others build complex systems of indicators or create their own.

There is also no right and wrong, there is only the logic of creating your own strategy that allows you to provide an adequate entry signal. It is obvious that even if in third place for relevance, the entry rules must aim at obtaining the best Statistical Advantage on the future transaction.

An entry signal must be CLEAR, at least for the one who created the Trading System. The reason that drives us to define that same signal must also be clear and not leave too much room for interpretation.

Let's assume I was convinced that a trending market must have RSI greater than 55 and price candles above the 200-period daily moving average. I should enter the market with long operations whenever these specific indications are presented to me. The reason why? Because this is how I defined it in my Trading System, and I considered it suitable for the specific market observed.

Once again, I want to give you some advice, at the beginning of this journey, it is advisable that you focus your attention on a single strategy. Don't make the mistake of thinking you can create 10 different strategies that work just because you've heard the broad outlines of 10 different indicators.

Create your first strategy, clearly define the rules that govern it, and only after 100 operations, at least, will you be able to evaluate its effectiveness. I guarantee you that you could either find yourself pleasantly surprised or receive a huge disappointment, the important thing will be to learn what worked well and what didn't, look for a new solution, and check everything again. What you want to achieve is not something trivial, therefore its construction will not be trivial.

> Didactic example:
>
> *I decide to enter only when the market is trending. To do this, I use the 200-period moving average to identify the state of the market. I carry out this check initially on the daily periodicity time frame and, subsequently, on the operational time frame with a periodicity of 4 hours. I will carry out long trades only if, on both time frames, the 200-period average gives me a good indication of the upward trend. I will not trade if the trend is not evident.*
>
> *I will apply the Heikin Ashi chart mode so that you can observe the moment of change of direction of the candlesticks more clearly.*

I decide to carry out purchase operations only and only if the price chart is above the 200-period average.

The buy signal will be given by the color change of the candles from red to green.

Stop Rules

The stop rules are used to define when the operation is to be considered compromised, therefore the negative outcome is accepted, closing it at a loss.

Doing this is important because having understood risk management well, we know that cutting losses suddenly will protect us from excessive Drawdowns of our Equity, preventing enormous difficulties in recovering capital.

When cutting losses, the most important thing is to have previously defined a Stop Loss, which must be identified even before placing the order, as it is more important than the entry point itself.

If I wanted to enter the market now and, analyzing the volatility of the instrument, I found that I was too far from a level of support or resistance, dynamic or static, I would have to abandon the operation or increase my level of risk. Attempting this operation, maintaining my specific risk level, would, in this case, be technically wrong as I would focus on wanting to carry out a Trade at all costs without adequately limiting the risk of losing execution.

Even when we define the Stop Loss, simplicity is very important, for this reason, the Trading System must clearly define how to set the level.

If the stop level feels vague, you are probably not on the right instrument or entering the market at the best possible time.

On the other hand, if through your method you can define the stop level with confidence and in the absence of emotions, you have probably found the correct method.

Let's take a closer look at a numerical example. If I put the stop at $9, entering a volatile market at $9 and 50 cents, in all probability, I will experience the operation governed by terror. Applying a Stop Loss so close to the entry point will put me in front of a high probability of occurrence, and I certainly cannot live in the hope that the market will go exclusively in the direction I wish.

An expert Trader sets up his operation with serenity and then leaves it to the market. You don't have to hope you're right, but be confident that you have a chance of success, and that must be enough.

If the operation closes in Stop Loss, your mind will be calm because something that you had already foreseen will simply have happened, and you will know, thanks to your Statistical Advantage, that the next operation could go better.

At the end of the 100 Trades, you will take some time to evaluate your strategy, and if too many operations will be at a loss and the results do not align with your expectations, you will decide if and where to intervene, making the necessary corrections and then start applying it again.

> Didactic example:
>
> *As a stop rule, I will use the Trailing Stop at regular risk intervals. Every time the price reaches the risk value R, I will progressively raise the Stop Loss level, first to break even and then to positive.*

Market Exit Rules

The exit rules are a bit the opposite of the stop rules, they are necessary to establish what are the conditions which, once verified, will make us deem it wise to exit the market.

The aim to pursue will be to identify a moment in the future in which everything went according to our plans, we achieved the profit that we had established, and remaining further in the market would represent more of a risk than an opportunity.

The first time I heard Tom Hougaard, this sentence stuck in my mind, "You will never achieve great results in Trading if you don't let profits run." This sentence expresses the enormous potential that arises from being able to define the rules for exiting the market.

Among the first mistakes I made as a novice Trader, there was of setting too large Stop Loss and placing take profits very close to the entry point, the result was that I earned and went in profit 90% of the time, but when I lost, the rare times that happened, my profit was demolished.

Having read this book has already taught you what my mistake was by not cutting losses immediately and taking profits too early, they certainly increased my chances of winning but with obvious bad results. I paid dearly for my ignorance of risk management.

Your strategy will have to foresee that the position can develop for as long as necessary and, if the risk/reward ratio has been defined correctly, losing one, two, or ten Trades in a row will not make a difference in the overall performance.

The risk/reward ratio will need to be asymmetrical and pre-determined like every other aspect of your Trading System. Predetermined does not simply mean a 1:2 or 1:3 ratio, which I have shown you, however, it is technically suitable for the purpose. It means identifying a relationship that is appropriate to the market condition.

If we were reasonably sure that we were in a trending market we could, for example, opt for the use of the Trailing Stop, which could act as both a stop rule and an exit rule, and there would be nothing wrong with a priori we wanted to establish, as a further rule, an asymmetric ratio. I would like to underline that applying the

Trailing Stop in sideways markets, characterized by insignificant volatility, can be very risky.

Taking profit is obviously more difficult than cutting losses, closing too early or too late can undermine your equity in the long run, especially when we are talking about static exit rules.

As we have already extensively illustrated, a good starting point for a novice Trader is to use a predetermined risk/return ratio of 1:3. Learn to master this first simple rule, pay attention to the financial instrument, your risk profile, the entry point and the Stop Loss.

If, from your analysis, you believe that the graph can actually give you the expected return, having already made all the appropriate choices in the most correct way, you can peacefully place the order on the market and wait for the position to close, for better or for worse.

> Didactic example:
>
> *As an exit rule, I will use the fixed limit equal to 3 times the R risk, therefore, I will exit the position whenever the prices reach the risk/reward ratio of 3, determined at the time of opening the position.*

The rules that define the Trading System

The rules of the strategy are what you have decided to do in various situations and include, but are not limited to, which financial instrument to trade, how to buy or how to sell when it is appropriate to operate.

If you have noticed it, the rules that we have described up to this point have identified which specific financial instrument to use but not how to proceed operationally. Starting from the reference market, we must carry out our personal assessments of the financial instruments contained therein, reasoning in more targeted terms.

If I have chosen the Crypto market, I will be able to invest in the Crypto index, Dominance, Bitcoin or one of the Altcoins, I will be able to decide if, at the moment, the DeFi sector, Decentralized Finance, can give interesting ideas or if I believe that the Metaverse will exploit in the future a specific token. I will choose an instrument in line with my knowledge.

We have identified a reference market, and perhaps we also have a specific instrument, but how do we buy and sell it?

For example, we can choose to buy Bitcoin directly through an Exchange and take it to our Hard Wallet, or we can always use an Exchange to operate on Bitcoin leverage, or we can still carry out exchange operations on the Bitcoin Future listed on the CME, Chicago Mercantile Exchange, and again we could go to a DEX, Decentralized Exchange.

We will then have to decide whether to operate directly on the financial instrument, i.e., buy or sell it, whether to carry out a spread operation, or again whether to apply an option strategy.

Each of these possibilities requires that there is a solid theory at the base, exactly what we have discussed in this text, but the specific instrument and the specific type of operation will inevitably bring further notions with them, from which you will not be able to ignore and which will then have to result in additional rules of the Trading System.

Let's say that you will find yourself in the situation of having followed the lessons of a course on different topics for a whole year, you will have developed some ideas critically and you will have reached the date of the exam, you will therefore have to make a choice based on the more probable topics, knowing that it is impossible to study everything perfectly and with the same attention in a short time. This choice of yours will be constantly tested with direct market experience.

Knowing how to define the rules of our Trading System will therefore allow us not to be surprised when we observe a specific configuration of the prices of a specific financial instrument. We will know a priori that when a specific condition occurs, we will have to operate in a specific way suitable to deal with that situation.

Rules help us deal with the freedom and uncertainty of the markets, looking for a specific weakness or strength to exploit. For some, this nature of the markets is a real tragedy, for others, it is what gives us opportunities. The rules will allow you to keep your reasoning in front of the amazing exploits of Mister Market and will make you a consistent Trader.

Uncertainty is the only sure thing about the behavior of financial markets. You will never, ever, ever have the mathematical certainty that by carrying out certain operations in the presence of certain configurations, you will have a precise result.

Being a Trader means being able to handle the odds and accept possible, and I would say inevitable, losses. To manage probabilities and therefore increase our Statistical Advantage against uncertainty, it is obviously mandatory to define a series of rational rules suitable for dealing with a specific situation.

> Didactic example:
>
> *Operations will be purely discretionary and will be based on the opening hours of the American market. I will opt for a broker who allows me to operate on instruments such as ETFs and gives me the possibility of operating with modest financial leverage if the strategy proves to be valid.*
>
> *I will record all profit and loss trades, keep track of them in a trading journal and, if I deem it useful, I will keep some screenshots of the best and worst trades to draw conclusions afterward.*
>
> *Every 100 Trades I will review the result of the strategy to decide on any changes and improvements.*

Now that you have enough notions to write your personal rules, take a sheet of paper or generate a text file, it's not important how but write them. You will have to read this set of rules every time you are about to observe the market, whether it is in the morning when the stock exchanges open or whether it is when a specific market opens, it doesn't matter, it all depends on the rule itself that you impose on yourself and which it is an integral part of your Trading System.

Also, remember that the first set of rules obviously isn't great, so take the time to do your own testing, play demos, and discover your system's strengths and weaknesses over time.

Knowing the six components of a complete Trading System is all you need. Thanks to them, you will be able to embark on your journey in this complex, interesting and, in my opinion, fascinating world.

I repeat, I strongly advise you to write your Trading Systems, try them for a good period in demo mode, track the results in your personal Trading journal, evaluate the win rate and the global profit/loss ratio and sum up after having made at least 100 Trades.

It is also very useful to carry out backtests on the financial instrument, extended over a fairly large period of time and such that it includes all phases of the market, including any collapses. Suitable study time windows range from 5 to 10 years.

In case you don't know, a backtest is studying the performance of your specific strategy based on past price movements. In simple words, you will test your set of rules on a specific Security, Asset or Currency of your liking, starting from an arbitrary moment in the past up to the present day. Your rules will dictate that you enter at a certain time and exit at a later time, generating a sequence of virtual Trades. Just as if they were real operations, you will evaluate the win rate and the profit/loss ratio, developing awareness of the validity of your idea.

If you are thinking that 100 Trades certainly do not cover such extended periods as five or ten years, know that the choice of 100 Trades arises from the need not to delay your entry into the market excessively, but obviously, the test will be all the more valid, the more Trades virtual run.

Remember that most Traders lose money on the markets and only a small percentage manage to be sufficiently profitable at the end of the year. Knowing this, you will have to aspire to be in this minority of profitable Traders because you will be capable of it, because you will have deserved it by eliminating emotions from your operations because you will have done your homework, and because you will have written a Trading System that is consistent and robust.

By consistent, I mean that it can generate profit over time, and by robust, I mean that it can withstand a series of losing operations without affecting your capital at risk too much.

Trading is a business model, it's like a company, if you open a shutter and hope, you will most likely fail. If, on the other hand, you have a business plan that contemplates what to do, how to earn, how to spend, and how to deal with difficulties, your probability of staying in business will grow exponentially over time.

A capable Trader must be confident because he knows his system, knows the instruments he wants to trade, and knows that he must be extremely disciplined in sticking to his ideas and plans.

If you rely only on your judgment skills, without objective evidence, you could be influenced by the moment and make hasty decisions when instead you should be careful and prudent.

Furthermore, having a Trading System will give you the possibility to objectively evaluate your performance, it will make you a greater awareness of the market on which you operate, it will make you receive signals that you otherwise would not have observed, and it will make you make choices that you would not have otherwise assumed.

Chapter 14:
Psychology in Trading and Winning Mindset

In this chapter, we will address one of the central themes in the formation of a Trader, the psychological component, i.e., that set of winning habits that must be acquired during the process to become a Trader.

Understanding the psychology of trading is perhaps one of the most important aspects a successful Trader must master. At the beginning of this text, we have already seen how the Three Cornerstones of professional trading determine the final result.

Having configurations that provide high-quality signals, and therefore with a high probability of occurrence, as well as operating with an adequate risk/return ratio, will unfortunately not be enough if you get tossed about by your emotions and the deceptions of the mind.

So far, we have focused on the technical part of the Trader development process, now it's time to lay the foundations for a solid personality, which is capable of executing what we have set ourselves.

If you have not yet experienced it on your skin, you must know that Trading on the financial markets is something very difficult, you can make mistakes with each operation, and there is the possibility that it will not bring the desired result even when the operation is technically perfect

The true nature of "Mister Market" is to be neutral. We call Mister Market the final result of millions of transactions, operated by millions of Traders through their own Trading Systems, automated or discretionary, largely based on the information and related emotions. Everything is absorbed into a single final result, the price beaten on the market. It doesn't matter if for a short time or for a long time, the price represents the definitive equilibrium of the market at a given moment.

Market behavior is nothing more than the result of this unrestrained technical and emotional competition, which reflects both the analytical and rational component of market operators and the more illogical, hidden, and profound component, driven by almost psychological reactions of all participants.

This changeability and ambiguity is the fundamental cause of the mistakes made by Traders. The market does not care that a Trader is able to interpret his behavior, in short, it will vary, and the Trader will be wrong.

Mister Market is, therefore, a mad and fickle creature that exalts and self-damages itself, which involves all those who participate in this struggle with itself.

It is a bit as if he can turn our best weapons, our strategies, against ourselves, regardless of the skills we can develop.

In the light of all this, you will ask yourself: *"Is it possible to survive this economic chaos and always come out of it in profit?"*

Unfortunately, despite our most important efforts, regardless of our commitment and the effectiveness of our ideas, the market will adapt, and what worked before will probably lose effectiveness over time.

However, there is a solution to survive all this, to develop a psychological advantage that allows you to face these variations with adequate calm and rationality.

A good Trading System with a good statistical edge can help you beat the market temporarily, but applying it over time requires tremendous concentration. The Trading System can be applied consistently and generate profit only if you decide to develop the Psychological Advantage.

Psychological advantage

Traders who manage to generate profits consistently and systematically have not developed magical indicators, nor are they custodians of economic secrets or inside the news. These Traders have simply been able to develop an adequate aptitude for trading, therefore, the psychological advantage derives exclusively from one's winning mentality.

Many Traders are constantly on the lookout for the "holy grail" of trading, a secret and mystical indicator that allows them to predict future market movements with disarming accuracy. This amazing indicator cannot exist, nor can it ever be produced due to the very nature of Mister Market, therefore you will not find indications for searching for it in this book, rather I will show you the real secret of Trading.

The secret of Trading is that there is no secret, everything is already known, and everything is already available and ready to be exploited. Everything is only to be researched, studied, applied, and improved. The secret of trading lies in your mindset.

Four types of operations

There are winning trades, losing trades, correct trades and wrong trades, and it is important to understand the differences between these four categories.

A fair trade is a trade that has been executed in compliance with a defined set of rules included in a Trading System.

A wrong operation is any other operation such that it is the result of an arbitrary choice.

In the rational world, a good deed should automatically correspond to a reward; conversely, a bad deed should correspond to a punishment. This would be true if everything on earth were the result of a logic of cause and effect but, unfortunately for us, the world is not at all fair, logical or rational and the financial markets replicate this fickleness even more clearly.

In Trading, it is correct to expect to execute our Trading System in an exemplary way, already suitably tested over time and therefore considered reliable, and equally to suffer a series of consecutive losing operations.

On the other hand, it is also possible to operate totally at random, with very serious and obvious errors regarding, for example, money management or the timing of entry and exit from the market, and yet close a series of operations profitably.

In the mind of a rational person, such as we want to be when dealing with the market, this randomness at the beginning can also be a cause of discouragement.

A Trader must learn to focus, from the beginning of his journey, on executing correct operations rather than achieving mere winning operations. This mental turn is the basis of Trader psychology. To do this, we will have to focus exclusively on what we are able to control: following our rules, following a predefined plan, cutting losses early, letting profits run, and so on.

By doing so, we create a solid foundation that nips harmful thoughts such as the pursuit of victory, the attempt to avoid a loss, chasing the sensational and alarming news, following random advice found on the net or comparing it with the results of other Traders.

By focusing on correct operations and not on winning ones, you will have the real possibility, even in the presence of losing operations, of achieving an overall positive result, obviously, as long as your Trading System continues to generate a Statistical Advantage and you correctly apply risk management.

Your Trading System will need to be evaluated on a large number of trades. Fifty or one hundred operations will allow you to issue a mathematical and flawless judgment on the effectiveness of what you are doing, useful for eliminating the emotional component.

Even if the result of this evaluation is negative, it will lead you to make decisions and measures in a much more rational and targeted way.

Goals

It is good practice, in trading as in life, to set goals. Many people do not understand the usefulness of defining a specific purpose, and Traders are no exception, they enter the market and want to make money in a vague, random, and generic way. An objective must always be achievable, measurable, and with a time limit. The greater its definition, the greater its effectiveness.

Example: *"In a month I want to make 30 trades and at least half must be in profit"*

Emotions

Our most important enemy is emotion. Our decisions as human beings are always made according to a combination of emotion, logic, and intuition. The rationale comes from our analysis of the state of the market, conducted by applying all the tools known to us. Intuition is mainly the result of the experience of the financial markets, and it grows over the years. Emotion, on the other hand, is something much deeper and more difficult to manage, it generates most of the problems during operations and keeps us awake at night. Emotionality causes us to overestimate possible benefits and underestimate the respective risks. Emotionality makes us make gut decisions and not with our heads on our shoulders.

Successful Traders always have several applicable strategies, calibrated on different markets and prepared to minimize the emotional contribution from their decisions. Some rely on their unshakable discipline and constancy, others instead exploit algorithms to completely free themselves from the decision-making weight, leaving everything to a calculator, while some manage to better manage their emotions and build on a performing system. However, all successful Traders always have one factor in common, they manage to find a way to integrate the emotional factor, when it is present, in a positive way.

Understanding our emotionality, and the internal landslides it causes, can give us the serenity necessary to manage its effects. All this contributes to building our "Psychological Advantage."

Unfortunately, each of us has an aggressive being inside us who fights, paws, and trembles to be right. We always wish we were right and feel physically bad whenever we are wrong, whenever someone proves us wrong and points out our mistakes repeatedly. In the financial markets, this happens constantly, it is slammed in our faces over and over again every day! Every time the Trade, even if correct, ends in Stop Loss! Every time the take profit is touched and then the price goes down! Every time we feel a blow to our wallet.

You will have to learn, in the shortest possible time, to accept and embrace this reality as something normal and inevitable. The market is able to dazzle you with surprisingly effective methods. It could make you believe that you are invincible just because, in a market markup, you luckily bought and managed to ride the trend temporarily.

This unshakeable self-confidence will grow until you collide with the fickleness of the market, but by now, strong in your great analytical skills, you will be mistakenly led not to close a position that is obviously at a loss just because you believe it will return to profit. You may even be strongly tempted to move and expand the Stop Loss to delay the painful moment of the loss, which, precisely because of this action, will be even more painful.

One of my first CFD Trading Systems, Contracts for Difference, had a win rate of roughly 90%, with only about 10% of trades losing. I do not deny that discovering that I was so capable a few weeks after approaching this world made me feel like a genius in Online Trading. Unfortunately, and also fortunately, I was making a classic and trivial beginner's mistake. The Trading System provided for narrow take profits and excessively large Stop Losses, moreover it was based on too short time frames, and I did not even remotely consider the idea of making a general overview of the market, taking advantage of wider time frames.

It was inevitable that this strategy would lead me to collapse. The self-assessment test on 100 Trade, which I did cautiously from the first moment, clearly showed me that, when I lost, I lost an average of $10, and when I gained, the profit did not exceed an average of $1.

The smart thing I did from the first moment was not to enter immediately with important capital, deciding, on the contrary, to practice for at least a year in demonstration mode. Let me tell you it was a very good decision and it saved me a lot of suffering.

Among the greatest challenges of a Trader is the fight against oneself, the fight against the desire to be right at all costs. In Trading, we do not make forecasts, we are not soothsayers but simple interpreters of a market. We make assessments for how it looks at a given moment, and if our strategy suggests a possible Statistical Advantage, then and only then do we decide to proceed with the operation. Furthermore, the moment we place our operation on the market, we are already aware that it could be both a winning Trade and a losing Trade. Every operation will be for us like Schrödinger's cat, until the operation is concluded, we can consider it both positive and negative.

Making a mistake in the market, and therefore losing money, is something inevitable, it is an investment cost that must be included in our general balance from the first moment. You will always have partial information, and therefore, the results will never be perfect, letting yourself be paralyzed by possibilities related to economic factors or technical factors, rising indicators, and fluctuating rates can only make your choice heavier.

To master a strategy and have positive results in the market, you will need to better separate the emotions related to the possibility of profit and loss. One of the most devastating emotions for a Trader is fear. Fear of losing money, fear of misdirection of the market, fear of missing a market trend, and fear of losing the current deal.

Fear of losing money

The fear of losing money is exactly what will lead you to wrong choices, such as those mentioned above and which I committed myself in my first Trading System, cutting profits too early and losses too late. This same fear has the power to paralyze you before entering the market and making a simple choice complex.

Fear of going wrong

Another mistake I made at the beginning was linked to this fear. I entered the position, and the prices went into the profit zone, suddenly they turned in the opposite direction, and then, believing I had made a mistake, I closed at a loss to immediately open a new position in the opposite direction, only to then observe the prices take the initial direction with renewed vigor.

They were trivial mistakes resulting from a mind that imagined that trading was something simple and did not require particular skills. I was confident in my abilities, but the market scared me, and as an inexperienced Trader, I let fear take control.

F.O.M.O.

F.O.M.O., Fear Of Missing Out, is one of the most subtle fears. In Trading, this acronym is used when the Trader feels a feeling of exclusion from a market that, momentarily, is having record performances. In his own mind, he thinks he is missing out on the Trade of the Century opportunity, perhaps on a cryptocurrency such as Dogecoin, almost unknown until a few months ago.

This fear originates due to the greed of people who observe the movements of a market from the outside and, without adequate evaluation, decide to get on a train that has long since left. These people rush, make risky decisions and jump on a train that has already reached 150km per hour, and then... they get hurt.

You are well aware that institutional operators carry out their operations in the lateral phases of the market, both at the beginning and toward the end of a trend. When a financial instrument has undergone an important price movement, we must carefully observe the trading volumes, which will be very different from the usual.

This means that large institutional Traders have sold many of their shares at a profit, placing many trades in a short period. Buyers, strengthened by the explosiveness of the movement, will expect to get an extra profit, dreaming of a parabolic and infinite trend. Unfortunately, every trend always has an end; as we have observed, the end depends on the progressive reduction of the purchase demand.

Here is an example that shows exactly why many inexperienced Traders get dazzled by these moments. On Dogecoin, a memecoin with little intrinsic value but much talked about, the price per share went from around $0.066 to a maximum of $0.44 in April 2021, after which it reversed to resume the race again, with peaks of 77 cents in May. A growth of 1066% in 40 days.

Obviously this growth, as obvious as it may seem to say now, is absolutely not sustainable and the price obviously then collapsed. Currently, Dogecoin is valued at around 0.12 dollars, and even if it may seem little compared to the previous explosion, remember that in practice, it has grown by 87% in less than a year, with unimaginable values on classic financial markets.

A Trader in F.O.M.O. will buy shares of projects such as Dogecoin, or shares of low value denominated in jargon Penny Stock, which momentarily show encouraging short-term performance.

The Trader of this type, ignoring the fundamental data of the market capitalization of the instrument observed and the historical price data, not going in-depth with the study of what he intends to buy and letting himself be dazzled exclusively by the price movement, will most likely expose himself to enormous risks. By purchasing at high price levels, he will be able to make only three choices, one worse than the other:

- A. Choosing to sell shares immediately, settling for a small profit or accepting a small loss. Emphasizing that executing trades under the pressure of fear or greed is certainly not a strategy, it is certainly the least painful of the three choices. Unfortunately, a Trader who gives in to the temptation of F.O.M.O. will be driven more often by greed rather than by the fear of losing money, therefore it is unlikely that it will suddenly exit the market;
- B. Choosing to stay at the window, believing that the market, now collapsed, can recover in a reasonable time. He will maniacally observe the graphs, day after day, seeing the enthusiasm of the recent past diminish, suffering from the passage of time. At the height of his suffering, he will give in to despair, accept losses of up to 98% of his invested capital and sell everything;
- C. Choosing to behave as a drawer or, realizing the now changed situation of the financial instrument, well aware of the devastating reality concerning the destruction of his own capital, the Trader waits years and years and still other years, no longer observing any type of graph and almost forgetting that he now has those market shares, keeping only in a hidden corner of his mind the hope of recovering one day, who knows when the losses suffered.

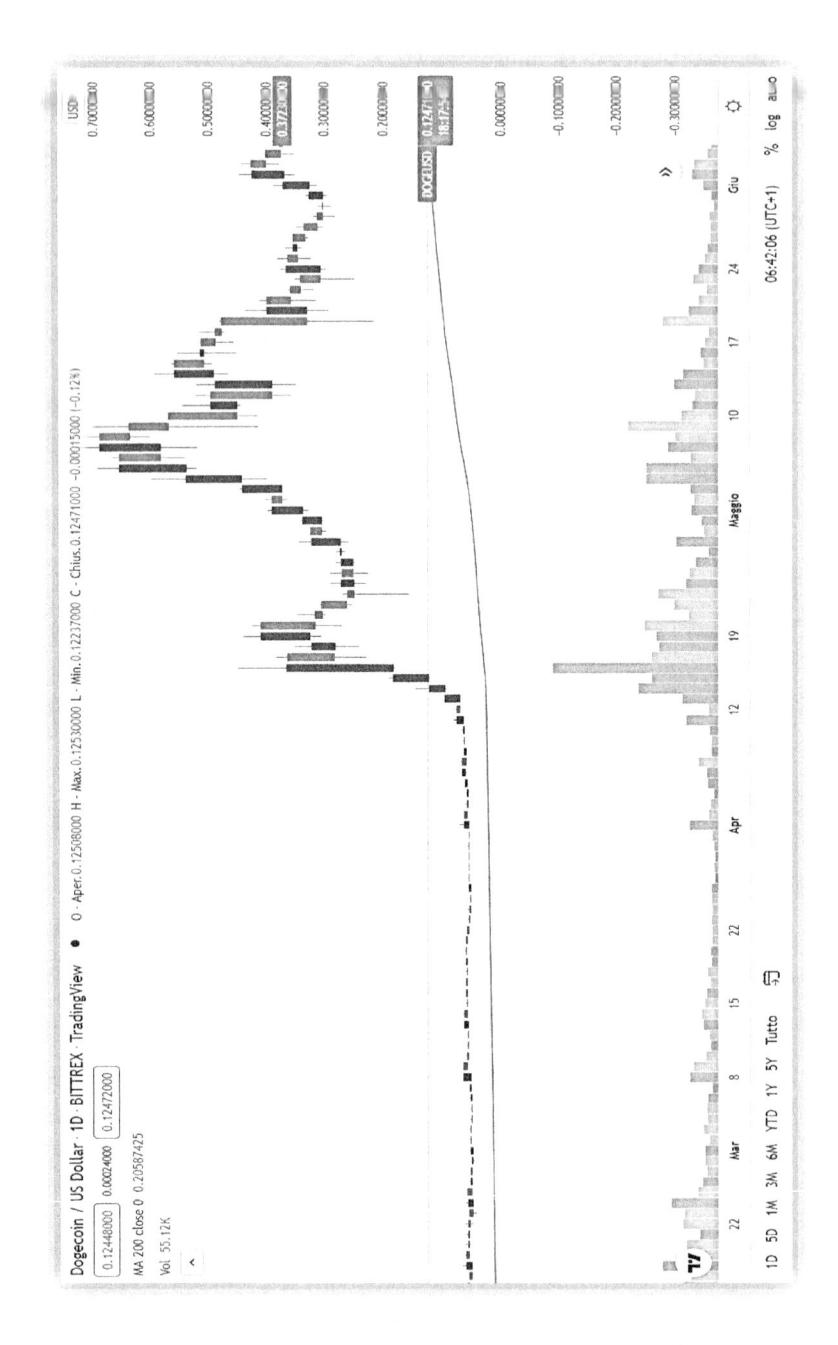

Illustration n.61– Chart of the Dogecoin Market April 2021

My advice is always to not enter a market without having clearly and preventively defined your rules and without having carefully assessed the costs and benefits of each operation.

Past negative events also increase fear, the greater the loss in a past operation, the greater our fear and reluctance to proceed with trading operations again. Our brain also associates lost profits with negative operations, therefore, our insecurity will generate fear of both direct and indirect loss.

Hope

On the other hand, hope is an extremely powerful emotion, almost on par with fear. Hope is what encourages one to undertake risky operations without adequately assessing the risks. Hope encourages us to delay losses beyond any level of logic.

Some Traders keep their losing positions open, beyond reasonable limits, in the very hope that one day, who knows when they will break even again. Hope can drive us to ignore our Trading Systems so we don't have to admit we have suffered a loss.

During the Dotcom bubble of 2000, many investors bought Tiscali stock, driven exclusively by F.O.M.O. Most of these succumbed to despair linked to the collapse, many others instead opted for hope, converting into drawers. Hope can do even more harm than despair. A Trader cannot rely on hope during his operation, he does not have the time, and he does not even have infinite capital.

Let's look at the Tiscali graph, from the Bubble to today's date, perhaps hope has rewarded the most devoted. What do you think about it?

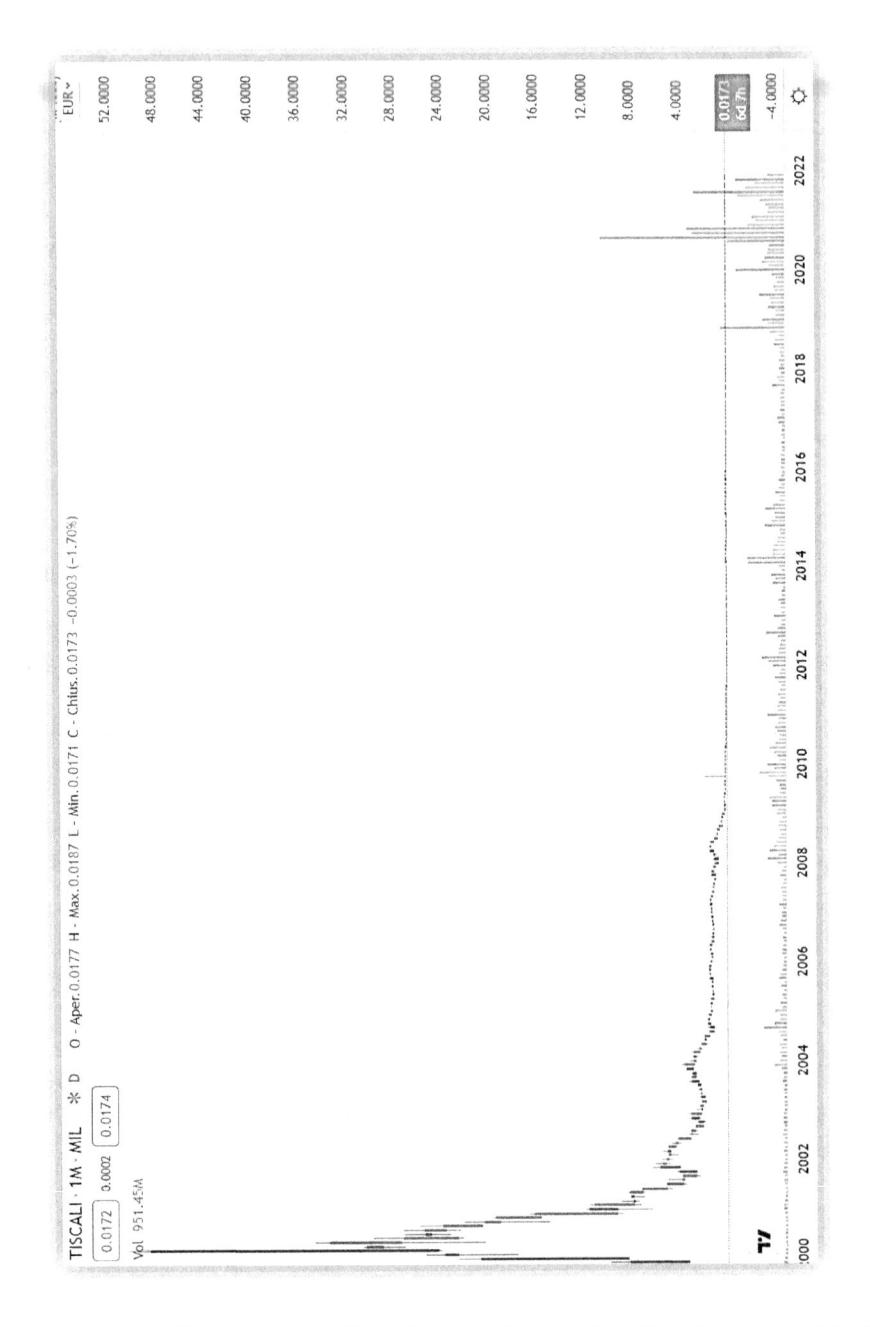

Illustration n.62– Graph of the Tiscali collapse in 2001

Manage your emotions

In order to be extremely disciplined and to be able to govern our emotions, we must first confront ourselves and do something contrary to normality. Subsequently, with the opening of each operation on the market, we will force ourselves to consider it totally wrong whether the Trade is technically correct. By doing this, we will be able to go one step further, making an effort to observe the development of the wrong Trade in all its evolution, understand its nature and finally identify the degenerating causes.

This leads us to also face the fear of loss. If, for every Trade I place on the market, I already start with the idea that it will make a loss, I will have a sense of joy when the result is positive. Conversely, when the Trade actually loses, in my mind, simply what has already been predicted will have happened.

You must convince yourself that losing trades are not a loss of the economic value of your account at all but something physiological, expected and natural, and they are exactly the price you pay to be able to participate in the market.

We will then have to develop the ability to resist the temptations of the market, further reducing the risk associated with a single position. We will operate with a fraction of the capital we would use to trade under normal conditions. For example, if a financial instrument does 100% in two weeks, instead of entering full F.O.M.O. with the maximum expected risk, let's say 2% of the capital, we could decide to further split this risk quota, let's assume 0.3%, and then progressively mediate the price until the maximum risk is reached.

To keep hope at bay, after having carried out a market transaction, we will have to constantly remember the conditions that led us to make that particular choice and why those reasons can still be considered valid or invalidated. If a financial instrument has behaved in a completely unexpected way and has created an unexpected scenario, we evaluate the possibility of closing everything, or we investigate the reasons why our ideas can still be considered valid. It is certainly useful to keep a written record of one's considerations, especially if one's memory is not always exceptional.

Intuition

You know well that the three elements that lead us to make an operational decision are the logic resulting from the technical and fundamental analysis of the markets, the emotion with which we constantly fight, and the intuition dictated by experience.

Intuition is something that distinguishes some of the most capable Traders, and it is something that has nothing to do with magic. The power related to intuition comes from countless hours of study and application of the concepts of financial economics and markets. We train over time to have a particular mindset that makes it easier for us to identify the essential information necessary to operate.

Building Trader intuition requires:

- A continued intentionality.
- Being able to focus on specific market structures.
- The execution of constant passionate work, repeated with an open-minded attitude towards Trading activities.
- The constant evaluation, objective and not partial, of the observed conditions.

As the masters of Kung Fu require their disciples to perform a technique thousands of times, with the aim of making them develop maximum naturalness and mastery of it, in the same way, those who want to aspire to be great Traders will have to repeat and study the subject with a practical and tireless approach, they will have to deepen every aspect by fixing it indelibly in their own mind. Only in this way will each choice also be the result of spontaneous instinct, what I will later explain as "Unconscious Competence."

Frequent Mistakes

There are several recurring mistakes that a beginner Trader can come across, one of these is certainly to focus too much on the money and equity of the account rather than concentrating on the execution of the Trading System.

Together with this first mistake, there is usually the tendency to focus excessively on obtaining short-term results, while by now, you know well that every Trading System must be observed in its overall development, on longer-term intervals, so that the relative Statistical Advantage can be revealed.

Some novice Traders, accused of losing their first operations, get angry and start making senseless operations. For example, they increase the specific risk of the Trade, which leads to non-compliance with the position sizing criteria. These inexperienced Traders imagine that, by operating in this way, they will recover their losses in a short time, forgetting the reason for which the correct sizing of the position is carried out. Remember that these choices protect capital from unrecoverable Drawdowns; therefore, let me emphasize it again: expanding the position will only be a way to further accelerate the much-hated losses.

On the other hand, other Traders accused of consecutive losses will become more fearful because they are deprived of their trust. It follows that they will no longer reactively follow the rules set by their own Trading Systems. Holding losing positions over the limit or, even worse, adding new ones in the hope that the price will move in the direction we assume will not help these Traders to perform better.

Another mistake that can occur is projecting one's faults onto others or looking for the reasons for our losses outside. Everything we do in the financial market, and in life for that matter, is directly caused by ourselves. We buy, we sell, we decide when, and we decide how much and what to exchange, driven by a reason identified by ourselves. It is important to be aware that, behind our every action, there is only and exclusively our responsibility.

Some Traders will be dazzled by advice and ideas found in books or by encouraging words from other Traders, accepting them as absolute truths without proving their truthfulness or placing them under the magnifying glass of their judgment. Even the tendency to compare one's economic results and performance with those of established Traders is part of this common mistake and generates unrealistic goals in the novice Trader.

Everything you read, everything you study, everything you apply, and everything you listen to will always have to be, and I always repeat, first screened by your mind, your beliefs, and convictions, you will always have to fit all the information with your previous culture, and only if everything seems to be congruent to you, you will be able to take certain statements as true and begin, in a cautious but methodical way, to experience what you have understood.

Chapter 15:
The 11+1 Habits of the Successful Trader

Having dealt with the subject of fears adequately, we now move on to the positive side of Trader Psychology. Although Trading is an extremely profitable activity for some, many of the Traders who try their hand in this world inexorably lose part of their capital. A question may then pop into your mind:

"What do Winning Traders do different?"

In this chapter, we address the 11 + 1 habits that differentiate profitable Traders from average Traders as well as how they manage their psychological attitude. If you have read the whole book carefully and have not skipped entire chapters, you will find many of my suggestions on these pages.

First Habit - Accepting that you don't have total control

The successful Trader focuses exclusively on the things he can control and accepts what he cannot control.

The profitable Trader knows that he cannot control market movements, periodic earnings, catastrophic announcements or even winning or losing a position. He is aware of his lack of power in all of this and accepts it with equanimity.

We carry out operations in environments governed by randomness and uncertainty, which is why a shrewd Trader will not build generic Trading Systems but create specific ones that adapt to his personality. He will strictly follow the self-imposed rules, setting plausible goals and leaving his emotions aside.

Everything you can control has the potential to increase your Statistical Advantage, therefore the potential to obtain enormous benefits and satisfaction from your Trading Systems is also in your hands.

Second Habit - Accepting uncertainty

Successful Traders feel comfortable making decisions based on partial and incomplete information. A beginner perceives bias as a threat and is convinced that he must know everything about the specific instrument he is about to trade. When beginners lose money, they become convinced that they have overlooked something in their analysis and have made decisions without all the necessary information. To avoid incurring new losses, the novice Trader puts more effort into making the overall picture more complete and spends more money and time searching for as much information as possible, obtaining, at most, a limited increase in his performance.

He reminds you that, even if you have all the necessary information, even if you execute a trade perfectly, you could always incur losses.

A successful Trader wastes no time creating complex analyses, rather he masters the game of probabilities, embraces uncertainty, evaluates the risk associated with the conditions he observes, and trades with confidence. A successful Trader is certainly not the most informed person about the instrument he is about to trade; he is simply methodical in his evaluations, making him self-confident.

In economics, it is said that the price of a financial instrument is the result of all the buying and selling operations carried out on the basis of all the information present on the earth at a given moment.

Put simply, the price discounts all the information and is the only fundamental and all-encompassing data to interpret. Building a good Trading System, and applying it well, is all that is needed for a Trader to interpret the price chart and, by extension, all the information present on the market at that moment.

Third Habit - Observing the Price Action

An average Trader has the tendency to make his own purchase or sale evaluations using only the price struck as a discriminating factor. It is important to be clear on this point, it is not possible to compare two different stocks in two different markets! The fundamental characteristics of the two companies would be extremely different. Do you think you can compare Poste Italiane's share price to Tesla's share price? Do you think Poste Italiane is cheaper than Tesla precisely because the price per share is accessible to you, as it is very low compared to that of Tesla? To be a successful Trader, you will have to immediately stop thinking that the price observed in the market is too expensive or too cheap for you.

The price per share will be an important entry barrier for a beginner precisely because of the caution that must be maintained initially. This world will not pamper you; at the first mistake, it will punish you!

Let's assume that you have taken all the steps, and now you are here, called to make the choice between these two companies. Both show fundamental signals and positive technical signals. What will you do?

Since the choices you will have to know how to make, as a Trader, will never be based on the price beaten but on the conditions present in the market at a given moment and on the basis of the possible return in terms of risk/return, you will operate on both companies respecting your Trading System.

Now I ask you another question, what is more, likely in your opinion, that a 2,000-dollar stock falls to 1,000-dollars or that a 3-dollar stock goes to a dollar and a half? This question is inherently wrong because market price volatility depends on factors such as market capitalization and the number of freely circulating market shares.

A company with a $2,000 share price but low liquidity due to a very small market capitalization will experience extreme price movements. Conversely, a company with a $3 per share price but a large market capitalization and ample liquidity will experience much less market shocks. Think of the FOREX market, an unregulated and highly liquid world market. The value of currency pairs almost never fluctuates excessively, and when it does, it depends on more exceptional causes and events than anything else, such as the war between Russia and Ukraine, which saw the value of the Russian Ruble collapse.

A successful Trader focuses exclusively on the Price Action and not on the price itself, observes the imbalance between supply and demand, and evaluates its opportunities.

Therefore, the advice you should follow is to ask yourself, always before operating, if, in the future, there will be someone who would pay more or less to hold the financial instrument you are observing and evaluating.

Fourth Habit - Variability of risk appetite

Inexperienced Traders have the habit of increasing their position after having undergone a series of losing operations, a tendency moved by the semi-unconscious hope of recovering the money sold to the market in a short time.

A Trader who has a professional approach will operate aggressively when he finds that he is performing well on the market and vice versa he will operate with greater caution and prudence when he sees that the situation is not momentarily favorable.

As mentioned in the chapter on sizing the position, risk capital becomes the modulator of the exposure. The exposure will increase, in absolute terms but not in percentage terms, when the market is favorable, while it will decrease until it stops completely, if necessary, after a series of loss-making operations that have clearly affected our capital.

An effective Trading System should always include proper position sizing planning. This planning should help you both by giving an incremental boost to positions when the Equity line is growing and by indicating a contraction of new positions when you face the inevitable Drawdown moments.

Keep in mind that in this type of business model, there are four essential choices to be made:

1. Take long buying positions;
2. Take short positions on sale;
3. Create a neutral trend-type position in Hedging, which is essentially a combination of opposing positions whose gain derives from the price spread, i.e., from the difference between them;
4. Take no position.

Regarding the last of the four choices, that of not trading when the market is uncertain and nervous, it can be a wise action in certain situations, therefore, you could use this rule within your strategy if it makes you less emotional and increases your market confidence factor.

Fifth Habit - Controlling Your Emotions

Every Trader has experienced that feeling of dissatisfaction and discouragement linked to having observed a market in which he would have liked to enter with his own strategy, a market that would have given him an excellent profitable operation, but not having entered it, he perceived the feeling to lose money. The F.O.M.O. springs from this feeling of loss, it makes the novice Trader imprudent, who torments himself with the loss of profit. Having observed this loss, he becomes convinced that he will be ready next time and that everything will go as planned. This reasoning erroneously leads to overestimating the pain associated with loss of earnings and greatly underestimating the pain that would result from a losing operation. Leaving behind the lost earnings, freeing up the necessary mental space, will give greater serenity to the neophyte Trader who can immediately focus on the next opportunity.

An expert Trader never gives in to F.O.M.O., he knows very well that the market will always offer other opportunities, and he will have to concentrate on them. He also knows well that it makes no sense at all to try to enter a F.O.M.O. market because it is nothing more than an excessively euphoric moment that will tend to end shortly.

He reminds us that the market will also be there tomorrow, so it doesn't make much sense to try to chase the planes in flight. You will see that over time you will be able to find hundreds of new planes stationary and waiting to take off on the runways, you just have to learn to recognize them, book your ticket in time and wait for the next take-off.

Sixth Habit - Knowing how to accept losses

A beginner Trader unconsciously carries the unfortunate belief that when a position starts to lose, it becomes cheaper and more convenient. Based on this belief, a very inexperienced Trader will add more money to the position, increasing the specific risk and exposing him to losses far greater than those initially estimated.

To be a good Trader, you just need to respect the rules of correct risk management, never increasing losing positions and, in general, never exceeding the value that you have set yourself as a specific risk.

Experienced Traders, when the market is against them and if this is in accordance with the rules of their system, may decide to exit completely from the losing trade and may also decide to re-enter the same market at a later time by opening a new position which is not said to be in the same direction initially envisaged.

Adding positions in a losing trade, thereby averaging the price down, is something that can only accelerate the drain on your account. Trading mainly consists of operations with a reduced time extension and is very different from long-term investments, where mediating the price downwards can also prove to be an effective strategy.

In the light of the above, when you see your Trade proceeding in the opposite way to what you assumed, accept the loss calmly, take some time to absorb its impact, calm your emotions, and go further.

Seventh Habit - Be clear about your Statistical Advantage

An expert Trader knows exactly what the Statistical Advantage is deriving from the individual strategies he puts into practice. In addition to this awareness, he is so clear about its advantage that he can explain why it makes sense and works in sixty seconds.

An inexperienced Trader has, on the other hand, the tendency to believe that he knows his Statistical Advantage because he has been able to obtain some good results, yet if I ask him to explain why he manages to be profitable, he will not succeed in any way to be brief.

If I have to explain to a third person that "When the 30-period average exceeds the 50-period average, and both are above the 200-period average, only when I experience high volatility if a retracement occurs and the RSI is above 55, etc.," you can well understand that the strategy is starting to be difficult even only in the illustration phase, therefore constant implementation will be quite difficult.

If you can't explain simply and clearly why you can make money in the market, you probably don't have an edge on it at all. Understanding and knowing your Statistical Advantage will help you enter and exit the market, applying an objective method without being influenced by external influences and, therefore, without conditioning your operations.

Physically writing your Trading System can prove to be very useful, especially if what you write down is clear, linear, and concise. Your Trading System will accompany you every time you want to enter the market, so you can apply it in an exemplary way, observe all its rules and evaluate its effectiveness from time to time.

Having written your personal system will not exempt you from its subsequent revisions, you will always have to look for its weaknesses in the various market conditions, but I assure you that, at some point, the revisions made will lead to a more robust system capable of generating a real Statistical Advantage on the market.

Eighth Habit - Limit Specific Risk

Some Novice Traders arbitrarily trade 100 shares per position in any single trade, others are capable of trading $10,000,000 to open a single position on a single company. These errors, generated by total ignorance of risk management, can do enormous damage in a short time.

Novice Traders often completely ignore the concept of specific risk and rely solely on their partial and non-objective judgment to determine how much to buy or sell.

Position sizing is an essential part of risk management in any Trading System, therefore, predetermining the maximum tolerable risk for a single operation well before deciding how much money to invest in a financial instrument is the only wise thing to do.

Experienced Traders apply position sizing as a basis for risk management, aware of its long-term utility. How large the position should be will be decided on the basis of risk appetite and not the price struck.

Ninth Habit - Focus on the result

Too often, we are tempted to want to see at all costs that our operation goes as imagined, just to demonstrate that we understand the market. This spasmodic desire to be right inexorably leads to maintaining operations on the market that no longer have a reason to exist just because the Trader's ego asks for satisfaction.

He reminds you that a market can have very extended rhythms, therefore, it can remain in the direction you consider "Wrong" much longer than it takes you to prove that you are "Right."

You don't fight with the market, you don't seek revenge, you don't try to prove anything in the markets. You look for a specific weakness and exploit it to your advantage. We must always operate with an open mind and follow what the market suggests. The market will confirm our ability, you don't have to.

The expert and aware Trader has learned to accept and admit the error he incurs and has developed the mental fluidity necessary to radically change position when the Trading System suggests it. He points to the overall final result, he doesn't care about being right or wrong about the single operation but about generating his own profit.

Tenth Habit - Patience and Precision

An inexperienced Trader will have to fight against himself constantly, he will perceive in himself, every time he places himself in front of the price charts, the irrepressible urge to make market operations, a sensation that will arise regardless of the observed market conditions.

This happens because he believes that Trading is like working in a classic way, if you do nothing, you will not be paid; therefore, even without a valid signal provided by his Trading System, he will feel he has to do something.

Experienced Trader also considers it part of their job to take the time to find good deals. He could observe the market even three weeks in a row without making any trades. The major activity in Trading does not consist in the mere act of placing orders on the market, but rather it is an enormous search for the conceptually correct Trades, obviously based on one's own Trading System, and only at the end of this search will we issue the order.

Successful Traders are a bit like snipers, they sit in a privileged position and patiently observe the market waiting for the right configuration. They don't shoot randomly every day just because they get bored. They know exactly why they are waiting and will only fire when the target is in sight, within shooting range and the probability of hitting is high.

Eleventh Skill - Knowing how to limit losses and maximize profits

As you may have already understood, an inexperienced Trader keeps a losing position open for a long time in the vain hope of seeing it return to positive, while when the position is in the positive zone, he gets agitated and does not wait for its conclusion and is satisfied with a small profit.

Obviously, an expert Trader will do exactly the opposite, he will be very patient in waiting for his position to reach the expected profit target, and instead, he will have strict and limited Stop Losses, such that they can be promptly executed if things go wrong different than assumed.

Successful Traders suffer a large number of small losses of controlled size, this is their way of reducing the damage and always having enough capital to move on to the next high-potential trade.

When the trade goes in the right direction, they never dampen it, they wait for the position to close in the predefined risk/reward ratio or their Trading System develops, giving a closing signal or, even more simply, they carry out Trailing Stop as long as that the trend is active and in your favor.

Quickly closing losing trades and allowing trades time to develop profits is among the most complex skills a Trader has to develop. Get used to losing often but always so that losses are already planned as part of your system as if they were a necessary cost to enjoy the profit derived from winning Trades.

Additional Skill - Keeping a Trading Journal

An expert Trader always keeps an updated register of all the operations carried out on the various markets, whether they are positive or negative, this register is called the Trading Journal.

If you are looking for a specific ability that can allow you to considerably improve your performance, this ability is exactly that of keeping your Trading Journal updated, the register where the essential information of your Trades is reported.

Keeping a register appropriately updated will enhance the Trader's ability to discern his own performance. By objectively reflecting on trading history, it highlights weaknesses, giving you the judgment needed to remedy them, thereby helping to increase your statistical edge in the market.

It will be virtually impossible for you to progress without having a clear record of all your operations. The Trading Journal will be your mirror, and you can use it to evaluate the actual profit obtained at the end of the year on each individual strategy. Through a Trading Journal, you can evaluate your performance mathematically and observe the mistakes made from another point of view.

Many Trading platforms autonomously maintain all the data of the previous operations, but my advice is to transpose them into an electronic spreadsheet to reprocess the data as you deem appropriate.

Chapter 16:
The Process of Becoming a Trader

In psychology, the four-stage process of developing skills is often used, applicable to any learning cycle and the acquisition of the ability to operate in the financial markets.

The process describes the stages leading to the transition from the condition of incompetence to the condition of competence in a given subject and skill:

1. Unconscious incompetence
2. Conscious incompetence
3. Conscious competence
4. Unconscious competence

Unconscious Incompetence

As a novice Trader, at the first stage of this journey, you will encounter the phase of unaware incompetence, where those who do not know the financial markets and lack any basis for dealing with them are placed.

Traders in this first sector have heard of Trading, and maybe they vaguely know some aspects of it, but in reality, they don't have the slightest idea of how to carry out operations on the market and, fundamentally, they can't even understand that this activity requires the development of specific skills and specific training.

They enter the financial markets recklessly, with complete self-confidence, and are sure that it is an easy way to make money, something that requires only a bit of luck in snatching the correct information on the net.

This is the stadium where we find people who think, *"I don't know and I don't care to know,"* the place that takes the greatest victims among inexperienced Traders. No matter how lucky these unknowing incompetents get, they may get good results in five or ten, or even a hundred trades, but in the end, they will suffer huge losses and find themselves painfully realizing that there is a lot to learn in order to make money in this world.

Many unaware incompetents will never invest in this world again, precisely because of the large wounds they have caused themselves, but for the remaining minority, made up of the most stubborn and resilient, there will be the transition to the second stage.

Conscious Incompetence

In the second sector there are still incompetent Traders who are aware of their current situation, unlike the previous sector. The Trader in this phase begins to form, recognizing that he does not have sufficient information, and, with the advance of his knowledge, he becomes progressively more cautious.

Placing himself in this stage, the Trader is aware of his current inability to operate successfully, aware of the intrinsic difficulty of this business model and therefore thinks, *"I don't know anything about Trading, but I'm interested in learning more."*

For these reasons, aware incompetents spend much time studying and developing the necessary skills. This is most likely your current stage. You are passionate about something that you do not fully understand yet, but you are working hard to fill this gap, because it is something that fascinates you.

Conscious Competence

In the third stage, that of competent and knowledgeable Traders, we observe all those resilient and stubborn Traders who have had extreme patience and diligence. They studied both techniques and theory, developed their own operating model, and finally started to be able to generate profits on a regular basis.

It took them years to reach this level of competence, working a lot on self-confidence and considering the Trading activity as a business model, not a game.

Despite their undoubted abilities, knowledgeable and competent Traders still have to spend a lot of energy to concentrate. The cause of this need arises once again from emotions, which force the Trader to develop constant self-control and an increasingly natural ability to govern himself. This phase includes all the people who by now have a clear understanding of what is at stake, and the rules of the game itself, therefore, they say to themselves, *"I am aware that I am capable, for this reason, I will pay even more attention."*

A Trader who has accumulated a large amount of experience in different markets, who has survived the stress deriving from operating in these first three phases, who are resilient and capable, who has developed suitable technical and psychological aptitudes, will move on to the last of the stages of the learning, the unconscious competence.

Unconscious Competence

In this stage of evolution, the Trader has accumulated all the practical and theoretical competence necessary to operate, he has committed himself with such constancy that by now, observing the markets and operating has become something natural, second nature, he no longer has any difficulty in deciding when to enter and exit and operates almost totally emotionless. It's the final level, the level of *"I know what I'm doing and I don't have to force myself to do it anymore."* His entire brain makes correct choices almost automatically.

When you drive a car, you perform a series of actions almost unconsciously: sit down, start the engine, engage the gear, press the clutch, etc. You don't have to consciously think about every single action, it's natural by now, you know how to do it so well that you don't have to think about it anymore or pay too much attention. A Trader in this phase possesses this level of ability, he is an expert and self-confident, he observes Trading as something simple and natural, which does not require too much effort.

Through these phases, the temper of the successful Trader is built, but do not think in the slightest that the achievement of the fourth and final stage is a matter of a few months. The evolution of the Trader takes years.

The time necessary for an unaware incompetent to develop self-awareness, and therefore reach the phase of the aware incompetent Trader, can also be considerably long, around 1 or 2 years, years in which he will build the very first basis of competence.

Having reached the second stage of development, it will generally take about four years to see the results of the new concepts learned, become a consistent Trader, and move on to the third stage of aware and conscious Trader.

In these years the Trader becomes technically and theoretically expert, he behaves to all intents and purposes like a professional Trader, but as I have already anticipated, all of this continues to require an enormous ability to concentrate, as naturalness has not yet developed.

The final stage of a competent and unaware Trader, which we can define as a successful Trader, is reached after having gone through all the possible existing market situations, therefore only when he has had direct experience of entire economic cycles.

Dealing with economic cycles will allow the Trader to develop the ability to feel at ease in any condition, be it of abundance or crisis. He will constantly feel at ease in the most difficult conditions, and generally, in phases of economic crisis, he will be able to obtain even better results than normal.

Consider the Trading Activity as a Business

The first advice I can give you is to consider trading from the outset, not as a pastime or a bet, but as a real business model.

We are not here to bet on victory or defeat, we do not throw coins in the air, but we must approach this type of business with the same seriousness and respect you would have in opening your own business.

In a classic business, you would build a solid structure, draw up a business plan, make a cost plan and keep it constantly under control, and evaluate which actions are taking you in the right direction and which ones are taking you away from your business goals.

Trading is exactly this, a professional activity with the advantage of not necessarily having to own a physical place to operate nor have employees, yet there are also fixed business costs to keep under control.

Treating Trading as any other business model will help you believe in the importance of properly developing Trading Systems, which are essentially your sectoral business plans. You will always have to set realistic, measurable, and achievable goals and accept losses as something physiological, as a necessary cost of the business.

Considering your system as an activity will help you assess the risks and reduce the emotion related to them. A business owner cannot control the economy of the country, he cannot control the tax systems, he cannot even control the rules of the contracts of his employees, but for these things, he does not despair, he learns how to manage what is in his power, how to choose which sectors to invest in, choose which activities allow him to obtain tax benefits and reductions, choose how many employees to hire and what skills and professionalism. A business owner focuses on what he can control. A Trader will focus on what he can directly control, measure, improve and manage, thereby eliminating all the background noise generated by what is not controllable.

The result of a good job in this sector can be seen in the long term by making progressive improvements and adjustments with constancy and patience. You won't do 1000% in one month, but you will focus on achieving consistent and positive performance year after year.

Invest Your Time Wisely

The second advice I feel like giving you is to invest your time in developing skills and studying. Take the time to learn, and take the time to develop the Trader mindset with heightened judgment and awareness of action. It also dedicates time to your operations and systems, leaving you the necessary space for evaluation aimed at improving your actions. Your systems require some time to demonstrate their effectiveness, only when you have enough data will you be able to make your assessments objectively, therefore you will have to hold back from the desire to change the system, even in the presence of a negative series, even when discouragement tries to knock you down.

I must warn you that this phase of learning and increasing your skills can last even years, and since you may not reach your profit goals at all, and you could probably incur losses, albeit controlled ones, you will have to constantly fight with yourself to resist to the easy temptations of the market. Know that it is highly probable that, despite the evident growth of your knowledge, your performance will continue to be really poor, so be prepared, this is absolutely normal.

Incurring continuous losses, even in the presence of strong motivation to study and commitment, can generate enormous frustration, leading you to mistakenly believe that Trading is not something within your potential. For this reason, you will fight with yourself, you will fight with that voice in your head that advises you to abandon everything and give yourself up to less demanding passions, you will have to make an effort to observe the positive side of this phase of your evolutionary process.

Set Realistic Economic Goals

Since the basis of trading, the raw material with which we work is capital, the third piece of advice is to set realistic economic goals. You will need to have a very large risk capital to generate significant profits. If you want a profit of $30,000 a year, it is unrealistic to think of investing the same amount or even less, counting on generating 100% or more profit every year.

To offer you a yardstick, institutional and professional Traders consider 25% per annum of invested capital to be a good return, and even Warren Buffet, the largest investor in history, has had an average growth rate of 20% over the years.

Starting with little capital for a Trader is extremely important. In the early stages of approach and growth, it is natural to make mistakes, therefore, it is equally logical to expect to lose money in these stages.

You will find that you learn much more from losses and the pain they cause than from success and happiness. You'll learn to be careful, trade cautiously, and protect your hard-earned capital. In the beginning, during the learning phase, it doesn't matter whether you earn or lose money, but it is important to always understand the reasons that led to that result.

A further necessary condition is to impose on yourself not to withdraw anything from your account for the first three years of operation. Focus on learning, not profit.

I recommend dedicating part of your savings to economic and financial training, making purchases, reading books, attending courses, and joining communities with expert Traders, they could give you good advice and perhaps follow you in some of your operations.

Create a Routine

Good advice is to create a routine, positive habits, aimed at increasing naturalness and confidence regarding financial markets and trading over time.

You will need to know exactly what to do on a daily basis before executing a Trade, but also on a weekly, monthly or quarterly basis, annually, and so on. You will have to push towards actions that, repeated constantly, will become inevitable habits of your daily life.

Positive habits can include anything that gets you in the best shape to trade in the financial markets. You could read, meditate, prefer nocturnal hours to observe the opening of the Asian markets, or on the contrary, sleep late to better follow the American market hours, despite being in Europe. It doesn't matter what the habit is as long as it is something that creates an advantage in terms of information, concentration, probability, and psychological terms.

A positive habit can also include studying past successful or unsuccessful operations, studying periodic earnings dynamics, or observing market openings.

There is a world of habits, and in order for them to be effective for you, you cannot copy them from other Traders but create ones that are appropriate for you.

Know How to Choose Your Broker

The last advice is certainly to choose a good broker, paying attention to commissions, expressed or hidden. For example, you may prefer a fixed commission broker rather than a percentage commission broker.

The choice of the broker based on the commissions is crucial in order not to weigh excessively on the overall performance of the year. It doesn't matter how you pay the established commission, but you should set a maximum annual expense, which could be 2% or 3% of your entire capital, and it is already a significant value. For example, over a full year of operation, out of $10,000 of risk capital, you shouldn't spend more than $200 or $300 in commissions.

You should also pay close attention to rollover costs, inactivity costs, custody costs, or rate changes that may occur over time.

A serious broker to rely on has ample resistance to economic conditions, such as giving all the security of depositing and withdrawing the desired amount of money at any time and offering guarantees on the deposited capital.

It is also important to choose the broker based on the type of financial instruments you want to trade, for example, there are many brokers who offer a wide range of choices between financial instruments, while others specialize in specific derivative markets, still others exclusively on the currency, and so on.

In choosing the broker, you will also have to pay attention to the two existing macro categories: Dealers, intermediaries that allow direct access to the market, and Market Makers who create the right conditions to operate with reduced capital.

Dealer-type brokers only create a bridge between the client and the market, therefore, in conditions of suspension of trading, they too will have to interrupt their operations.

Market Maker brokers purchase packages of financial instruments from the market with the aim of facilitating the injection of liquidity within their platforms. This activity will then be charged in the form of the difference between the purchase price and the sale price, effectively creating a commission between the real price of the financial instrument and the price traded within the platform. Since they buy and hold shares within the platform, they will not be strictly bound by the opening hours of traditional markets.

The ability to manipulate the spread, the difference between the purchase price and the sale price, means that these brokers earn higher commissions on illiquid markets because, to generate adequate liquidity, they will necessarily have to expose themselves to greater risk, while they will have reduced spreads on very liquid markets, such as FOREX for example.

When you operate with small capital, you are almost forced to move toward brokers of the Market Maker type, therefore, if this is your case, I advise you to pay close attention to the spreads of financial instruments because they will make a difference in your pockets.

Conclusion

By reading this text, you have understood how your passion for Trading requires considerable commitment and perseverance. In the pages of this book, I have guided you through the most important topics essential for starting your course of study.

As a novice Trader, you are now well aware that you will have to commit to consolidating all the concepts expressed in the various chapters of this text, and applying them directly to the financial markets. From the beginning, I asked you to draw up a list of financial instruments, therefore I hope you have had the patience and diligence to observe the corresponding concept on the respective price charts, with each new concept exposed.

Now you have no excuse to say that you don't understand charts or are unable to find good price levels to buy or sell. You know exactly which configurations are most effective and frequent, you understand what indicators really are and how they should be used, and you also know how to identify the phases of a market cycle, both to operate in trend and with breakout strategies.

You know how to determine the specific risk linked to each of your operations, therefore you will be able to build your personal and unique Trading System with the tools I have shown you.

Finally, you realize that despite the technical knowledge you can accumulate, there is a greater enemy to fight, your mind. You are aware that, in order to aim to become a Trader worthy of the name, you will have to face concepts that, at the moment, seem contrary to logic, you will have to form new beliefs and consolidate new habits.

Every day you will have to believe, despite everything, that you can succeed. Every day you will have to repeat inside your mind, "I BELIEVE IN YOU!" and with these words, I want to say goodbye and wish you the best:

"I BELIEVE IN YOU!"

Luigi Mele

Review this Book

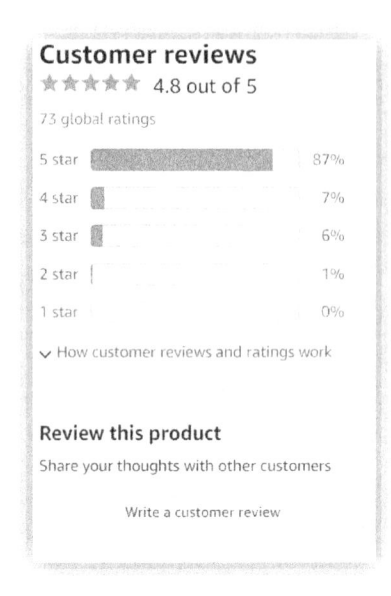

I would be extremely grateful if you would take 1 minute of your time to leave a review on Amazon regarding my work.

Bonus Contents

Inside the shared folder, reachable via the QR code shown below, you will find some content that will allow for a better and easier reading of the text.

I intend to share, without having to reduce the quality, all the charts in the text and an example of Trading Journal.

My intention is to add new content, over time and progressively, deemed useful for your Training.

To be enabled for access, simply send an email to the following address: lmele.trading@gmail.com

In the text, you will only include your name and surname, and possibly, if you deem it appropriate, your comments on the book.

References

Bibliographical references:

- Technical Analysis of Financial Markets – J. J. Murphy

- Technical Analysis of Financial Markets – M. J. Pring

- The Intelligent Investor: A Book of Practical Counsel – B. Graham

- The Stock Exchange is beautiful, a pity when it goes down – S. Graziano

- Easy Trading with Moving Averages – S. Lowry

- The Unger Method: The winning strategy of the 4 times World Trading Champion – A. Unger

- The Disciplined Trader – M. Douglas

- Technical Analysis of Stock Trends – R. D. Edwards, J. Magee

- Smart Investing: How to invest in shares successfully - A. Moretti

- Japanese Candlestick Charting Techniques - S. Nison

- Technical Analysis Explained – M.J. Pring

- New Concepts in Technical Trading Systems – J. Wilder, Jr. Welles

Printed in Great Britain
by Amazon